GLOBAL CURRENTS

GLOBAL
CURRENTS

MEDIA AND TECHNOLOGY NOW

EDITED BY

TASHA G. OREN AND **PATRICE PETRO**

RUTGERS UNIVERSITY PRESS

New Brunswick, New Jersey, and London

II

CIRCULATION
CULTURES, STRATEGIES, APPROPRIATIONS

ACKNOWLEDGMENTS

As with the previous collections in this series, New Directions in International Studies, this volume evolved from an international conference, "Transmissions: Globalization, Technology, Media," held in April 2002 at the University of Wisconsin–Milwaukee and sponsored by the Center for International Education. In these brief acknowledgments, the editors would like to extend their sincere thanks to the many individuals who made the conference and then this volume possible.

We would like first to thank the College of Letters and Science and Dean Richard Meadows for their crucial and ongoing support of the Center for International Education. We would also like to thank Professor Lane Hall for lending continual inspiration, interest, and advice on cutting-edge artistic work engaged in reflections on globalization. Finally, we would like to thank the staff at the Center for International Education. Here, as in the past, Amy Kuether deserves special mention. She has once again done an exceptional job at all stages of this project. Not only did she help organize all aspects of the conference, but she also served as in-house copy editor and facilitator for this volume. The editors are also grateful for the outstanding work of Center staff members Sara Tully, Anne Banda, and Rachel Schrag.

Leslie Mitchner, editor-in-chief at Rutgers University Press, has been an invaluable advisor and supporter, both of the series New Directions in International Studies and of this volume. We would also like to thank Bobbe Needham for her meticulous attention to all the essays gathered here and for her excellent and ongoing work as copy editor on this and other volumes in the series.

GLOBAL CURRENTS

INTRODUCTION

TASHA G. OREN AND PATRICE PETRO

This volume sets out to explore the complex relationships among media, technology, and globalization. Our title, *Global Currents*, also serves as our conceptual framework to suggest new and contemporary ways of thinking about mobile media forms and technologies—notably film, television, music, and the Internet—within the complex dynamics of global circuits and the multivalent processes of globalization. Rather than a set of binaries or confrontations, this collection conceives of these relationships through the guiding metaphors of currents, flows, journeys, passageways, and transmissions.

The inspiration and impulse for this volume was a conference we organized at the University of Wisconsin–Milwaukee's Center for International Education in April 2002. Interdisciplinary in scope and international by design, this conference aimed to expand the dialogue about the contemporary character of technology, communication networks, and the mediated arts, in an effort to show how each has been affected by worldwide trends, now often designated by the all-encompassing shorthand term "globalization." Participants from a wide variety of scholarly and professional fields (including film studies, cultural studies, economics, communication, anthropology, computer science, law, software design, musicology, and rhetorical studies) were invited to reflect on recent developments within their own disciplines and fields—and to engage in a cross-disciplinary dialogue about the changing roles of technology and media within new social and cultural configurations in our increasingly integrated, mobile, and globalized world.

This cross-disciplinary exchange served not only to energize the conference but also to transform the essays gathered here. For instance, now-commonplace issues in studies of global media and technology (e.g., the digital divide, cultural democracy, citizenship, the role of minority publics, cultural policies, Internet activism, and innovations in computer hardware and software) were examined in a fresh light as scholars, artists, and computer scientists joined together to push beyond accepted definitions, and to consider media and new technologies theoretically and historically, and as fodder for policy, invention, and art. Although the approaches taken and conclusions reached are by no means uniform, all contributors begin from the assumption that to speak of the global is necessarily to speak about media, understood not as technological essence or formal system but by way of media circulations, institutions, and multiple meanings and effects.

What distinguishes this collection is thus its truly cross-disciplinary engagement with now-conventional assessments about the promises, potentialities, and failures of contemporary technologies and media practices. Indeed, the contributors to this volume, both collectively and individually, endeavor to move beyond the tendency either to celebrate the resistances supposedly inherent in media forms or to condemn the "global media" entirely as cultural imperialism triumphant. New technologies, they argue, do not simply destroy older forms of communication (in this logic, the Internet supercedes television, which put an end to film). Rather, they call into being new relationships and mobilities while solidifying older ones, creating new and ever-changing circuitries of commodity exchange and media flow that require conceptual and theoretical approaches as innovative, interdisciplinary, and expansive as the developments they seek to understand.

These approaches, moreover, insist on moving media studies from the realm of technological identity (or ontology) to the realm of judgment and practice (or epistemology). Put another way: In the ontologically defined terrain of so much of media studies, various technologies produce (are indeed responsible for) particular global flows and effects; thus is film study separated from the study of television or music or the Internet to establish their particularities, identities, or intended effects. For the contributors to this volume, this kind of ontological understanding is hardly the point. Rather, they insist that media technologies must be understood in terms of practice, both institutional and aesthetic, and within larger global processes, in which media forms converge and in ways that are polyvalent, uneven, and nonsynchronous.

To capture and build upon this interchange of ideas and cross-disciplinary dialogue, and thus to build upon an understanding of global media that necessarily involves judgment, intervention, critical thinking, and critique, this collection is organized into two broad overlapping and interrelated categories. The first, entitled "Institutions: Nationalism, Transnationalism, Globalization," focuses on systems—material, legal, political, or discursive. The second, entitled "Circulation: Cultures, Strategies, Appropriations," takes up questions of representation and textual practices. While the first section looks directly at the media within global economies and emerging corporate and legal policies, the second section focuses on media technologies in their textual, theoretical, and experiential dimensions. The distinctions between the two sections, however, are more heuristic than absolute or practical, for although they mark a subtle difference in emphasis (from systematic structures to cultural texts and practices), both sections are best understood as guiding terms for a much more expansive discussion about the relationships among texts, contexts, and institutional frameworks. Indeed, whether in textual practices, legal systems, or distribution networks, the media and contemporary technologies of representation are organized in ways both formal and informal, textual and institutional, caught up in circuits of global media flows often opaque to traditional modes of theorizing—and found in places and spaces where the textual, institutional, political, and aesthetic interact and overlap.

This thematic grouping reflects the essays' collective attention to the questions, issues, and challenges that currently surface at the meeting point of global processes and technological possibilities. However, we also include an alternative table of contents that assembles the essays by technological and media-specific categories. This more traditional organization—with modules on the Internet, television, film, and music—may be of use to students in the classroom or to scholars interested in a particular media format. In any case, and regardless of how readers choose to make their way through the volume, it will quickly become clear that the convergence of media forms in processes of globalization is something that all the essays explore and underscore.

The first section of *Global Currents* takes on the question of globalization directly by analyzing media practices both within and outside changing definitions of the nation-state, the global system, and established disciplinary models for their understanding. It is of course a near cliché in globalization discourse to credit technology, and media technologies in particular, with a rapidly shrinking and seemingly homogeneous world. Whether or not technologies can be thought of as initiating formations, they are, primarily, powerful tools in the hands of producers, corporate owners, and users. Indeed, it is through that relationship that their impact on our changing environment can best be felt, articulated, and analyzed. As the essays in this first section of the volume make clear, understanding global media requires systematic examination of institutions and the strategies they employ to control and shape media technologies and their subsequent use. In this sense, this first section most clearly articulates the book's fundamental contention that it is not technological innovations that shape global changes but rather how (and by whom) they are put to use, developed, and delimited. Lenny Foner puts the issue succinctly in his essay "Crypto Regs: Fear, Greed, and the Destruction of the Digital Commons," which opens this volume. "While dependent upon technology," he writes, "the main issues in our current worldwide information systems are political, not technical. Thus, pursuing a purely technical solution to these problems is unlikely to succeed." In his detailed and timely contribution, Foner, a technologist at the MIT Media Lab, offers an insider's view of the mounting threats to freedom, use, privacy, and exchange in the digital sphere. These threats, as Foner argues, are not the price we pay for a wired world but rather the result of active collusion between corporate and political interests. As he details the extent and possible reach of such infringements on user freedoms, Foner nonetheless insists that they are reversible; developments that fulfill rather than impede the potential in information technologies are within our grasp through popular political agency. In this sense, Foner informs us, the arguments that traditional understanding of rights and protections are diluted or complicated by developing technologies are strategic, deliberate, and, most importantly, wrong—aimed at deflecting attention from political action by configuring emerging questions about global media as somehow purely "technological" in nature.

In "What We Should Do and What We Should Forget in Media Studies: Or, My TV A–Z," Toby Miller also takes aim at "commonsense" understandings of media as a transformative force. In this pointedly provocative essay, Miller provides a survey critique of contemporary television studies that still labor under received epistemologies about "effects" and "power." As he argues, the same paradigm that structured narrow conceptualizations of television research in the past now dominates attempts to study television in the global context. By revealing how studies about the latter draw deeply from ingrained assumptions in the former, Miller points us toward a new and more fully integrated approach to global media studies. As Miller puts it: "The best political economy and the best textual analysis can work in tandem through the imbrication of power and signification at all points on the cultural continuum. Ideally, blending the two approaches can heal divisions between fact and interpretation and between the social sciences and the humanities, under the sign of a principled approach to cultural democracy."

Peter Sands continues this examination by looking to educational institutions and their deployment of the Internet as one such example of strategic understandings of technology. In his essay "Hybridity," Sands examines the discursive constructions of the Internet as surrogate space, illustrating how such constructions inform and galvanize the recent institutional embrace of distance education. Working through the reifying power of certain concepts that enjoy hypercirculation in discourses about technology and globalization (from science fictions to educational policy), Sands demonstrates how hybridity together with understandings of the Internet as a space (location) that transcends place and physical presence has particular problematic dimensions for higher education today.

Like Sands, Steve Jones examines the origins and consequences of understanding the Internet in spatial terms. In his essay "@henryparkesmotel .com," Jones uses the trope of Internet surfing as tourism to explore the conceptual possibilities and limits of the once metaphoric and now commonplace understanding that casts a computer protocol for shared representation and communication between remote servers as a "space" made up of "places." His analysis of the Internet, so closely aligned with understandings of the global gives new weight and resonance to notions of home, mobility, location, and, most importantly, territory and ownership.

To be sure, the local/global axis of understanding media technologies has been particularly visible in both popular and scholarly engagements with television. In his essay "Is Television a Global Medium? A Historical View," Jérôme Bourdon reexamines the claims for television as either a powerfully globalizing or an exemplarily local technology as he argues that considerations of national television histories demand reconciliation between the two narratives. Through an analysis of early television industries, Bourdon offers a new perspective on recent claims about the rapid globalization of television, pointing to regionalism and patterns of ownership as crucial elements in global media scholarship while maintaining that the nation is still its organizing principle. His analysis highlights the role of international relations that remain too complex for isolationist accounts of television and too particular for narratives of global sweep.

While in most discourses about global media, the United States occupies the position of dominant and homogenous aggressor, Susan Ohmer's essay "The Land Grab for Bandwidth: Digital Conversion in an Era of Consolidation" seeks to complicate this casting with her account of the struggle over the emerging consolidated media technology of digital television in the U.S. context. Ohmer illustrates how local interests, corporate conglomerates, policy interventions, and conceptions of television as a public arena play out through the same set of debates as their global counterparts. By focusing her analysis on the United States, Ohmer points out the false dichotomy that often equates the United States unproblematically with "global" media power poised against the "locality" of another populace.

In her analysis, large and diversified media corporations stand against fragile legal defenses that define "local voices" in problematic and increasingly ineffective ways. Ohmer's essay raises the question of whether media forms are exchangeable or equivalent in their public, local meaning once the means of their delivery—through digital technologies and software—minimize their particular, material differences for owners and producers. How, she asks, do the abilities to inform the public and represent local interests change with developing and converging technologies? Like that of other contributors to this volume, Ohmer's main concern is with media policy and its ability to effectively protect local interests in rapidly shifting media environments. This point is particularly poignant and timely in light of the recent FCC relaxation of media ownership laws in the United States.

The interaction between the realms of law and technology is also the subject of Sandra Braman's essay "Posthuman Law: Information Policy and the Machinic World." In her analysis of the current state of the field, Braman illustrates how computer technologies have increasingly become not only the object of legal preoccupation but also its subject and, increasingly, its executor. As Braman shows, legal engagements with technology increasingly delegate decision-making processes to automated systems of data collection, storage, analysis, and evaluation. The widespread interest and institutional investment in such posthuman agency, writ large on a global scale through the vast interconnected network of computers, code exchange, and databases, have, as Braman argues, far-reaching but generally unaccounted-for consequences in both legal discourse and its wide applications in the social world.

The question of human agency in the domain of technology is further addressed in the second section of this volume, "Circulation: Cultures, Strategies, Appropriations." Taken together, the authors in this section consider how cultural products gain and shift in meaning through their circulation in various media formats or localities. While fully cognizant of far-reaching corporate, legal, and institutional systems and controls, each essay nonetheless argues for specific meaning-making trajectories in the circulation of media texts, thus reminding us of the critical importance of particularity and of looking and thinking beyond received notions of globalization and media. As each author emphasizes through a case study, understanding contemporary media practices in circulation requires a consideration of a distinctive blend of politics, technology, aesthetics, and textuality. In each case, these embedded systems define and shape cultural products in specific and thought-provoking ways

In "Piracy, Infrastructure, and the Rise of a Nigerian Video Industry," Brian Larkin takes up one such embedded system, media piracy in Nigeria, and explores the connections between systematic organization and media formats as they help define everyday life and textual practices. As Larkin demonstrates, this mode of media circulation, born of necessity, is not merely an alternative mode of distribution, but a cultural practice with its own formal characteristics and experiential qualities. Organized according to the same logic of technology that produces the overall marketplace, this system of piracy, as Larkin illustrates, has itself spawned an original media industry. This account of media piracy further reminds us that dispersal of, and access to, "global" media is fundamentally unequal and that such viewing practices characterize a large portion of encounters with mass media around the globe.

Following upon Larkin's account of local traffic in global media, Annabelle Sreberny turns her attention to the equally charged political reception of Eastern images and their consumption in the West. Her essay "Unsuitable Coverage: The Media, the Veil, and Regimes of Representation" takes up the veil as a shifting signifier in the politics of gender and image making. From the *burqa*'s deployment as an after-the-fact inducement to war to its endless symbolic circulation (in the text of an Internet petition, for instance) as an empty cybergesture of click politics, Sreberny's critique focuses on the patriarchal nature of state politics and what she argues is a cynical deployment of gender in Western war propaganda. Through this analysis, she revisits the often-repeated dichotomy that regards the Internet as a political medium and television as its conservative, commercial, and stodgy forerunner. As Sreberny argues, recent changes and innovations in television programming have brought the two media into closer proximity and thus necessitate a new focus on their interconnections in fueling activism in global politics.

Anne Ciecko picks up on this theme of cross-media circulation but focuses her analysis on the role of multimedia cross-pollination in the Asian film industries in her essay "Muscle, Market Value, Telegenesis, Cyberpresence: The New Asian Movie Star in the Global Economy of Masculine Images." As part of her project to "recenter" the global Asian film industries and focus attention on the various traditions, market structures, and conventions that make up these industries without the constant presence of global Hollywood as the navigational seat of discussion, Ciecko examines the particular position of the Asian movie star as a multimedia presence. Illustrating how notions of celebrity are reconfigured through changing and melding media technologies, Ciecko argues for a necessarily intertextual understanding of this model of global stardom. Drawing directly from local and diasporic experience, this model extends notions of cinematic narratives, international celebrity, and fandom in new and intricate ways.

Diasporic experience is also at the center of Anna Everett's essay on the ongoing growth and political activism of African digital communities. In this essay, "The African Diaspora Speaks in Digital Tongues," Everett traces African diasporic consciousness through to the digital era and points to virtual collectives such as the Nigerian Naijanet and its political offshoot, ANA-net (Association of Nigerians Abroad), as productive examples of a new digital reconfiguration of postcolonial political agency. As Everett argues, African netizens and the political communication of on-line diasporic activists are contributing to the formation of "new Africanities" and productive cybernationalisms that, given current political realities, are made possible precisely through their digital relocation.

The complexities of private consumption practices within proscribed economic and ideological structures are at the heart of the essay that concludes the volume, Timothy D. Taylor's "Some Versions of Difference: Discourses of Hybridity in Transnational Musics." In the marketing of the "global" itself as a commercial product, no industry has been successful than the record industry, with its impossibly broad and equally lucrative category of "World Music." Taylor analyzes how the twin discourses of authenticity and hybridity dominate this strategic category not only in the marketing of non-Western popular music in the West, but also in the ways critics and audiences approach and make sense of it. As Taylor illustrates, this practice, far from realizing Homi Bhabha's "third space" of resistance, often works to reify power relations and to deny actual cultural mobility to both music and to the artists who create it.

Taylor's concern to uncover the connections between corporate practices and cultural circulations define this volume as a whole. And just as Taylor moves beyond narrow conceptions of authenticity and hybridity in globalization discourses to envision a comprehensive, multidimensional approach, so do the authors in this collection aim to think about the media within the many embedded structures that animate them. As each contributor to this collection has emphasized, the current moment of highly corporate, transnational ownership and integrated media systems demands such a new analytical paradigm. In combination, the essays in this volume move us toward such a cooperative, entwined, and nuanced approach to the study of contemporary media—and thus to new ways of apprehending the dynamic practices, cultural texts, and contemporary developments that make up the global currents of media and technology right now.

INSTITUTIONS

NATIONALISM, TRANSNATIONALISM, GLOBALIZATION

CRYPTO REGS

FEAR, GREED, AND THE DESTRUCTION OF THE DIGITAL COMMONS

LENNY FONER

Introduction

The increasing globalization and integration of the world's information systems promises a host of benefits, but there are significant perils to these promises. This essay examines the tradeoffs involved, summarizes the current state of the world, and makes suggestions for what we can do to maximize the likelihood of outcomes that enhance global freedom, creativity, and civil liberties.

While dependent upon technology, the main issues in our current worldwide information systems are political, not technical. Thus, pursuing a purely technical solution to these problems is unlikely to succeed. My analysis therefore focuses on evaluating current and potential political interactions with information systems, leaving the technology involved as, essentially, a black box. I will lay the groundwork for why we should care about the increasing politicization of technology and its implications for global control and global civil liberties. I first touch upon some of the promises of globalization and of modern information and communication systems, paying particular attention to the global Internet. Next, I investigate contemporary and likely future political effects on worldwide civil liberties, almost all of which are deeply threatening. Finally, I suggest ways to influence the political discourse in the direction of greater freedom.

THE PROBLEM OF TECHNOLOGICAL UTOPIANISM

While many who study technology are prone to assume a technologically inspired utopian vision of the future, the political forces I address here suggest otherwise. They are primarily driven by government and corporate interests, and these entities are far more concerned with *control*—at almost any cost—than is assumed by the technological Utopians. Governments want control because it gives them power over their citizens and because it may give them power over other governments as well. Both reasons are part of why governments, even democratically organized governments, are formed. Corporate interests also want control, because it gives them power that can be translated into profits—and such profits may often be translated into further control, of individuals or even of their own governments, as the rise of both lobbying and multinational corporations have vividly demonstrated.

This desire for control thus leads to prohibitions over what citizens may and may not do with technology. Powerful governmental forces push to strip citizens of any shred of privacy—after all, you might do something illegal with that privacy—at rapidly increasing costs to civil liberties and the very concept of civil society itself. Further, a cowed society is a complacent society, one that will not be as dangerous to the status quo, and any government entity already in power seeks to maintain that status quo so as to maintain its power. Thus, the trend among modern governments has been to make privacy hard to obtain: by denying access to strong cryptography, by expanding the use of and sharing between databases, and by weakening the procedural safeguards against misusing this access to oppress their citizens.

Equally powerful corporate interests are pushing the original idea of copyright—a grant of limited rights, for a limited time—to become an absolute, all-encompassing, inescapable straightjacket that treats all possible users of information as thieves, assumes that all possible profit must be squeezed out of every bit, discounts the value to the public of any information not so controlled, and then bribes governmental entities that are complicit in creating laws that criminalize any attempt to wriggle out of these controls. And since information now controls just about everything, such control can (and has!) been used even to stifle competition in its crib—take, for example, the true story of an ink-cartridge manufacturer prevented from making cheaper refills for a different company's laser printer because the latter uses *copyright* and *legal prohibitions against violating that copyright* to absolutely prevent anyone else from making refills.

A PERSONAL STAKE, AND THE LIMITS OF TECHNOLOGY

As a technologist who has been following civil liberties issues for decades, these forces have directly affected my research agenda. For example, as part of my doctoral research at the MIT Media Lab, I created a system designed to form instant coalitions of people who share similar interests, and to enable them to have secure, private conversations amongst themselves, even though none of them knew any of the others a priori.[1] This application must handle a large amount of personal information, yet do so without creating a civil liberties quagmire. It does this by ensuring that there is no single point at which everyone's information may be collected—*there is no central server anywhere.* Without such an aggregation point, there is no location at which an intruder may gain access to everyone's data. Also, since there is no central point, no one could be successfully subpoenaed to provide information about anyone they were not already corresponding with, because the information would never be in their possession in the first place. Even if I, its creator, were subpoenaed, coerced, or bribed, I could not reveal anything about someone that they hadn't already sent personally to me. It accomplishes this feat via a *decentralized architecture*, which matches the Internet's fundamental organizational principle. And it protects its users' data in transit and in storage from eavesdroppers via *strong cryptography*, used in many places in its design—a technology that has been under constant attack by various governments for decades.

I built such a system to serve as an example of how to do it right—how to handle a large, shared collection of personal data, and make effective use of it, without giving a toehold for unscrupulous individuals, corporations, or governments to use it as a means of repression and control. But, while such technological systems can serve as exemplars and be useful to their users in their own right, they will not by themselves stop the tide of disastrous corporate greed and misguided government policy that threatens to make such technology either illegal or unavailable. Essays such as this are an essential alternative step, educating policymakers and the general public about why such attempts at control are dangerous to a free society and thus encouraging readers to try to stop such policies in their tracks.

A ROADMAP TO THE INTERCONNECTEDNESS OF IT ALL

I mention many disparate elements in this essay, but they form a related whole. To help guide a first-timer in making sense of this morass of interlocking political and technological forces, it is helpful to have a high-level view of how they fit together. (This view is discussed more completely in the section titled "Threats.")

Note, by the way, that my focus is relatively U.S.-centric—it draws most of its examples from the way the United States views the network and the rest of the world, and makes specific connections to U.S. law. However, since U.S. technology and law often exert a strong forcing function on the rest of the world, this seems defensible for the purposes here.

I start with the fundamental assumption that *modern information systems have a profound effect on the world as a global entity.* Chief among these information systems is *the Internet itself,* which promises worldwide equality and effectively instantaneous communication, but which both threatens existing power structures and enables unprecedented levels of both control and surveillance. To attempt to contain this threat, government and corporate interests exert influence via a variety of mechanisms.

The United States is ostensibly a free society, so direct attempts to control technology, especially the software that makes up an increasing amount of *all* technology, are difficult. However, great success was achieved in the 1980s and early 1990s via *export controls*, which make certain kinds of software (such as cryptography, used primarily to keep secrets and to prevent tampering with data by outsiders) impossible to export to the rest of the world and therefore uneconomic to incorporate into products (the section of this essay entitled "Export Controls" goes into substantial detail on this point). In the latter part of the 1990s, and continuing until today, *copyright* has grown explosively into a tool of control, via a variety of mechanisms, including effectively infinite terms (recently upheld by the U.S. Supreme Court and prohibition against circumvention *even for fair use*!).[2] These topics are addressed more fully in the section "Copyright and the New Threats to Crypto." Finally, in "The Empire of U.S. Policies," I discuss yet another aspect of globalization, in which the U.S. government, as prime offender, engages in a sort of incremental baloney-slicing attack by which policies unpopular at home may first be pushed via treaties on other governments, then used as justification for an unpopular or misguided policy at home in the guise of honoring the treaty so developed.

The remaining parts of this essay address certain other structural and civil liberties problems, including the universal panopticon of surveillance enabled by this technology; additional intellectual property issues which bear on a structural defect in the Internet—namely its use of the *domain name system*, which forces reliance on a single point of control, consequently inviting abuse and political manipulation; and *venue shopping*, in which the ambiguous overlay of the Internet on real physical geography enables some players to game the system in deciding which legal jurisdiction should be employed in intimidating their rivals. Finally, I touch on *genetic diversity*—a threat brought about by having too many machines running similar software which are all vulnerable to the same pathogen. Like relying on a single strain of wheat, this threat is a disaster that can only happen to a ubiquitous implementation—and as with wheat, this very ubiquity is often brought on by monopolistic control employed by very large corporations in totally dominating their market segments.

But first, let's investigate the promises of modern communications technology—specifically, the Internet—to see what's at stake, and to get a sense of what these corporate and political forces threaten to destroy.

Promises

The Internet's fundamental architecture is one of equality—every endpoint looks exactly like every other endpoint. Viewed up close, there are small variations. For example, not all nodes have equal bandwidth, though paying more—buying faster infrastructure, and paying fees to connect that faster infrastructure to some other part(s) of the network—generally raises what is available to any degree required. Similarly, latency—the time it takes to get a packet from one place to another—varies based on where those two places are, yet is typically much less than a second between any two points on Earth.

From an architectural standpoint, then, the Internet is fundamentally egalitarian. The network infrastructure does not care what a packet says, who sends it, or how much political or economic clout the originator or the recipient of the packet possesses. Devices that span at least nine orders of magnitude in computational power speak to each other transparently, and the network can equally well connect endpoints on the same tabletop or many light-hours apart across the solar system.[3] It is an economy of abundance—unlike bookstore shelves or newspaper boxes on street corners, there is no shortage of physical space in which to put information. Unlike radio broadcasts, where there is controversy over whether spectrum scarcity is a law of nature or evidence of political bungling in the development of technical standards, the Internet has no way to have a shortage of spectrum.[4] Thus, viewed from the standpoint of routing a packet from one place to another, the Internet can favor one speaker over another only if considerable engineering effort is invested to force that outcome—such as deliberately blocking packets from a given source or bound for a particular destination. Were the Internet left unfettered, everyone using it would have an equal voice.

The fundamental Internet architecture enables a large number of social goods. For example, worldwide information-sharing and collaboration between people and organizations need not take geographical distance, nor the boundaries of sovereign governments, into account. And while differences in human languages may tend to disrupt communications across different communities of speakers, this problem does *not* afflict communications between computers themselves, if properly engineered. The rise of machine translation efforts also promises to help, if only a little bit, with the current problem of human-to-human differences in language. This makes geographical details irrelevant, for the most part, in determining who may talk to whom, and how the network is used.

Because no speaker is, in principle, favored by the infrastructure itself, everyone may own their own printing press. (Speakers whose views turn out to be extremely popular may benefit from buying more bandwidth, or arranging for other sites to share some of the load, but this turns out to be a relatively minor engineering point.) Even extremely early in the history of the network, this equality of representation led to electronic mail and large-scale discussion lists, the Usenet news system, various online bulletin-board systems, the Internet Relay Chat system, shared virtual worlds such as MUDs and MOOs, and a panoply of other information-sharing and conversational tools.[5] Later, it led to the development and widespread deployment of more unidirectional, publishing-like environments, such as the World Wide Web.[6]

The shortage of physical and economic barriers to entry thus enables a vast profusion of different voices. The principal scarcity on the Internet is *attention*—getting someone to actually notice whatever it is you have to say. The traditional roles of editors, journals, and anthologies of similar materials—evolved over centuries of print publication and face-to-face interaction—are just as relevant and needed on the Internet now. However, unlike in the previous world (where the capital equipment required to run a printing press or a broadcast station, the distribution network required to move physical objects from producers to consumers, and the physical space required to warehouse and display these objects served to disenfranchise those who cannot get their words approved by a large set of intermediaries), the Internet allows *anyone* to at least make their views potentially receivable by anyone who is interested in them and knows where to look. Placement on a prominent website, posting to a well-read newsgroup, or being easy to find by a search engine certainly help to make those views more popularly accessible, but even marginal views are still available and may occasionally become well known through word of mouth and alternate distribution channels. In general, this is infeasible without the environment of the Internet, because of the existing barriers to entry in the physical world.

This elimination of traditional barriers to large-scale communication and the irrelevance of physical geography have driven a number of interesting sociological developments. For example, the open-source movement, in which programmers freely share and redistribute their work, improving others' programs and sharing them again, now has the potential to displace commercial production of software in many domains. It has become such a potent force that the richest producer of software in the modern world, and a proven monopolist, has nonetheless determined it to be a threat that must be stamped out as soon as possible.[7] While open-source software as a movement existed before the rise of easy accessibility to large-scale networking (for example, programmers traded magtapes of code in the early 1960s to the same ends), "the net" has vastly accelerated it.[8]

Similarly, mass activism on a global scale is now much easier to arrange, whereas it was previously quite difficult. Why? Because activism usually implies marginalized views by those engaging in it, and existing nonnetwork communications infrastructure allowed those with the capital investment, FCC broadcasting licenses, and distribution agreements to act as gatekeepers, locking out politically unpopular or economically unprofitable viewpoints. But using the Internet as a communications medium allows unprecedented global coordination by finessing or bypassing the previously ubiquitous chokeholds.

Yet many forces threaten this rosy view of worldwide egalitarianism. As I argued at the outset, these threats are entirely political—the technology itself at best enables them, and at worst makes them harder to carry out. Just because the technological architecture was not necessarily designed to enable these particular political policies to come to pass does not mean that they will not—only that they may take longer.

Threats

The global egalitarianism promised by the fundamental architecture of the Internet faces several major threats. Among them are those imposed by limitations on the free use of cryptography and their concomitant effect on free speech; the privacy implications of the universal panopticon enabled by ubiquitous surveillance; concentrations of power created by modern trends in intellectual-property and international copyright law; the problems posed by jurisdictional shopping; and issues of computational genetic diversity and its effect on security and choice. I will investigate each of these topics in turn.

CRYPTOGRAPHY

The ability to speak freely implies the ability to restrict the audience for one's speech. Not everyone wishes everything we say to be potentially perceivable by everyone in the world. This is why the concept of "speaking in private" exists. Yet on the global Internet, the potential for ubiquitous surveillance of all traffic makes this impossible, unless those involved use cryptography to make their communications private.

Furthermore, many interactions demand that those involved have some confidence that they are actually speaking to whom they think they are. Since all bits look alike, speaking without using cryptography invites spoofing—having a third party masquerade as one of the participants. Modern cryptographic-based authentication systems allow reasonable assurances that the person you *think* you're talking to really *is* that person, even if the communications themselves are in the clear and observable by others (this is what's meant by "signed plaintext" in cryptographic circles).

Yet the ability to use cryptography on the net has been under continuous attack for at least two decades. Governments generally have a strong incentive to spy on their citizens and those of other governments, whether for law enforcement, military empowerment, the enforcement of a repressive regime, or government-sponsored industrial espionage. And since government actors can make law, they can attempt to restrict the use of cryptography by law, and threaten fines or incarceration for violations of their policy.

EXPORT CONTROLS

In the United States, it is difficult to threaten the use of cryptography directly—or the act of transferring knowledge about how it works—because of constitutional issues. The First Amendment provides for very strict checks on fetters to dissemination of knowledge of any sort, and also makes prior restraint of publication extremely difficult, as argued in the Pentagon papers and the *Sullivan* and *Progressive* cases.[9] Instead, the U.S. Department of Commerce used a different tactic, classifying forms of cryptography that were sufficiently hard to break (*strong* cryptography) as *export controlled*, just like advanced military systems, and hence nonexportable without permission from the Commerce Department itself. Because this was implemented as an Executive Order, the International Traffic in Arms Regulation (ITAR)—later transferred to the Bureau of Export Control (BXA) and called the Export Administration Regulations (EAR)—the executive branch had wide latitude in its interpretation.[10] There was no set of rules by which one could guarantee an export license would be granted—instead, it was a matter of "submit an application, wait a random number of months or years, and perhaps be granted or denied at the end."

The usual rubric used to justify these restrictions was "to prevent other governments or terrorists from acquiring strong cryptography," but this was a transparent defense strategy—*books* about strong cryptography could not be export controlled, due to the First Amendment (after a court case in 1996, anyway)[11]—even though *floppies* of the same content *could*—and it depends on the incorrect assumption that only Americans understand strong crypto in the first place. Instead, as was often expressed by administration officials and others, the purpose was to prevent U.S. commercial manufacturers from incorporating strong crypto into their own products. After all, if a vendor had to make two versions—a weak one for export, and a strong one for domestic use—and if the market wasn't clamoring for the strongest crypto available, there were significant economic disincentives to investing the effort required to create and distribute two separate products—especially when (a) a slip-up in which version went where could subject the company to massive fines and/or seizure of the product; and (b) the two versions would not interoperate with each other anyway, unless the strong version deliberately stepped down its strength to match that of the weaker one. Hence, ITAR/EAR effectively denied *domestic, U.S. consumers* access to commercial implementations of strong cryptography for about 15 years, and this was the intent of such regulations. They were designed to protect the U.S. government from being unable to decrypt the majority of eavesdropped traffic *to and from its own citizens.*

EAR, while officially on the books, has been weakened substantially in recent years, due mostly to political pressure from those wishing to do commerce on the Internet. It had become extremely obvious to all in the field that ITAR/EAR's restrictions on key length were dangerously small—for example, a machine was built in the late 1990s that could crack one exportable key, every day, for an initial investment of $250K—and no amount of stonewalling by, for example, the FBI could any longer avert the clamor that massive frauds were about to be enabled solely because customers could not use sufficiently strong cryptography to protect themselves.[12] In addition, even the National Security Agency, the original promulgator of ITAR, had reversed itself, claiming that lack of strong crypto made U.S. infrastructure vulnerable, for example, to fraud, spoofing, and manipulation of critical networked systems such as the air-traffic control system or the electric power grid. Finally, it was generally recognized that there were plenty of ways of acquiring evidence or catching malfeasants via good old-fashioned methods (such as intercepting keystrokes of a passphrase as they are typed, or video surveillance, or the tried-and-true methods of human intelligence and good detective work), such that breaking the actual cryptography involved could be finessed. Thus, under the new rules, even strong crypto is now (usually) exportable, as long as the code implementing it is registered with the BXA at the time of export (no preapproval required). This is a requirement commonly met, among open-source software developers in the United States, by CCing the BXA on their software patches when they send mail to the relevant development mailing lists.

Even though the situation is rosier for strong crypto than it has been, EAR is still officially in place, and is still causing problems. The battle is not yet over, though its force has been blunted. For example, *Bernstein v. United States* is *still* challenging the constitutionality of ITAR/EAR's export restrictions; this case was originally brought in 1993. Despite a series of delaying tactics by the U.S. government (and a series of court defeats for it during the various steps of the suit), the case continues to drag on, and export restrictions for cryptography could be brought back in full force via the stroke of a pen.

Adding more aggravation to this issue, there has been a rise in calls to try again to restrict strong crypto in the wake of the attacks of September 11, 2001 (most recently by Louis Freeh, former head of the FBI). A massive increase in surveillance and accompanying decreases in Constitutional protections against improper search, surveillance, and detention have been facilitated by the USA PATRIOT Act. Nonetheless, it appears reasonably certain that the strong-crypto genie has been permanently released from its bottle.

COPYRIGHT AND THE NEW THREATS TO CRYPTO

In the last few decades, there has been a dramatic shift in power from the *author* of a piece of intellectual property (a human being) to its *owner* (typically a corporation, and, in the case of music and video, often a large, multinational corporation). Comparatively few works these days are copyrighted by individuals, with the exception perhaps of the billions of electronic-mail messages generated yearly—the automatic copyright upon creation that applies to fixing almost anything in tangible form means that all of these messages are, like it or not, copyrighted. But the economic value of these individual creators is typically very low, each taken individually. Further, each is by definition decentralized, making the political power that they can bring to bear negligible compared to the giant corporate interests that own the copyrights on virtually all other intellectual outputs. Individuals, even small groups of individuals, do not have the resources to pursue copyright-infringement cases, nor can they effectively lobby Congress. But large corporations are *designed* for these tasks.

The rise of giant corporate interests in copyright and its use as a tool of social control thus means that the latest threat to the ability of everyone to keep secrets has, surprisingly, come from the publishing industry. Very strong interests, such as the Recording Industry Association of America (RIAA), the Motion Picture Association of America (MPAA), and corporate "content" giants such as Disney, pressured Congress in passing the Digital Millennium Copyright Act (DMCA), ostensibly to protect their copyrighted content from trespass. This is a deeply flawed law, which has received enormous—but belated— coverage because of the degree to which it tries to bend copyright law to serve the will of a few large special interests.

In the United States, there is no such concept as a "creator's moral rights," unlike in Europe and many other places. This means that a creator of a work, once that work has entered the public domain, has no say in its use. Instead, copyright is granted for a (theoretically) limited term, during which the owner of the work has great power to grant or refrain from granting rights to use the work. The last several decades, however, have seen a continuous expansion of both the scope of what can be copyrighted (ship hull designs, for example, were but one part of the DMCA,[13] and many other types of works have been ruled copyrightable in recent decades) and of the terms available to copyright. When the Copyright Act was first enacted in 1790, the term was 14 years. However, the term now is typically on the order of 90 to 125 years, depending on whether the owner is a human or a corporation, and has been lengthening by 20 years every 20 years—just fast enough, as many have quipped, to guarantee Disney that The the Mouse never, ever enters the public domain. Indeed, thanks to lengthening copyright and to *the retroactive extension of copyright to certain previously public-domain works,*[14] *nothing created in the twentieth century* has yet entered the public domain. This exacts an enormous cost to public life. Consider, for example, that Disney's own empire was built on works that had entered the public domain when Disney was founded. Yet the increasing concentration of power among the major copyright interests, and consequently Congressional changes to copyright law, have fundamentally tilted what was formerly a more even balance of rights between creators and those who might eventually use their work unfettered. The balance has now swung so far that recent analyses have indicated that the depreciated "value" of a given copyright now assigns 99.8% of *all* the value it will ever have to the owner, and 0.2% to anyone who may ever be able to use that content[15]—almost a century and a half after it was created.

This has led to some unfortunate tragedies of the commons, as well. For example, most early films are copyrighted. Yet they are so old that no one knows who owns those copyrights. Thus, their copyright cannot be cleared, and the films cannot be reproduced. Since they can't be reproduced, even to save them from deterioration—much less to accrue some economic profit that might motivate their restoration and reproduction—almost all early films have simply rotted in their cases, never to be seen again. We have lost an irreplaceable history of how modern film came to be, simply because their copyrights lasted too long. Surely this is not the state of affairs envisioned by the Founders when they created copyrights. (Note once again, of course, that I'm being U.S.-centric in talking about the authors of the U.S. Constitution. But unfortunately, this state of affairs is becoming less and less confined to the United States, as the United States pushes its intellectual-property mania on the rest of the world through venue shopping, WIPO [World Intellectual Property Organization], and not-too-subtle attempts to strong-arm other governments into adopting laws similar to the DMCA.)

But it is not the sheer, unprecedented bloating of the rights granted to owners, versus the rights granted to the commonwealth that concerns us here—although it is a very serious problem in its own right. Instead, it is the culture of control—and decades of always getting their own way—that has emboldened the major copyright owners. Since modern politics demands access to mass media, the major mass-media holders can exert tremendous control over elected officials, and this, in addition to good old-fashioned lobbying and campaign contributions, is in part why Congress has been so willing to grant laws further enhancing their power. But the latest example of such legislation, the DMCA, grants this power in a totally unprecedented fashion.

Major content producers now distribute a great deal of their content in digital form. The very ease with which this content may be copied has alarmed them—for example, no longer is it the case that photocopying an entire book is more trouble than simply buying it (for low-value paperbacks, at least). Various publishers have attempted to distribute content in ways that restrict what their consumers may do with it, but these attempts have typically met with market resistance—since they made the product harder to use—and were often circumvented. Worse, barring so-called "trusted hardware" and a way of enforcing its use, anyone who could circumvent whatever copy protection existed on the product could then redistribute it to the entire world: This has been known as "break-once, read-anywhere." A continuous, technologically driven arms race has resulted, with most publishers until recently realizing that the best they could do was to deter only casual copying, while simultaneously alienating their best customers.

The passage of the DMCA changed all that.

The DMCA, for the very first time, *criminalized designing or building a device that might circumvent copy control*, even if *no actual infringement takes place*. Thus, merely telling someone how to circumvent a copy control, or building a device that could do so, is suddenly a criminal (not civil!) offense, with potentially long jail terms and very high fines (five years and half a million dollars, per violation!). With this stroke, the arms race was over—anyone who dared to break any protection scheme, no matter how flawed, simplistic, or onerous, could simply be locked up. Further, since this is a criminal offense, the U.S. Department of Justice could be prevailed upon to spend its own money and time pursuing the conviction, freeing content producers from the pesky (and politically embarrassing) expense of suing their own customers.

The DMCA had immediate effects even in academia. There was a well-publicized case, for example, when Princeton professor Ed Felton, and the entire Usenix conference committee, were threatened with a lawsuit should he present a paper detailing how he has broken the encryption on a trial-balloon copy-protection system—*even though the creators of that system had publicly solicited such efforts!*[16] Indeed, Felton has been quoted as advising his graduate students that, because of the risk of prosecution under the DMCA, those who are interested in studying computer security (which often involves breaking systems that can protect copyrighted content, thus determining how such systems might be improved) should either change fields or pursue their studies out of the United States. Some non-U.S. security researchers have declined to attend U.S. conferences for fear of arrest, and their fears appear well justified—a Russian programmer was arrested on U.S. soil for violating the U.S. DMCA because he described the creation,[17] while he was in Russia, of a program that was completely legal in Russia and could be used to back up an electronic book in case its original media were lost. This arrest led to Russia's issuing a travel advisory warning its citizens against travel to the United States[18]—a curious and ironic state of affairs in a land once known as the land of the free.

There are some curious carve-outs in the DMCA, but they are insufficient. For example, security researchers are explicitly exempted—but this did not save Felton. Also, the preservation of copyrighted content by libraries is allowed—but the act of breaking the encryption to use the content on whatever machinery might be "modern" at the time is still illegal. Thus, fifty years from now, when current DVD players are all obsolete and gone, a library may be in the situation of having a DVD that it is allowed to show but be prohibited from building a DVD-player emulator to show it with.

The DMCA is a manifestly unfair law. It prosecutes inventors, rather than infringers. Furthermore, by criminalizing *any* unauthorized use, it perverts the original meaning of the copyright act. Copyright explicitly states that not all uses are "authorized"—some are considered *fair use* and may be indulged in without obtaining prior permission from the copyright holder. These include certain scholarly uses and quoting of small portions in, for instance, critical reviews. However, by making it impossible to *obtain* any bits of the work without using a mechanism controlled by the content's owner, fair use is thwarted. For example, timeshifting a broadcast, by recording it on videotape and watching it later, was explicitly authorized as fair use by the U.S. Supreme Court in the Betamax decision, when major movie studios were trying instead to kill the entire VCR industry using copyright law. The shortsightedness of this attempt is obvious, of course, now that the industry derives so much of its revenue from videotape rental (and, these days, from DVD rental), but they had no collective imagination on the issue and never dreamed that they might be able to change their business models slightly to capitalize on a new invention. Such shortsightedness has not changed since the days of piano rolls, but this has not stopped them from trying. What else might we expect from an industry that apparently treats all of its best customers as criminals? Yet the content industry is currently pushing for a "broadcast bit" that, when set, will prevent modern hardware from recording any show that is broadcast with this bit set. They have no incentive—and no regulation—not to leave this bit set all the time, hence disabling recording off the air completely. This clear violation of both the spirit and the law of the Betamax decision is nonetheless the current trend—and the DMCA allows them to enforce it, and any number of other violations of both law and common sense, by imposing criminal penalties on anyone who would circumvent it.

Further, many of the technological controls now imposed on media take no account of the fact that—in theory, anyway—*works eventually enter the public domain.* For example, if it has been properly designed according to the specifications of the content industry, a DVD player will refuse to disgorge the unencrypted bits of a DVD under any circumstances. However, at *some* point, any given DVD must become a part of the public domain, simply because it is too old. But there is no way to tell the DVD player that two hundred years have passed and that it is time to let the consumer at the data. Further, the very act of *creating* a DVD player that does this—even if applied to a DVD that has entered the public domain—is a criminal act, because it *could* be used on a DVD that is not yet old enough and hence is still copyrighted. Thus, the DMCA's punishment of the inventor, not the infringer, completely defeats attempts at fair use, and should fail Constitutional muster because of this. But until the Supreme Court rules on it, the DMCA continues to damage the commons, by interfering with legitimate research and with legitimate unauthorized ("fair") use, and by enabling an absolute control that, as a matter of law, was intended to be a limited-time compromise.

THE EMPIRE OF U.S. POLICIES

The focus on the United States in the previous sections should not lull those in other countries into a false sense of security. Many other governments worldwide are following the U.S. lead in these areas, for several reasons. The most obvious, of course, is that many countries are signatories to treaties of the WIPO, as well as the World Trade Organization (WTO), and many have attempted to "harmonize" their laws with those of WIPO. Indeed, many of the most egregious recent changes to U.S. copyright law came in the guise of this harmonization; however, if one examines them closely, one finds that the United States seems to only attempt harmonization for some of WIPO's provisions, while ignoring others.

However, this is far from the only factor at work. During the height of the ITAR/EAR export-control regime, the United States had a so-called "crypto ambassador," David Aaron, whose admitted purpose was to cajole or threaten other nations into going along with U.S. ideas on export control. The Electronic Privacy Information Center (EPIC) and others attempted, mostly without success, to use the Freedom of Information Act to obtain his travel records in order to discover which countries were having the most pressure applied to them;[19] the Administration was notoriously unforthcoming about his activities.

Further, there is a certain quid pro quo when it comes to international surveillance. For example, while it was (at least before the PATRIOT Act) theoretically illegal for entities such as the Central Intelligence Agency or the National Security Agency (NSA) to spy on U.S. citizens on U.S. soil, they were free to do so against foreign nationals. Similarly, U.K. intelligence—Government Communications Headquarters (GCHQ)—was prohibited from spying on its own citizens. Yet, as confirmed by recent embarrassing revelations about the worldwide Echelon surveillance program, it was apparently a matter of common policy that the U.S. NSA would spy on U.K. citizens, and then hand over the data (in some cases) to the U.K. GCHQ—and the British would likewise return the favor.[20] Thus, while domestic surveillance by such entities was theoretically constrained, the actuality was quite different—they had gamed the system of U.S. law, such that ubiquitous surveillance of their own citizens was nonetheless the order of the day.

These sorts of reciprocal arrangements, whether via coercion or mutualism, have thus helped to ensure that there are very few places on Earth to hide if one would like to escape either ubiquitous surveillance or power-mad control grabs by the large copyright interests.

THE UNIVERSAL PANOPTICON

Surveillance has become an increasing part of daily life. While I have referred in various ways to many of these issues, let us now delve a little deeper. I will avoid the obvious single-issue examples (such as the incredible rise of security videotaping systems in the United States, the United Kingdom, and elsewhere) and deal with more systemic trends, especially as they relate to the global Internet.

One of the major reasons why surveillance is so easy to carry out on the net, of course, is the lack of deployed cryptography of *any* sort—strong or not. In large part, this is because the United States was quite successful in its export-control policy by having it in place at a critical time. New technologies often have a sharp upswing in their usage, and this point is commonly called "the knee in the curve." Changes made before this knee are far easier to spread widely, because relatively fewer devices are in use before the knee than after it. Hence, by denying the easy deployment of widespread cryptography, especially strong cryptography, early in the knee of Internet adoption, the thousand-fold expansion of the net that took place in the 1990s did so virtually without any encryption whatsoever. And now that all of this infrastructure is in place, adding crypto is difficult. Had crypto been in place at the beginning, on the other hand, it would be ubiquitous now. Virtually the only common use of cryptography on the network is in SSL-secured web transactions, and virtually all of *those* are to protect a user's credit-card number—itself a trivial secret unworthy of such strong protection. (This is true both because its security in the real world of carbons, waiters, and point-of-sale terminals is much lower, and because many merchants obtain the number via a strong-crypto connection, and then proceed to *store* that number on vulnerable systems where insiders or Internet-based crackers may easily obtain the cleartext information directly from their disks.)

This lack of crypto for everyday use—such as obscuring *all* web page fetches, or routinely encrypting *all* email traffic—makes using any crypto very difficult because of the operational issues of getting to critical mass. Just as having the only telephone isn't very useful, not being able to secure one's connections with the majority of one's correspondents makes it less likely that one will secure *any* of them. Furthermore, it makes those connections that *are* protected extremely vulnerable to traffic analysis—if crypto is very rare, then any encrypted link that one finds via routine surveillance is probably worth noticing. Even if the conversation itself remains forever secure, simply knowing *who* is using crypto is quite valuable—such people may be labeled potential troublemakers (or, these days, potential terrorists), and their very use of cryptographic envelopes around their otherwise plainly readable Internet postcards could subject them to more-intrusive observation or even to outright interrogation. While this is becoming more and more likely in the United States due to the fallout from 9/11, it has already been a fact of life for years under other, more repressive, governments.

Commercial interests also enable universal surveillance. The lure of data mining is ever present, and nearly every commercial entity's marketing department would like nothing better than to know *everything* about every customer, potential customer, and competitor. From supermarket loyalty cards to "Know Your Customer" efforts at banks to location-based SRS spam via tracked cell phones, there is unrelenting pressure to collect, store, and process every possible bit of information about everyone who might spend money. The constant, giant sucking sound of so many databases hoovering up everyone's personal information only makes such extensive data mining a more obvious target for government intervention and civil subpoenas.

The threat of subpoenas is a serious one. The *Wall Street Journal* once reported, for example, that Federal Express gets several hundred subpoenas *a day* for its shipping records.[21] Why? Because tobacco companies, in the midst of potentially ruinous litigation, were sniffing around to see which of their researchers might be leaking information to reporters and prosecuting attorneys. As another example, take the sort of tracking commonly employed by so-called Intelligent Traffic Systems, exemplified by EZ-PASS and similar electronic toll-collection systems. While it would have been possible (and, actually, easier) to design the system to function with transponders that worked like DC Metro passes (e.g., electronic money), most such systems instead work like a telephone system—they keep track of who passes each tollbooth, and when, and then send a bill at the end of the month. And, while it was obvious from the start to me and to many others in the field that this was a disaster waiting to happen, it wasn't until the first of a rapidly growing spate of divorce-court lawsuits that the general public realized that being able to have a third party know exactly where and when you might have gone somewhere in your car might be a problem.

Worse, there are unholy combinations waiting to spring out at us. Take the telephone 911 emergency system, for example. Recent Federal Communications Commission policy decisions have required the creation of the E911 system, by which cellular phones may be tracked to within fifty meters or better, ostensibly to enable the timely arrival of emergency personnel when needed. While a good idea in theory, details of its implementation are extremely troubling. For example, the requests for proposals have typically made no nod to privacy at all, and do not require, for example, that the system *only* report such high-precision accuracy when requested by the user. Absent such mechanisms (such as a phone that *cannot* be accurately tracked unless the user tells the phone to do so), we have a rapidly growing infrastructure that is ripe for abuse by a large variety of actors. Government surveillance of citizens' locations to such a high precision could easily be interpreted as interfering with their right of free assembly—for wouldn't knowing everyone who was at some particular meeting deemed "subversive" be extremely interesting to a government increasingly interested in such control? (Such speculations are hardly outlandish when one considers both passive infiltration and active disruption of civil-rights groups in the 1960s by the illegal actions of undercover FBI agents.) And even if one assumes that the U.S. government would never again stoop to such tactics, consider that the United States is the world leader in telephone-equipment manufacture. Could we in good conscience assume that such technology would never be exported to a more repressive regime?

But it need not take widespread government misbehavior for E911 to be a serious threat to personal privacy. Consider how many businesses would like nothing better than to know, with a high degree of accuracy, if a potential customer is mere steps from their door. Even if they couldn't call the customer at that moment, or send a text message to the customer's phone, they could always accumulate the information and either use it to send all sorts of customized solicitations to them, or sell that information to the highest bidder, who might do anything it likes with such information. And since such information is deemed "transactional," it is subject to much lower protection (often zero) preventing its misuse by anyone who obtains it. If you think email spam is a problem now, wait until cell phone location–based spam starts happening for real.

INTELLECTUAL PROPERTY AND THE
DISASTER OF THE DOMAIN NAME SYSTEM

I have covered many of the threats posed by modern power grabs in the intellectual property arena already. And while the DMCA and the "infinite Mickey" are themselves potent and serious threats, there are others that also threaten both the global Internet and the social commons more generally.

Take, for example, the Domain Name System (DNS).[22] This is the system that maps human-comprehensible machine names on the Internet to router-comprehensible addresses in the Internet Protocol (IP). There is, in general, no particular reason why the system must operate in a mode of scarcity—for example, it tries to guarantee a uniqueness of naming that is unrealistic in the real world and never seen there. But as a happenstance of history, it was started amongst people who weren't, themselves, power hungry, and who thus weren't thinking about potential politically motivated power grabs. This left a vacuum, into which subsequent bungling—such as the creation of the Internet Corporation for Assigned Names and Numbers (ICANN) and the Commerce Department's mishandling of authority over the system[23]—has sucked in a variety of shortsighted players and policies, yielding a system that has a single, highly coveted root, and domain names that are essentially short words in a global namespace. There are other ways in which this issue could have been handled, but for the foreseeable future, we are stuck with it.

Why is the current system so bad? Because it enables stockpiling and abuse of the "good" names at everyone's expense. In the DNS, there can be only one obvious "Acme," even though there may be ten thousand Acme Hardware stores scattered around. Furthermore, the tree-based allocation of names—and, worse, the tree-based allocation of domain servers—means that the DNS serves as one of the Internet's only true concentrations of power. There is little structural redundancy in the design of the DNS—which means that he who controls the root, rules. (This is *not* true at the level with which packets get routed from one machine to another—no single entity could effectively control the entire network—and if people could easily remember 32-bit numbers or the DNS had been designed differently, we would not have the DNS problem, either.) Because this artificially-produced chokepoint exists, actors with a natural desire for absolute control have moved in and attempted to extract monopoly rents—not to mention the perpetuation of their own control—on various subparts of the DNS and on its root as a whole. Neither ICANN nor Network Solutions has any incentive to give up any of the power that they were handed, for free, by the U.S. Commerce Department, and neither organization has a reputation of being effective, fair, or desirable.[24]

Furthermore, because the current system produces a false environment of scarcity, it encourages trademark fights and other litigious attempts at control of the namespace. Thus, we not only have fights over who has the "right" to particular names (no matter that many legitimate entities may share the same name—and that, before the DNS, trademark law applied to *particular geographic regions* and *particular industry segments* in an attempt to disambiguate some of the inevitable collisions), but we also have fights over names which are clearly designed to enable speech and which are instead falsely accused of generating "confusion" (the threat for which trademarks are the supposed solution). Hence, the Foo Corporation can be reliably expected to sue the owner of the Foo-Sucks domain, no matter how unsupported by case law, common sense, or the First Amendment. And because both ICANN and trademark law strongly favor the party with the deeper pockets, such suits often exercise a chilling effect on those who would criticize richer opponents.

VENUE SHOPPING

While the Internet promises to obliterate accidents of geography, it also enables a curious, pathological flip side, namely venue shopping. Legal thought recognizes a concept known as "personal jurisdiction," which, briefly stated, says that if one does business in Montana, and has no contact with someone in, say, Utah, the entity in Utah cannot sue in Utah—no relationship has been established with the entity from Utah.

The Internet turns this on its head. What, exactly, is the jurisdiction for a company based in California that sells goods to an individual in Massachusetts and uses an intermediate server in Texas? Does it matter whether the packets went through a router in Ohio? What if the most efficient way to send a packet happens to be via another country—does international law now apply? How about if the two parties involved happen to use an Internet service provider (ISP) that routes through Havenco, off the coast of the United Kingdom—does the International Law of the Sea now apply?

Unfortunately, the confusion that this scenario engenders presents two serious problems. The first typically plays out in some individual being sued in a state he has never set foot in, simply because some, possibly trivial, part of some transaction he was involved in happens to pass through that state.

The second is even more serious—it concerns the liabilities of someone who makes any content available in one jurisdiction that might be actionable in another, even if the person making the content available has no personal knowledge that the information is going somewhere it shouldn't, or even any effective way to stop it. This latter case was exemplified by a couple in California who made available imagery that was deemed obscene in Tennessee. Even though they had no effective way to know that someone from Tennessee might view it (for example, if someone fetches the content from AOL, there is no way to know where the viewer resides—only where the AOL proxy server was), they were nonetheless extradited from California, sued, and imprisoned in Tennessee.[25]

This awful outcome means that what is safe to put on the Internet devolves to what is safe *everywhere,* a sort of lowest-common-denominator race to the bottom that threatens to make only the most noncontroversial content available at all—or to chill a Constitutionally guaranteed right to the point where it is nonexistent. Who, in reality, would want to risk prosecution under "community standards" by a community one has never set foot in?

GENETIC DIVERSITY

The final problem I will address is one of genetic diversity. By analogy with its biological meaning, I will investigate both corporate control of the majority of communications in the world, and the computational effects of the concentration of power in the operating-system and applications market.

Over the last several decades, there has been an enormous consolidation of the worldwide media market, made possible by globalization, economies of scale, and modern communications systems. Thus, we have nearly all audio recordings produced by only five companies worldwide, and a similar situation exists in movie production. Three companies—Clear Channel, Emmis, and Infinity Broadcasting—now own over 90 percent of all commercial radio stations in the United States—a startlingly recent development, taking place almost completely in the 1990s. And, due to changes in FCC policy regarding cross-ownership rules (brought about by the laissez-faire attitude of recent Commissioners and the inescapable conclusion that there just aren't that many actually independent players in the marketplace any more), one corporation can now own several television and radio stations in any given city, *and* several of its major newspapers as well. The resulting homogenization of opinion—not to mention sheer brute force in control of the communication channels people need not only to live, but even to know anything about those they are expected to elect—is extremely dangerous to democratic discourse.

Similarly, the vast majority of desktop software now used worldwide is made by one company—Microsoft. This single-source provider means that architectural failures in design are replicated across hundreds of millions of machines, without variation. (It is not my intention to single out Microsoft per se—but since it controls the vast majority of desktop systems, *any* argument about genetic diversity must, unavoidably, do so.) And, just as even a mild blight can cause a famine if everyone plants the same strain of wheat, we now see viruses and other security failures that can affect tens of millions of machines overnight. Indeed, recent research indicates that a patient, careful, but not even particularly bright programmer could create a fast-propagating *flash worm* that, with a few weeks of careful computation up front, could own nearly every machine on the Internet in *seconds*[26]—far faster than human response could ever possibly handle.

Because of the speed and reach of current viruses and theorized versions of flash worms, the abysmal track record of Microsoft in fielding secure systems, and the ubiquitous deployment of these systems, we must take such a threat very seriously indeed. Given the world's dependence upon desktop computing, such attacks could do enormous damage even if major infrastructural systems (such as electric power grids) were completely unaffected. Thus, this lack of genetic diversity is a global security problem, and leads directly to threats of a global economic problem as well.

This similarity of implementation also leads to cognitive blinders—for the vast majority of people on the planet, what a computer *is* means precisely what a Microsoft operating system makes a computer appear to be: How the user interface works, whether it uses a desktop metaphor at all, whether computers "just crash all the time anyway," and so forth. Thus, they mistake a specific implementation for the general, and, lacking any counterexamples, simply assume that this is the nature of computation by definition. This is a dangerous situation to be in, when one considers its impact on worldwide creativity and technological advancement. This homogeneity of the user experience thus acts to suppress radical views of how people and computers might meaningfully interact.

The State of the World, and What We Can Do

I have thus laid out a situation of:

Fear—and the resulting crypto restrictions and ubiquitous surveillance;

Greed—and the copyright power grabs that result; and

Monopoly—leading to a computational monoculture that threatens worldwide stability.

The situation for the global commons is not good. Can we do anything about it? In the following sections, I point out some ways to proceed. But be warned—the prognosis is not hopeful.

WHY TECHNOLOGY IS ONLY A PARTIAL SOLUTION

The problems discussed so far are primarily political ones. Yet sometimes technology can trump politics. For example, it became easier not to keep human slaves once their mechanical analogs were cheap enough, and there can be little argument that public policy and politics would be very different if our technological infrastructure were also very different. Without modern technologies of mass communication, for example, political campaigns would not operate in the way they do. Why, then, is it unlikely that a purely technological fix can be applied to these problems?

First, good technology does not always win. It is well known that the company with the better marketing, rather than the better product, often wins in the end. Further, in technology-intensive arenas, there is often the problem of technological lock-in: Once enough people do something in one particular way, any competing approach, no matter how good, must first climb two hills. One hill is that of an entrenched user base. These users might have to be retrained or worse, might have to frame the entire problem in a different way—and conceptualizing a solution differently is often very hard, no matter how valuable the change of viewpoint may eventually be. The second hill is the problem of interoperability—if some technological artifact is incompatible with its predecessor, it is hard to adopt it without retooling everyone. This is possible in some industries, where the devices one company uses can be mostly independently designed from those of another. But communications-intensive industries, and things like the Internet itself, tend to enforce a uniformity of protocols so that everyone can talk to everyone else and read everyone else's files. Even if a far better telephone were invented tomorrow, it might be a very long time indeed before it was adopted if it required throwing away the existing investment in telephones first.

Second, law can force the outcome, no matter what the technology. The starkest examples in the previous discussion concern crypto export controls and the DMCA. Both of these are attempts to enforce—by the raw power of a sovereign state—what one may and may not do with a computer, regardless of how clever one may be with its technology. Such fiats are extremely difficult to overturn technologically; historically, the best one might expect is an arms race, with the technologists on one side attempting to invent technologies that sidestep any particular set of laws, and the legislature on the other passing increasingly onerous laws in an attempt to contain the damage. This is not a situation we should be encouraging.

Yet sometimes technology can help. For example, the long history of open-source software (going back to the very start of computing itself) has in the last few years become a much more visible force, thanks in large part to the power of the Internet and the Web in accelerating communication, and thanks to political activism by thousands of programmers against the sorts of legislative and commercial controls imposed by current governments and monopoly software vendors. The results are beginning to threaten even entrenched, government-declared monopolies such as Microsoft, which has been growing increasingly strident in its attempts to squelch free operating systems such as Linux—and leading to wry commentaries such as this, from science-fiction author Bruce Sterling, during his keynote address to the "Computers, Freedom, and Privacy" conference in April 2002: "The supposed explosion of digital creativity on a million websites and a thousand channels. . . .Well, come 2002, it boils down to 95 percent market share by a single ruthless feudal empire! . . . A thing like Linux, . . . that isn't a competitive free-market innovation, it's a slave revolt!"

Decentralized computing also promises at least the hope of an end run around some of the more draconian attempts at centralized control. Whatever one might think of the dubious legalities of using vast clouds of machines to evade copyright restrictions, their use in evading censorship by repressive governments—by making it hard to get rid of information forever, and by making it easy to hide details of authorship—surely deserves attention. Over time, rarely is information generally considered better locked up than open, and the U.S. First Amendment also argues strenuously that one must think very hard before attempting to restrict almost any sort

of expression. Thus, efforts to guarantee the permanent, uncensorable availability of *all* viewpoints—no matter how potentially offensive to a particular
individual or government—are likely to be seen through the lens of history as
the right idea.

One particular example of technological assistance against repressive
regimes concerns recent work using data-intensive analysis of victims of
state-sponsored violence. A recent case was used in testimony at The Hague
against Slobodan Milosevic, demonstrating that Kosovo refugee flows were
strongly correlated with internal police violence and uncorrelated with NATO
bombing.[27] While these sorts of technological success stories are important
for demonstrating that *some* political problems are at least partially repara-
ble via the use of technology (if only for eventual use in legal proceedings),
its use does not help most of the political problems mentioned above.

POLITICAL ACTIVISM

The Internet has a long history of social and political activism, enabling as it
does minority speakers and allowing coordination across long distances with
minimal resources. In the United States, some of the most influential players
in this field include organizations such as the Electronic Frontier Foundation
(EFF), the Electronic Privacy Information Center (EPIC), the Center for
Democracy and Technology (CDT), and the American Civil Liberties Union
(ACLU).[28] Each of these organizations has its own policy bent and mode of
operation (inside the Washington, D.C. Beltway versus outside, for example);
those interested in pursuing political solutions via alliances with these
organizations are urged to investigate their web presence and make contact
with them directly.

Direct action in the courts has been threatened for many of the problems
mentioned here, such as crypto export restrictions, but has been surprisingly
thin on the ground. In the export regime in particular, the Federal government was particularly unwilling to actually see any case come to trial, and it
was popularly believed that this was because the government would have had
such an uphill battle on First Amendment grounds. ITAR/EAR were much
more effective when the rules they promulgated could be hidden behind
unauditable and anonymous review committees; when threatened with the
possibility of public exposure and defeat, the entire export-control mechanism instead ran out of steam—but it is not yet officially dead. While not a
strategy that will work for everything (the DMCA, for example, has had a

depressing number of courtroom victories for the government side), litigation is nonetheless potentially effective for what is, after all, a problem created by law in the first place.

Unfortunately, one of the reasons for the ascendancy of legislative actions that have favored the entrenched copyright interests and those most interested in surveillance is that civil libertarians—and particularly technologists—have not been nearly so effective at lobbying Congress. This root problem, while fundamentally important, requires political organization rarely seen outside of that funded by corporate interests with deep pockets. It is possible that the more outrageous fallout from laws such as the DMCA may finally provoke this kind of reaction; for example, we are already seeing protests from various parts of the electronics industry, which fears that overzealous copy controls may damage the market for their products. It remains to be seen whether this will serve as effective motivation for the sort of political organization that must be mustered to mount an effective counter-lobbying effort.

SOCIAL ENGINEERING

There are a number of Internet-based attempts to engineer a new sociology that might help ameliorate some of these problems. For example, the Creative Commons initiative is attempting to produce an easy-to-use compromise that allows people to easily (and without paying for lots of attorney time) specify that they would like to voluntarily give up some rights to their creations—thus helping the commons[29]—without necessarily putting their works entirely into the public domain. Similarly, the EFF's Open Audio initiative seeks to make it easy to release music with less-restrictive copyright restrictions than is typical in the industry,[30] and thus to lead by example in demonstrating that absolute control over all published music is not necessarily a good long-term strategy, either from the viewpoint of the commons or from the viewpoint of business models.

The Chilling Effects Clearinghouse, by contrast, focuses on documenting examples of people whose free expression has been chilled by threats of lawsuits, typically from corporations intent on denying appropriate venues for critical speech (e.g., "Foo-Sucks" websites).[31] By making available hundreds of examples of threatening letters—and by providing both easy-to-understand knowledge of the relevant laws, and working strategies for countering such nasty grams with a minimum of time and money—the site hopes to make such typically-unfounded threats less likely to succeed and thus less likely to be launched in the future.

Finally, of course, educating those who are not constantly in the heart of these controversies is of paramount importance.

The Internet promises a vast commons of expression and utility, but the politics of greed and fear have worked against these aims. While the situation is not hopeless, current political realities are difficult to escape, and will require both constant vigilance and the application of tremendous resources—technical, political, and economic—if the full potential of the Internet is to be globally realized for *all* people, and not just for a privileged and powerful few.

NOTES

1 Lenny Foner, "Political Artifacts and Personal Privacy: The Yenta Multi-Agent Distributed Matchmaking System," Ph.D. diss. MIT Media Lab, 1999; available at http://foner.www.media.mit.edu/people/foner/PhD-Thesis/Dissertation/; for additional information and other papers, see http://foner.media.mit.edu/people/foner/yenta-brief.html.

2 See *Eldred et al. v. Ashcroft*, 537 U.S. 2003, http://www.supremecourtus.gov/opinions/02pdf/01-618.pdf or http://supct.law.cornell.edu/supct/html/01-618.ZS.html; see the *Digital Millennium Copyright Act of 1998*, http://www.loc.gov/copyright/legislation/dmca.pdf.

3 Jeffrey Davis, "Vint Cerf Is Taking the Web into Outer Space—Reserve Your .mars Address Now," *Wired Magazine* 8, 1 (January 2000).

4 Kevin Werbach, "Spectrum of the World Unite," http://www.thefeature.com/index.jsp?url=article.jsp?pageid13539.

5 Mark Horton, "Standard for Interchange of USENET Messages," RFC1036, http://www.faqs.org.rfcs/rfc1036.html; www.platopeople.com; J. Oikarinen, "Internet Relay Chat Protocol," RFC1459, http://www.faqs.org/rfcs/rfc1459.html; Pavel Curtis, "Mudding: Social Phenomena in Text-Based Virtual Realities," *Proceedings of DIAC*, Berkeley, Calif., 1992.

6 Tim Berners-Lee, "Hypertext Transfer Protocol—HTTP/1.0," RFC1945, http://www.faqs.org/rfcs/rfc1945.html.

7 See *United States of America v. Microsoft Corporation*, Final Judgment, Civil Actions 98-1233 (TPJ), U.S. District Court for the District of Columbia, June 2000, http://usvms.gpo.gov/ms-final2.html; "The Halloween Documents," October 1998, http://opensource.org/halloween/.

8 Scholarly Societies Project, University of Waterloo Library, http://www.scholarly-societies.org/1960_1969.html. (The Digital Equipment Corporation Users Society formed in March 1961 and members immediately began swapping software on magnetic tapes through the mail.)

9 See "The Pentagon Papers Case," *Issues of Democracy (the Electronic Journal of the U.S. Information Agency)* 2, 1 (1997); *New York Times Co. v. Sullivan*, 376 U.S. 254 (1964); *United States of America v. Progressive, Inc., Erwin Knoll, Samuel Day, Jr., and Howard Morland*, 467 F. Supp. 990 (1979).

10 "International Traffic in Arms Regulations," *58 Federal Register 39, 280* (1993) (to be codified at 22 C.F.R. 120–128, 130); Export Administration Regulations, 15 C.F.R. 730–774; see also http://w2.accesss.gpo.gov/bis/ear/ear_data.html.

11 *Daniel J. Bernstein v. United States Department of State, 1996.* See also http://cr.yp.to/export/1996/1206-order.txt; http://www.eff.org/Privacy/ITAR_export/Karn_Sheier _export_case/floppy-2nd.response.

12 Electronic Frontier Foundation, *Cracking DES: Secrets of Encryption Research, Wiretap Politics, & Chip Design—How Federal Agencies Subvert Privacy*, O'Reilly & Associates, May 1998; http://www.eff.org/Privacy/Crypto_misc/DESCracker/HTML/19980716_eff_des_faq.html, http://jya.com/hir-hear.htm, and http://www.computerprivacy.org/archive/03171998-4.shtml.

13 *The Digital Millennium Copyright Act of 1998*, HR 2281, Public law 105-304, http://www.loc.gov/copyright/legislation/dmca.pdf.

14 *The Sonny Bono Copyright Term Extension Act*, S 505, Public law 105-298, 105th Cong., 2d sess. (January 27, 1998); see also http://www.loc.gov/copyright/legislation/s505.pdf.

15 http://cyberlaw.stanford.edu/lessig/blog/archives/2002_10.shtml#000531 and of Lessig's Supreme Court brief in *Eldred v. Ashcroft*, 6 note 6, http://eon.law.harvard.edu/openlaw/eldredvashcroft/supct/amici/economists.pdf.

16 http://www.eff.org/Legal/Cases/Felton_v_RIAA; http://www.cs.princeton.edu/sip/sdmi/announcement.html.

17 http://www.eff.org/IP/DMCA/US-V-Elcomsoft/.

18 Jennifer Lee, "Travel Advisory for Russian Programmers," *New York Times*, http://www.nytimes.com/2001/09/10/technology/10WARN.html.

19 *Electronic Privacy Information Center v. U.S. Department of State*, C. A. No 97-1401 (D.D.C); see also http://www.epic.org/privacy/litigation.

20 Nicky Hager, "Exposing the Global Surveillance System," *Covert Action Quarterly* 59 (winter 1997); see http://mediafilter.org/caq/echelon/.

21 *Wall Street Journal*, April 11, 1995, B1.

22 P. Mockapetris, "Domain Names—Concepts and Facilities," RFC1034, November 1987, http:// www.faqs.org/rfcs/rfc1034.htm.

23 http://www.icannwatch.org.

24 Ibid.

25 *United States of America v. Robert Alan Thomas and Carleen Thomas*, 1996 Fed App. 0032P (6th Cir.), 94-6648/6649, http://www.law.emory.edu/6circuit/jan96/96a0032p.06.html.

26 http://www.silicondefense.com/flash/.

27 Jane Asher, Patrick Ball, Wendy Betts, Jane Dudokovich, and Fritz Scheuren, "Killings and Refugee Flow in Kosovo, March–June 1999," Science and Human Rights Program, American Association for the Advancement of Science, http://hrdata.aaas.org/kosovo/icty_report.pdf and http://shr.aaas.org.

28 http://www.eff.org/; http://www.epic.org/; http://www.aclu.org.

29 http://www.creativecommons.org/.

30 http://www.eff.org/IP/Open_licenses/eff_oal.html.

31 http://www.chillingeffects.org.

WHAT WE SHOULD DO AND WHAT WE SHOULD FORGET IN MEDIA STUDIES

OR, MY TV A–Z

TOBY MILLER

> *It is with fear and trembling that the author approaches the controversial subject of television.*
> —Barrett C. Kiesling, 1937

The audiovisual media are everywhere, spreading their reach even as they undergo unprecedented textual, technological, and political transformations. Meanwhile, the *study* of the media is an evolving, contested domain that crosses the humanities and social sciences. Consider television. The field of television studies encompasses production and audience ethnography, affects research, policy advocacy, political economy, cultural history, and textual analysis. It borrows from and contributes to media studies, mass communication, critical race theory, communication studies, journalism, public policy, media sociology, critical legal studies, queer theory, science and technology studies, psychology, film studies, economics, cultural studies, feminist theory, and Marxism. The intersections between these disciplines and approaches are not always easily negotiated, but that negotiation is ongoing. I wish to trace the dominant strands of the history to TV studies before distilling from it some agenda items, specifically for working on the Internet, and a TV A–Z.

"Television" existed as a material idea long before you or I did—even before "it" did. Before the emergence of television sets and services, people fantasized about the transmission of image and sound across space. Richard Whittaker Hubbell made the point by publishing a book in the 1940s entitled *4000 Years of Television*. As TV came close to realization, it attracted particularly intense critical speculation. Rudolf Arnheim's 1935 "Forecast of Television" predicted that the new device would offer viewers simultaneous global experiences, transmitting railway disasters, professorial addresses, town meetings, boxing-title fights, dance bands, carnivals, and aerial mountain views—a spectacular montage of Broadway and Vesuvius. A common vision would surpass linguistic competence and interpretation. "[T]he wide world itself enter[ing] . . . our room" via TV might even bring global peace with it, by showing spectators that "we are located as one among many."[1] But this was no naive welcome. Arnheim warned that "[t]elevision is a new, hard test of our wisdom." The emergent medium's easy access to knowledge would either enrich or impoverish its viewers, manufacturing an informed public, vibrant and active—or an indolent audience, domesticated and private.[2]

In the same year as Arnheim's paper, Hollywood offered *Murder by Television,* in which every conceivable large media corporation wants to obtain the new technology.[3] Each is confounded by its inventor, the kindly old Professor Houghland, who wishes to keep television free from capitalist despoliation. Houghland refuses to obtain a patent because he wants to cordon television off from conventional notions of property so it can become "something more than another form of entertainment." As per Arnheim's forecast, a grand demonstration of the new invention joins people across the United States "without the use of relays." The professor takes us live to Paris, London, and an unnamed Asian city. But at his moment of triumph, when TV seems set to assure "the preservation of humanity" and "make of this earth a paradise," Houghland is killed on-screen. A doctor secretly involved with "foreign governments" (a cable to him in code is signed 'J. V. S.'—anyone for Stalin?) uses his office telephone to radiate waves that merge with those from the TV to create what Bela Lugosi later informs us is "an interstellar frequency, . . . a death ray." Television is shown to incorporate the best and the worst of human thought and guile, and the mystery of the modern: Great spirals emanate periodically from the set, suggesting a trancelike condition that never quite departs the film.

Meanwhile, in the *Daily Worker* of 1930, Samuel Brody drew this divide in political-economic rather than liberal-citizenship terms. TV was one moment in the multiplicity of war-directed capitalist inventions. In the United States, its political uses would involve campaigning for elections and pacifying audiences through "the same authentic lies" as did documentary cinema and the fiction film. Conversely, the Soviet Union would deploy television to "build socialism and a better world for the laboring masses."[4]

Not long after these predictions, the Second World War halted experimental television broadcasts in Britain, Germany, and the United States. But once the war ended, television's uptake was spectacular. Over the next ten years, it spread across the United States and Europe, then into the third world, as newly free peoples emerged from colonialism and claimed TV as a rite of passage and a right to communication. By and large, the growth of television mirrored the emergence of radio. Countries with sizeable commercial radio networks developed similarly commercial TV systems (Australia and the United States stand out), and countries with large public-service radio structures brokered them into television (India and Britain, for example). The United States was unique in eschewing public television until its commercial system had matured, while Australia was unique in its spread of private and public TV from the very beginning. TV was regarded as a means to profit in the United States and, mostly, a means of civilizing the population elsewhere. Pierre Bourdieu refers to these rather graceless antinomies as "populist spontaneism and demagogic capitulation to popular tastes" versus "paternalistic-pedagogic television."[5] In state-socialist and fascist countries, such as Poland and Spain, restrictions on information were greater than those in most Western European nations, which permitted their public broadcasters relative autonomy from political oversight.

This all changed in the 1980s, when the decline of state socialism in Europe and of fascism in Latin America coincided with a deregulatory fervor that gripped public policy making in capitalist democracies and international organizations, exerting a major impact on communication infrastructures. States that had regarded TV as too influential to be left to commerce were persuaded by this new cult to sever their allegiance to public ownership in the name of efficiency, effectiveness, and freedom. Countries that already had extensive commercial networks diminished regulatory controls on private TV. At the same time, new technologies made television less easily controlled by national governments, as viewers were able to draw signals from beyond political boundaries via satellite, and to domesticate their movie tastes, thanks to video. Today, we have a worldwide system that mixes public and private, but on an unequal basis. The former increasingly scrambles for funding and legitimacy, while the latter is rampant.

Most TV has always been dedicated to entertainment, and that focus, along with the ease of use and the double pull of vision and sound, has long produced embarrassment and even shame from some viewers. Consider this Ivy League professor recalling his New Haven follies of 1953:

"In those days a Yale faculty member who owned a television set lived dangerously. In the midst of an academic community, he lived in sin. Nevertheless, in an act of defiance, we put our television set in the living room instead of the basement or the garage where most of the faculty kept theirs, and we weathered the disapprobation of colleagues who did not own or would not admit to owning this fascinating but forbidden instrument."[6]

Or this exchange in Alfred Hitchcock's *Dial M for Murder*, from 1954:

TONY: You write for the radio, don't you?
MARK: No, television; for my sins.

No wonder U.S. producer David Susskind confided to 1950s readers of *Life* magazine that he was "mad at TV because I really love it and it's lousy. It's a very beautiful woman who looks abominable."[7] If we can transcend the crass sexism of this reifying metaphor, it resonates with Arnheim, Brody, and Houghland a quarter of a century earlier, sustaining the seemingly ineradicable binary opposition of televisual uplift versus televisual degradation. Meanwhile . . . in

September 1956 many Sydney residents had their first opportunity to experience first-hand contact with the new mechanical "monster"— TV—that had for the last seven or eight years been dominating the lounges of English and American homes. Speculation on its effects had run high. On the one hand it was claimed: it would eventually destroy the human race since young couples would prefer viewing to good honest courting; children would arrive at school and either go to sleep or disgorge half-baked concepts about the Wild West and the "gals" who inspired or confused the upholders of law; it would breed a generation of youngsters with curved spines, defective eyesight, American vocabulary but no initiative; it would result in a fragmentation of life whereby contact among, and even within, families would be reduced to the barest minimum. On the other hand, supporters claimed that it would initiate a moral regeneration of the nation by enticing straying husbands home to see "Wagon Train" and "The Perry Como Show"; it would encourage dead-end kids to explore the richness of books and of life in general; and it would unite the family by offering common goals and common interests.

Television and the Australian Adolescent (the 1962 source of this quotation) finds its authors, W. J. Campbell and Rosemary Keogh, worried about the "habits of passivity" that television might induce, and the power of particular genres to "instill certain emotions, attitudes and values." The upshot of all this, they feared, might be "a generation of people who are content to be fed by others."[8]

Seventy years after Arnheim, Brody, and *Murder by Television*, with Susskind (and *Life* magazine) a bare memory and the "Australian adolescent" facing retirement, the same questions preoccupy students of television. Broadly speaking, two critical tendencies predominate. One examines audiences; the other addresses programming. Horace Newcomb glosses these trends as a concentration on "the factors that go into [television's] making, distribution, and reception, . . . the forms it takes[,] and the appeals and threats it presents to potential viewers and users."[9]

What is the source of this focus on TV's social impact? In the nineteenth century, it was taken as read that audiences were active, given their unruly and overtly engaged conduct at cultural events. But the emergence of public education in the West, which took as its project empowering and hence disciplining the working class, shifted that rhetoric.[10] It did so via the missions of literary criticism (distinguishing the aesthetically cultivated from others) and psychology (distinguishing the mentally competent from others). The origins of social psychology in the late nineteenth century can be traced, for example, to anxieties about "the crowd" in a rapidly urbanizing and newly literate Western Europe. Elite theorists from both Right and Left, notably Vilfredo Pareto, Gaetano Mosca, Gustave Le Bon, and Robert Michels, feared that newly literate publics would be vulnerable to manipulation by demagogues.[11] This notion of the suddenly enfranchised being bamboozled by the unscrupulously fluent has recurred throughout the modern period. It inevitably leads to a primary emphasis on the number and conduct of people seated in front of televisions: where they came from, how many there were, and what they did as a consequence of being present. These audiences have been construed as empirical entities that can be known via research instruments derived from ethnography, demography, psychology, political communication, and marketing. Such concerns are coupled with a secondary concentration on content: What were audiences watching when they, et cetera. And so texts, too, are conceived as empirical entities that can be known, via research instruments derived from sociology, linguistics, and literary criticism.

Overall, contemporary television studies is subject to seven principal influences:

- the application of political economy to examine ownership, control, regulation, and international exchange
- the borrowing of ethnography from sociology and anthropology to investigate the experience of watching
- the use of psychological method to establish cause-and-effect relations between viewing TV and subsequent conduct
- the adaptation of sociological method to undertake content analyses of programming in search of generic patterns, such as representations of violence
- the call from social movements to interrogate stereotypes, exclusions, and power inequalities
- the rearticulation of evaluative criteria from the study of literature and film—same discourse, different object
- the adoption of structuralist Marxism and linguistics to identify the ideological tenor of content

Clearly, it would be misleading to propose a singularity to all this activity: "There's no unity in the *study*, any more than there is in *television*, since analysts speak different languages, use different methods, in pursuit of different questions."[12] The Jewish Bible/Old Testament tale of Babel, in which peoples with many languages who sought to collaborate in building a tower that stretched to heaven could not communicate effectively and hence were buried when it collapsed, suggests limits to the commensurability of certain approaches. But it is hardly an argument against uncovering what can and cannot be linked.

The most socially significant part of TV studies, as measured by funding, publication, influence, and public concern, is effects and ratings research. It traverses the culture industries, the state, and criticism. John Hartley suggests: "The energy with which audiences are pursued in academic and industry research . . . [is] larger and more powerful than the quest for mere data; . . . it is the search for . . . knowledge of the *species*."[13] There is something quite eerie about audience research and researchers—they have their own cults, of numbers, neurones, neuroses, and negativity. Many discussions of the audience are signs of anxiety, as per the elite theorists of nineteenth-century Europe. Consider contemporary U.S. laments over a decayed civic culture that correlate increasing violence and declining volunteerism in civil society with heavy TV viewing.[14] This melancholia animates scholarship as much today as when the Payne Fund Studies of the 1930s inaugurated mass social-science panic about young people at the cinema when researchers boldly set out to gauge youthful emotional reactions by assessing "galvanic skin response."[15] The continuity draws on academic, religious, and familial icono-phobia, and the sense that large groups of people consuming popular culture lie beyond the control of the state and the ruling class and may be led astray. In the U.S. context, the key variable that correlates with these anxiety attacks is immigration. In the early film period, assimilation and Anglo dominance were on the minds of the Payne Fund sociologists, and the same is true of their earnest communitarian descendants today.[16]

The audience as consumer, pupil, felon, voter, and idiot engages the state, psychology, Marxism, neoconservatism, the church, liberal feminism, and the many others who view it as what Harold Garfinkel calls a "cultural dope." In the eyes of such moral critics, this mythic figure "produces the stable features of the society by acting in compliance with pre-established and legitimate alternatives of action that the common culture provides"—whether that common culture is the dominant social order or, in this case, its representation on-screen. The "common sense rationalities . . . of here and now situations" used by ordinary people are obscured and derided by this categorization.[17] When the audience is invoked by the industry or its critics and regulators, it immediately becomes a "dope," for example, via the assumption that "[c]hildren are sitting victims; television bites them."[18]

Two accounts of the TV "dope" are dominant in academia, public policy, and social activism. In their different ways, each is an effects model, in that they both assume television *does* things *to* people, with the citizen understood as an audience member at risk of becoming a "dope," abjuring both interpersonal responsibility and national culture.[19] The first model, dominant in the United States and exported around the world, derives from the social sciences and is typically applied without consideration of place. I call this the domestic effects model, or DEM. It is universalist and psychologi-cal.[20] The DEM offers analysis and critique of such crucial citizenship ques-tions as education and civic order. It views television as a machine that can either direct or pervert the citizen-consumer. Entering young minds hypo-dermically, TV can both enable and imperil learning and may even drive the citizen to violence through aggressive and misogynistic images and narra-tives. The DEM is found at a variety of sites, including laboratories, clinics, prisons, schools, newspapers, psychology journals, TV-network research and publicity departments, everyday talk, program-classification regulations, conference papers, parliamentary debates, and state-of-our-youth or state-of-our-civil-society moral panics. The DEM is embodied in the nationwide U.S. media theatrics that ensue after mass school shootings, questioning the role of violent images (not hyper-Protestantism, straight white masculinity, or easy access to firearms) in creating violent people. The DEM is exemplified in Dorothy G. Singer and Jerome L. Singer's febrile twenty-first-century call for centering screen effects within the study of child development:

> For the first 60 years of the twentieth century, conceptions such as Freud's . . . theory of a fundamental aggressive drive or instinct pre-dominated. . . . [C]ritical analyses and careful research on social learn-ing . . . and literally scores of psychophysiological and behavioral empirical studies beginning in the 1960s have pointed much more to aggression as a learned response. . . . [C]an we ignore the impact on chil-dren of their exposure through television and films or, more recently, to computer games and arcade video games that involve vast amounts of violent actions?[21]

The second means of constituting TV "dopes" is a global effects model, or GEM. The GEM, primarily used in non-U.S. discourse, is specific and political rather than universalist and psychological. Whereas the DEM focuses on the cognition and emotion of individual human subjects via observation and experimentation, the GEM looks to the knowledge of custom and patriotic feeling exhibited by collective human subjects, the grout of national culture. In place of psychology, it is concerned with politics. Television does not make you a well- or an ill-educated person, a wild or a self-controlled one. Rather, it makes you a knowledgeable and loyal national subject, or a duped viewer ignorant of local tradition and history. Cultural belonging, not psychic wholeness, is the touchstone of the global effects model. Instead of measur-ing responses electronically or behaviorally, as its domestic counterpart does, the GEM interrogates the geopolitical origin of television texts and the themes and styles they embody, with particular attention to the putatively nation-building genres of drama, news, sport, and current affairs. GEM adherents hold that local citizens should control TV networks because their loyalty can be counted on in the event of war, while in the case of fiction, only locally sensitized producers make narratives that are true to tradition and custom. This model is found in the discourses of cultural imperialism, every-day talk, broadcast and telecommunications policy, unions, international organizations, newspapers, heritage, cultural diplomacy, and postindustrial service-sector planning. The GEM favors "creativity, not consumerism," in the words of UNESCO's "Screens without Frontiers" initiative (Tricot). It is exemplified by Armand Mattelart's stinging 1970s denunciation of outside media influence on the third world:

> In order to camouflage the counter-revolutionary function which it has assigned to communications technology and, in the final analysis, to all the messages of mass culture, imperialism has elevated the mass media to the status of revolutionary agents, and the modern phenomenon of communications to that of revolution itself, . . .
>
> . . . an element in a total system answering to the imperialist me-tropolis's conception of the role of the superstructure in the counter-revolutionary struggle in third world countries, i.e. that of smuggling in its models of development and social relations.[22]

These two positions shared what Wilbur Schramm, the doyen of cold-war media analysis, referred to as the dominant ethos of "communication research in the United States, . . . quantitative, rather than speculative."[23] This was in contradistinction to more populist, qualitative theorists like Mar-shall McLuhan, who argued for an intense conceptual differentiation between media. Whereas radio, McLuhan said, was a "hot medium" because it contained a vast array of data that led the audience in a definite direction that was explicitly defined, TV was "cool," as it left so much up to the viewer to sort out.[24]

Let's run through the problems with the two effects models. The DEM suf-fers from all the disadvantages of ideal-typical psychological reasoning. It relies on methodological individualism, thereby failing to account for cul-tural norms and politics, let alone the arcs of history that establish patterns of imagery and response inside politics, war, ideology, and discourse. Each massively costly laboratory test of media effects, based on, as the refrain goes, "a large university in the Mid-west," is countered by a similar experiment with conflicting results. As politicians, grant givers, and jeremiad-wielding pundits call for more and more research to prove that TV makes you stupid, violent, and apathetic—or their opposites—academics line up at the trough to indulge their contempt for popular culture and ordinary life and their rent-seeking urge for public money. The DEM never interrogates its own conditions of existence—namely, that governments and the media use it to account for social problems, and that TV's capacity for private viewing troubles those authorities who desire surveillance of popular culture.[25] As for the GEM, its concentration on national culture denies the potentially liberatory and pleasurable nature of different takes on the popular, forgets the internal differentiation of viewing publics, valorizes frequently oppressive or unrepresentative local bourgeoisies in the name of maintaining and developing national culture, and ignores the demographic realities of its "own" terrain.

Interest in audiences has generated one other paradigm that discerns an omniscient viewer. It sees our contemporary moment as the electronic transformation of a long history of surveillance under modernity. This history extends from the panoptic prison designs of Jeremy Bentham to the all-seeing gaze and internalization of closed-circuit security and virtual home cinema.[26] Today, new forms of computer-aided television reception allow viewers to elude commercials—at the cost of permitting software companies complete knowledge about their tastes. In this case, the consuming/creating viewers are themselves viewed, and hence subject to policing by the state and business.[27] These perspectives offered research a way in, too, via three other model TV audiences that continue to animate the DEM-GEM: the all-powerful consuming viewer (invented and loved by policy makers, desired and feared by corporations); the all-powerful creating viewer (invented and loved by utopic cultural critics, tolerated and used by corporations); and the all-powerful policing viewer (invented and loved by the state and corporations, feared and loathed by dystopic cultural critics).

These models have a common origin. In lieu of citizen building, their logic is the construction of consumers. Néstor García Canclini notes in this context: "We Latin Americans presumably learned to be citizens through our relationship to Europe; our relationship to the United States will, however, reduce us to consumers."[28] In the name of the consumer, ideas of the national popular are eschewed. Consumer choice becomes an alibi for structural-adjustment policies imposed by international lending institutions that call for privatization. Another tradition of audience studies, related to the consuming viewer, picks up on Garfinkel's cultural-dope insight and takes the reverse position from rat-catching psy-doomsayers. Instead of issuing jeremiads, this line claims that audiences, like neoclassical economics's consumers, are so clever and able that they make their own meanings, outwitting institutions of the state, academia, and capitalism that seek to measure and control them.

This position has been elevated to a virtual nostrum in some cultural studies research into fans, who are thought to construct parasocial or imagined social connections to celebrities and actants in ways that either fulfill the function of friendship or serve as spaces for projecting and evaluating schemas to make sense of human interaction. This counter-critique attacks opponents of television for failing to allot the people's machine its due as a populist apparatus that subverts patriarchy, capitalism, and other forms of oppression (or diminishes the tension of such social divisions, depending on your politics). Popular TV is held to be subversive/functionalist because programming is decoded by viewers in keeping with their own social situation. The active audience is said to be weak at the level of cultural production, but strong as an interpretative community, especially via imagined links to stars.[29] Umberto Eco suggests that fans can "own" a text, psychologically if not legally, by quoting characters' escapades and proclivities "as if they were aspects of the fan's private sectarian world." This world is then opened up to other followers through such shared experiences as conventions, Web pages, discussion groups, quizzes, and rankings. References to segments of an episode, or to the typical behavior of an actant, become "catalyzers of collective memories," regardless of their significance for individual plotlines.[30] As Joanne Woodward once remarked of the difference between film and TV: "When I was in the movies I heard people say, 'There goes Joanne Woodward.' Now they say, 'There goes somebody I think I know.'"[31] This level of identification is assumed by Jane Wyman's children in *All That Heaven Allows* when they buy her a TV set to cathect onto in place of her hunky gardener, Rock Hudson.[32] But can fans be said to resist consumer capitalism when they interpret texts unusually or dress up as men from outer space?

We can distill from this potted history the need for an economic and political account of the media. Most popular and significant media texts are commodities whose appeal lies in their meanings. These meanings derive from the interplay between sound, image, narrative, and subjectivity on the one hand, and audience interpretation and social intertextuality on the other. As commodity forms, practices, knowledges, and contexts, they are clearly mediated through capitalist and governmental forms of production, distribution, and reception.

The media can be understood through twin theoretical prisms. On the one hand, they are a cluster of culture industries and hence subject to the rent-seeking practices and exclusionary protocols that characterize liaisons between state and capital. As such, the media must be evaluated for their representativeness (i.e., whether they involve a representative sample of the overall population in production). On the other hand, they are the newest component of sovereignty, a twentieth-century addition to ideas of patrimony and rights, whereby images of identity sit alongside such traditional topics as territory, language, history, and schooling. As such, the media must be evaluated for their representations (i.e., whether they evoke a representative sample of the population).

Given this background, critical political economy should be a natural ally of textual analysis in studying the media. But a certain tendency on both sides of the divide has maintained that the two are mutually exclusive, on the grounds that one approach is concerned with structures of the economy, and the other with structures of meaning. This need not be the case. The best political economy and the best textual analysis can work in tandem through the imbrication of power and signification at all points on the cultural continuum. Ideally, blending the two approaches can heal divisions between fact and interpretation and between the social sciences and the humanities, under the sign of a principled approach to cultural democracy. This merger necessitates a focus on the contradictions of organizational structures, their articulations with everyday life and textuality, and their entanglement with the polity and the economy. Such a move refuses forms of analysis that oppose the study of production and consumption, or that fail to address axes of social stratification. We must avoid reproducing things called, for example, "film theory," "TV studies," or (urrgh) "new media studies" and instead interrogate the media, *regardless of disciplinary boundaries.* (That doesn't mean transcending the narcissism of small divisions between art historians and littérateurs, but reaching out to visual anthropologists, critical sociologists, law-school progressives, and communication-studies radicals.) The need for such an agenda is apparent from the history and historiography of the Internet.

The Internet

The Internet generated many smiles in the humanities. It promised a kind of Marxist-Godardian deliverance, whereby consumers became producers. They went fishing in the morning, made love in the afternoon, and inhabited autonomous collectives at night. A veritable cyborgian world was available, thanks to the adoption, adaptation, and rejection of multiple subjectivities delivered through touch. The rhetoric of new media was inflected with the phenomenological awe of a precocious child who can be returned to Eden. A redeemed version of the screen would heal the wounds of the modern, reconciling public and private, labor and leisure, commerce and culture, citizenship and consumption. The result? The drab and dreary economism of ownership and control forever compromised, and the exciting world of the active audience forever underscored by these new developments. Significantly, these touching fantasies met the wild origin myths of the technology.

Who invented the Internet? When he's not busy claiming the status of a role model for *Love Story*, Al Gore sometimes includes this achievement in his CV. He is not alone—chain bookstores feature memoirs by all manner of white entrepreneurial men making similar assertions. The truth is out there, though, and it lies in the realm of government action—with major cultural ramifications.

For while Al, his girlfriend, Tipper, and his roommate, Tommy Lee Jones, were padding around Ivy League dorms during late-night ice cream feasts, the U.S. Air Force's RAND Corporation was busily devising means of waging the Vietnam War. Its consulting services didn't end there, of course. Our friends over at the corporation also addressed the question, What if the Soviet Union managed to strike at the heart of the domestic U.S. communications system? A successful attack would leave the country disabled, unless a devolved network could be introduced. The packet system of today originated with that desire to decentralize computing through nodal, semi-autonomous sites. In keeping with those origins—state-driven cold-war consultancies—the Internet, as we all know, grew up nested within public institutions of government and education, and the associated warfare-welfare parabureaucracy of publicly funded but ostensibly independent research by private universities and firms. How, then, did what I'll call "cyber-tarianism" emerge as an origin myth of individual inventors/investors working to free communication from states and corporations?

Libertarian individualists such as the Electronic Frontier Foundation in the United States (libertarians need to organize?) today view the Internet as a technologically entrepreneurial zone. It is said to permit human ventriloquism, autonomous subjectivity, and a breakup of state power—all thanks to the "innate" properties of cyberspace. Hence the term "cybertarian." Cybertarian mythology rests not simply on a flawed, albeit touching, account of the person as a ratiocinative, atomistic individual who can exist outside politics and society. It equally assumes that what (a) was born of warfare consultancies and "big science," (b) was spread through large institutions, (c) was commodified for a tiny fraction of computer users, and (d) is moving toward comprehensive corporate control can be claimed, now or ever, for the wild boys of geekdom. A typical foundation myth, dependent on banal U.S. fantasies about the autonomous subject breathing life into the world.

The expansion of entertainment conglomerates into the Internet will not, of course, end the technical capacity of Web users to make their own sites. But it *will* minimize their significance. Today, hackers happily turn up at FBI conventions on Internet security, aiding the state and business to uncover errors and openness in operating systems. Crucial portals take up the traditional corporate role of policing zones and charging tolls. The fastest, easiest, most accessible search systems linked to browsers direct folks to the "best" sites—which are not those of cybertarians.

A far older subject is lurking here—older than the cybertarian, older even than the libertarian. This is, of course, the citizen. Whereas the cybertarian is a monad, happily sitting at the controls of his life, the citizen is intersubjective, keen to link her life with others in solidarity, as well as in conflict. In Internet terms, citizenship encompasses discussion groups, ventriloquism, physical space and hardware for collaboration, and access by *non*citizens, such as temporary workers and refugees (topics that are core issues for the public-sphere activists at Sarai in New Delhi, for example). The New International Division of Cultural Labor and the Internet will interact in ways we can only imagine, as cultural labor is internationalized on an uneven basis that favors north over south and capital over labor.[33] We are seeing some signs in the United States of a new drive toward unionization, as lapsing cybertarians and burst-bubble dot-commers find an end to vested shares, salaries, and health care if they got on board too late, added no real value, or confronted global competition for work.

What are we to make of the coming epoch's promises of digitally generated actors, desktop computers that produce and distribute feature films, simultaneous production work on TV programs across the world, and dial-up home-video access? The past half-century has seen television programs dominated by norms of narrative continuity in which one shot relates to another in sequences that build to a resolution. The digital era's commercial dictates are steering us toward storytelling and news driven by special effects, as analog's tendency to privilege overt signage identifying time and space transitions is supplanted by new notions of discontinuity via hypertextuality and video clips (although evidence from cognitive theory and analysis suggests there are limits to audience pleasure derived from hypertext).[34] The lucrative games market is constructed around interactivity, so it differs from the linear stories of most TV drama.[35] The technophilic magazine *Wired* dubs this new era "Hollywood 2.0," troping the language of software upgrades to argue for a sea change from the narrative and industrial organization of "Hollywood 1.0." Meanwhile, optimistic artists foresee a world where electronic audience subscriptions finance new projects, and high-capacity connections and multimedia computers find consumers downloading texts following electronic fund transfers, even as Web cameras are adding to and subtracting from their purchases.[36] While the idealized "digital individual" may have his or her persona defined through computerized forms that offer some freedom of representation inside screen space, these technologies also subject the person to surveillance and definition via governmental and corporate identification, and their control remains financially restricted to the upper social echelon.[37] Fears are expressed that broadcast television and mass-market video and film will continue to be what they are today for many people around the world, "a consolation prize."[38] And they will have a very different phenomenology, because the bodies in front of those screens will be unemployed or laboring for low wages.

We are faced with the claim that television has had its day, that the Web is the future. That may be. But it is worth remembering that Web TV has not been a great success, that interactive television has been around for thirty-five years without achieving real popularity, and that the digital divide that separates the poor from the Internet is not changing. Two billion people in the world have never made a telephone call, let alone experienced the frisson of assuming exotic personalities on-line.

The future may involve a transformation of television, rather than its displacement. TV started in most countries as a broadcast national medium dominated by the state. It was transformed into a cable and satellite international medium dominated by commerce—but still called "television." A TV-like screen, located in domestic and public spaces and transmitting signs from other places, will be the future. It may even be that "television" as a word will take over what we now call "new media." So there is intellectual and political value in using the knowledge gained from TV studies to assess this transformation and to intervene in it—especially if we borrow from the right traditions.

The questions asked of television today illustrate this continued relevance. For example, leading bourgeois economic maven Jagdish Bhagwati is convinced that TV is partly to "blame" for global grassroots activism against globalization:

> [S]ources that today are propelling the young into anticapitalist attitudes can be found in new technologies: cable television and the Internet. These innovations help explain the dissonance that now exists in many of globalization's critics between empathy for the misery of a distant elsewhere, and an inadequate intellectual grasp of what can be done to ameliorate that distress.[39]

Ah, I get it. Television makes people identify with those suffering from capitalism. This is bad, because that identification does not lead to rational action (i.e., subscription to the neoclassical economic policies that caused the problem, because in the long run . . .). But actually, I don't get it. Just a few pages further on in Bhagwati's essay, cable is suddenly a savior. There is no need to litigate against companies that pollute the environment or to impose sanctions on states that enslave children to become competitive in the global economy, because "in today's world of CNN, . . . multinationals and their host governments cannot afford to alienate their constituencies."[40] Come on down, Rudolf Arnheim, Samuel Brody, and the late Professor Houghland, and claim your prize—the "Australian adolescent" of the twenty-first century, same as it ever was. Once more, TV is Susskind's "very beautiful woman who looks abominable." The tie between the medium as a heaven and *a* hell is as powerful as ever, with the Internet its twin.

Conclusion

Television is an alembic for understanding society. "Television" stands for so many things, in so many contexts, for so many different people, that defining it could take a dozen books. A shortlist might include: fun, boredom, public service, profit, sport, action, news, men, the United States, movies, color, and disaster. Rick Maxwell offers the following additions: "An appliance, a piece of furniture, and then: rotting piles of wire, glass, plastic, poisonous heavy metals and noxious emissions polluting sidewalks and landfills around the world. A job, cut hands, long hours, broken backs, cheap parts, bad lungs, blood-shot eyes."[41] TV is first an object produced in factories and distributed via transportation; then it is a fashion statement, a privileged (or damned) piece of furniture—a status symbol; and finally, it is a piece of outmoded junk. In short, television has a physical existence and *a* history as an object of material production and consumption, as well as serving as a site for making meaning. Here is my television A to Z:

Advertising—texts that interrupt television, or are the best television, or enable television

Broadcasting—when TV went through the air and was aimed at everyone

Culture—what television was not.

Drama—once characterized television and has *always* characterized its internal workings and debates about it

Effects—measuring the impact of worrying about TV on politicians, family-power dynamics, and the careers of psychology and communications professors

Flow—the movement of Raymond Williams backward, forward, and sideways on a transatlantic liner

Government—the space between TV as a vast wasteland and a toaster with pictures

Hegemony—how TV forms consent. Of course this isn't functionalist. Not a bit.

Ideology—what people who live outside plutocracies and militarized states no longer believe in

Journalist—extinct species, formerly common in the United States

Knowledge—used to disagree with people who refer to an "information society"

Liveness—plausible, in the case of sports coverage

Media—subject for corralling undergraduates and teaching them that what they enjoy is also good for them

News—RIP, September 11, 2001

Ownership—a topic that used to matter but is no longer important because people in villages apparently interpret TV programs in accordance with their local rituals

Production—invisible, other than as what media-studies undergraduates prefer to do rather than their essays

Quality—it's not quality, it's television.

Race—a Grand Prix

Sex—only on satellite and cable

Technology—sold to public by offering sports exclusively on latest innovation

Uses and Gratifications—Jeremy Bentham watching *Survivor*

Violence—to be derided, other than when done by the state to foreigners

Women—a market segment

X-cess—media-studies academics writing about wrestling, Madonna, people behaving badly in public, or their children's viewing experiences

Youth—spectators learning how to be responsible consumers

Zworykin—fabled TV inventor from RCA who "liberated" an already patented invention

In the spirit of this list, studying the media today requires interrogating the commodification of textuality, the global exchange of cultural and communications infrastructure and content, the suburbanization of first-world politics, and the interplay between physical and visual power.[42] This can be done, in my view, by combining political-economy and cultural-studies tendencies into a critical media studies.

The intellectual genealogy of these two tendencies is formidable. They emerged from a need to address monopoly capital, racial inequality and racialization, class domination, technological change, industrial organization, public-policy dilemmas, cultural imperialism, conditions of production, textual meaning, gendered aesthetic hierarchies, audience interpretation, epistemology, and pleasure. Each formation has been at once scholarly and committed. Consider the significance of Dallas Smythe's contribution to political economy. He began as a U.S. government statistician and then an economist with the Federal Communications Commission, before shifting to academic life in Canada, where his development of political economy applied to the media influenced generations of radicals seeking to make a difference in policy terms.[43] And on the cultural-studies side, think of how encoding-decoding emerged from Eco's 1965 consultancy for RAI TV in Italy and Garfinkel's 1967 critique of the "cultural dope" paradigm, following a merger with Marxist and Gramscian analysis by several scholars, notably Frank Parkin, Stuart Hall, and Todd Gitlin.[44] This hybrid stimulated a critical audience ethnography.

Of course, emergent discourses always suffer the slings and arrows of critique. The *Village Voice* dubs TV studies "the ultimate capitulation to the MTV mind, . . . couchpotatodom writ large; . . . just as Milton doesn't belong in the rave scene, sitcoms don't belong in the canon or the classroom."[45] But much more potent is the position enunciated by the British government's Quality Assurance Agency for Higher Education, which argues for the centrality of an education in critical media literacy as equipment for citizenship and "mapping the contemporary." At the same time, major risks come with the medium specificity of, for example, film studies. It exemplifies the perils of creating a discipline in a reductive way that loses its social critique by compromising its openness to the social in return for a limited and limiting set of *données* about a limited and limiting object. Media studies must stay open to developments in both the social field and associated knowledge, if it is to be lively and successful.

John D. H. Downing has criticized hegemonic traditions of media research because "[p]olitics and power . . . are often missing, presumed dead."[46] The absence of these pesky twins in the study of the media is no longer sustainable. The new formation, a hybrid critical media studies, cannot accept the old shibboleths that separate political economy and cultural studies. It should realize that "TV programs [do] not fall out of the sky," so we must understand their material conditions of production; and equally, that the meanings of those programs are far from "explicit and unambiguous," so we must understand their materiality as texts.[47] This suggests the need for an analytic alliance to understand both the media's division of labor and their forms of reception, and a political alliance between media workers and progressive scholars. The three basic questions asked by undergraduate students of the media (Will this get me a job? Is television bad for you? How do we get that show back on?) in fact connect text and context, cultural studies and political economy, for the respective answers are: If you know who owns and regulates the media, you'll know how to apply; the answer depends on who is asking the question and why; and if you know how audiences are defined and counted and how genre functions, you'll know how to lobby.[48]

Whatever happens to the media in the next few years, we must bear in mind that they form a service industry, predicated on communication as a good. The Internet's history, as we have seen, is not a tale of visionary inve(n)(s)tors finding means to satisfy the existing curiosity of audiences—a consumer-driven market—but an uncertain dance of law, the state, education, science, monopoly capital, labor, performance, and interpretation that reveals complex, shifting power relations. Media policy is dominated by neoliberalism, with neoclassical economists saying there should be no governmental barriers to the exchange of texts and no state subvention—the market as a site of magic. This position is opposed by advocates of national-cultural institutions, such as public broadcasting. These critics argue that local audiences should be exposed to locally produced material, rather than to cheap imports.[49] Neoclassical economic discourse is also of great moment in such areas as cross-sectoral ownership, anti-union activity, control of distribution, hidden public subsidies, the rhetoric of technological determinism, and the NICL (New International Division of Cultural Labor). Public understanding of these topics is governed by economists, business journalists, corporate lobbyists, and agents of the state. Research is needed that addresses this hegemony, via a critical engagement with the analytic, financial, and governmental power of the DEM, the GEM, and neoliberalism. That might provide counter-discourses. Such work can draw on what I see as the strengths of critical media studies. Making a radical-democratic future depends on analysis and activism of this kind. Attaching electrodes to Psychology 100 students to examine their neurons, or observing that people shout a lot on daytime television, does something else.

NOTES

The epigraph is taken from Barrett C. Kiesling, *Talking Pictures: How They Are Made How to Appreciate Them* (Richmond: Johnson, 1937), 278.

1 Barrett C. Kiesling, writing two years later for a more popular audience, suggested that the advent of television would "some day end war" (ibid., 248).

2 Rudolf Arnheim, *Film as Art* (London: Faber and Faber, 1969).

3 Clifford Danforth, *Murder by Television*, 1935.

4 Samuel Brody, "Television: A New Weapon for the New Imperialist War," reprinted in *Jump Cut*, no. 33 (June 1988): 106.

5 Pierre Bourdieu, *On Television*, trans. Priscilla Parkhurst Ferguson (New York: New Press, 1998), 48.

6 John R. Silber, "Television: A Personal View," in *The Meaning of Commercial Television: The Texas-Stanford Seminar*, ed. Stanley T. Donner (Austin: U of Texas P, 1968), 113.

7 Wilbur Schramm, Jack Lyle, and Edwin B. Parker, *Television in the Lives of Our Children* (Stanford: Stanford UP, 1961), 3.

8 W. J. Campbell, assisted by Rosemary Keogh, *Television and the Australian Adolescent: A Sydney Survey* (Sydney: Angus and Robertson, 1962), 9, 23.

9 Horace Newcomb, "Preface to the Sixth Edition," *Television: The Critical View*, 6th ed. (New York: Oxford UP, 2000), xi.

10 Richard Butsch, *The Making of American Audiences: From Stage to Television, 1750–1990* (Cambridge: Cambridge UP, 200), 3.

11 These observers had populist predecessors, of course, notably Charles MacKay, whose musings on the subject remain popular with our egregious friends in business schools.

12 John Hartley, *Uses of Television* (London: Routledge, 1999), 18.

13 John Hartley, *The Politics of Pictures: The Creation of the Public in the Age of Popular Media* (London: Routledge, 1992), 84.

14 Robert N. Bellah, Richard Madsen, William M. Sullivan, Ann Swidler, and Steven M. Tipton, *The Good Society* (New York: Knopf, 1992).

15 Mark A. May and Frank K. Shuttleworth, *The Social Conduct and Attitudes of Movie Fans* (New York: Macmillan, 1933); Edgar Dale, *The Content of Motion Pictures* (New York: Macmillan, 1933); Herbert Blumer, *Movies and Conduct* (New York: Macmillan, 1933); Herbert Blumer and Philip M. Hauser, *Movies, Delinquency, and Crime* (New York: Macmillan, 1933); Henry James Forman, *Our Movie Made Children* (New York: Macmillan, 1933); Alice Miller Mitchell, *Children and the Movies* (Chicago: U of Chicago P, 1929).

16 Ellen Wartella, "The History Reconsidered," in *American Communication Research: The Remembered History*, ed. Everette E. Dennis and Ellen Wartella (Mahwah, N.J.: Erlbaum, 1996), 173.

17 Harold Garfinkel, *Studies in Ehthnomethodology* (Cambridge: Polity Press, 1992), 68.

18 Schramm, Lyle, and Parker, *Television in the Lives of Our Children*, 1.

19 These models were developed in Toby Miller, "Television and Citizenship: A New International Division of Cultural Labor?" in *Communication, Citizenship, and Social Policy: Rethinking the Limits of the Welfare State*, ed. Andrew Calabrese and Jean-Claude Burgelman (Lanham, Md.: Rowman and Littlefield, 1999), 283–285.

20 For useful summaries and debates, see George Comstock and Erica Scharrer, *Television: Whats On, Who's Watching, and What It Means* (San Diego: Academic Press, 1999); Jib Fowles, *The Case for Television Violence* (Thousand Oaks, Calif.: Sage, 1999); David Gauntlett; and Cynthia A Cooper. For the urtext, see Surgeon General's Scientific Advisory Committee on Television and Social Behavior, *Television and Growing Up: The Impact of Televised Violence. Report to the Surgeon General*, U.S. Public Health Service (Washington: U.S. Government Printing Office, 1971).

21 Dorothy G. Singer and Jerome L. Singer, "Introduction: Why a Handbook on Children and the Media?" in *Handbook of Children and the Media*, ed. Dorothy G. Singer and Jerome L. Singer (Thousand Oaks, Calif.: Sage Publications, 2001), xv.

22 Armand Mattelart, *Mass Media, Ideologies, and the Revolutionary Movement*, trans. Malcolm Joad (Brighton: Harvester P/Atlantic Highlands: Humanities P, 1980), 9, 17.

23 Wilbur Schramm, "Communication Research in the United States," *The Voice of America Forum Lectures 1962: Mass Communication* 4 (1973).

24 Marshall McLuhan, *Understanding Media: The Extensions of Man* (Aylesbury, U.K.: Abacus, 1974), 31.

25 John Corner, *Critical Ideas in Television Studies* (Oxford: Clarendon P, 1999), 4.

26 Norman Denzin, "The Birth of the Cinematic, Surveillance Society," *Current Perspectives in Social Theory* 15 (1995): 99–127.

27 David Burke, *Spy TV* (Hove, U.K.: Slab-O-Concrete, 2000).

28 Néstor García-Canclini, *Consumers and Citizens: Multicultural Conflicts in the Process of Globalization*, trans. George Yúdice (Minneapolis: U of Minnesota P, 2001), 1.

29 D. Horton and R. Wohl, "Mass Communication and Para-Social Interaction: Observations on Intimacy at a Distance," *Psychiatry* 19, (1956): 215–229; John Fiske, *Television Culture* (London: Routledge, 1987); Laura Leets, Gavin de Becker, and Howard Giles, "Fans: Exploring Expressed Motivations for Contacting Celebrities," *Journal of Language and Social Psychology* 14, 1–2 (1995): 102–123; Henry Jenkins, *Textual Poachers: Television Fans and Participatory Culture* (New York: Routledge, 1992).

30 Leets, de Becker, and Giles, "Fans," 102–104; Umberto Eco, *Travels in Hyperreality: Essays*, trans. William Weaver (London: Picador, 1987), 198.

31 McLuhan, *Understanding Media*, 339.

32 Douglas Sirk, *All That Heaven Allows*, 1955; thanks to Manuel Alvarado for reminding me of this sequence.

33 Toby Miller, Nitin Govil, John McMurria, and Richard Maxwell, *Global Hollywood* (London: British Film Institute; Berkeley: U of California P, 2001).

34 Greg Boiarsky, "The Psychology of New Media Technologies: Lessons from the Past," *Convergence* 3, 3 (1997): 107–126.

35 Robert Rosen, "Teaching Film in a Company Town: An Agenda for Discussion in the Digital Age," *Metro* 112 (1997): 55–59.

36 Peter Krieg, "Docs Go Digital," *Dox* 11 (1997): 12–13.

37 Douglas Gomery, "In Search of the Cybermarket," *Wilson Quarterly* 18, 3 (1994): 9–17.

38 Todd Gitlin, "TV and American Culture: Flat and Happy," *Wilson Quarterly* 17 (autumn 1993): 48.

39 Jagdish Bhagwati, "Coping with Antiglobalization: A Trilogy of Discontents," *Foreign Affairs* 81, 1 (2002): 3.

40 Ibid., 4, 6.

41 Rick Maxwell, personal communication.

42 Hartley, *Uses of Television*, 13.

43 Dallas Smythe, *Dependency Road: Communications, Capital, Consciousness, and Canada* (Norwood, N.J.: Ablex, 1981); Janet Wasko, Vincent Mosco, and Manjunath Pendakur, eds. *Illuminating the Blindspots: Essays Honoring Dallas W. Smythe* (Norwood, N.J.: Ablex, 1993).

44 Tod Gitlin, *Media Unlimited: How the Torrent of Images and Sounds Overwhelms Our Lives* (New York: Metropolitan Books, 2002).

45 Norah Vincent, "Lear, Seinfeld, and the Dumbing Down of the Academy," *Village Voice,* February 8, 2000.

46 John D. H. Downing, *Internationalizing Media Theory: Transition, Power, Culture: Reflections on Media in Russia, Poland, and Hungary, 1980–1995* (London: Sage Publications, 1996), x.

47 Justin Lewis, *The Ideological Octopus: An Exploration of Television and Its Audience* (New York: Routledge, 1991), 23, 25.

48 This point is made nicely by Wes Sharrock and Wil Coleman, "Seeking and Finding Society in the Text," in *Media Studies: Ethnomethodological Approaches*, ed. Paul L. Jalbert (Lanham, Md.: University Press of America, 1999), 4.

49 Eli Noam and Joel C. Millonzi, eds., *The International Market in Film and Television Programs* (Norwood, N.J.: Ablex, 1993).

HYBRIDITY

PETER SANDS

While distance education promises—or threatens—to eradicate the geo-spacial gulf between higher-education sites and potential students around the world, it does not appear to be connecting the first world with the rest in terms that match the hyperbole of its cheerleaders. At the same time, "hybrid-ity" is fast becoming a key concept in emerging approaches to technology-enhanced higher education, as faculty and administrators approach a middle ground between the completely on-line delivery of modular, numbers-driven distance education and the completely on-campus delivery of faculty-driven traditional courses.

Contemporary uses of "hybrid" in educational settings refer to a kind of course in which seat time is reduced but not eliminated, and the work of the course is distributed, with all its attendant senses in both space and time, through the global computer network.[1] The most striking difference between distance and hybrid models is the way hybrid forms preserve a physicality that distance models attempt to transcend but cannot. Ultimately, hybrid forms of education offer a way out of a gnostic error that lies behind—and not very far behind, at that—the push toward distance education. Bricks-and-mortar universities are dependent on location and material wealth—on the physical, as it were. Distance education, so vaunted among educational tech-nocrats, is dependent on the metaphor of transcendence from the physical into the virtual, with a concomitant absence of cultural or other heterogene-ity, owing to the near-complete dominance of Western metaphors, language, and curricula in virtual space. Hybrid models of education offer a radical reinscription of the heterogeneous bodies and cultures of the world in a globally connected educational system.

"Hybrid," in the sense employed by curriculum designers, enjoys a certain transparency, referring as it does to the simple admixture of two forms of "content delivery." Hybridity is both a reality and a metaphor on the Web, and it behooves us to pay attention to the metaphors we choose. As the cultural theorists Andrew Herman and Thomas Swiss of Drake University have it, "at the core of the magical powers of rhetorics about the Web is the use of metaphor, especially those of symbolic equivalency and exchange intended to make them meaningful in the social imagination," which surely applies to the hybridity metaphor.[2] Accordingly, I wish to challenge the transparency of the metaphor, tracing the term back through several variants of its usage, splitting it rhizomatically into its components and roots, seeking what may be found at the other end of the semantic line. As a concept, hybridity occupies a significant position in a number of fields, especially postcolonial studies and the biological sciences. In this essay, I seek simply to situate hybridity by examining its use in science-fiction texts, its presence in the multidisciplinary field of utopian studies and, by analogy, with postcolonial theory in the context of the global push toward greater use of information and communication technologies in the university. The fortuitous deployment of "hybridity" outside its more familiar contexts opens a door to ways of thinking about efforts to globalize education, particularly along a very Western model, which may have both positive and negative local consequences, much as colonialism itself has been seen to have had both positive and negative consequences. In the model I am drawing, distance education, with its U.S.-centralized delivery systems for on-line content, represents a latter-day colonial enterprise, transmitting ideology to the colonies at the other end of the digital pipeline. Distance education itself is fraught enough that even the World Bank says of it on its Web site devoted to distance learning: "One of the most sensitive policy issues of the present day concerns the role of distance teaching institutions in teaching in foreign countries, and the response of national educational authorities to this encroachment." This is not to say that the purveyors of global distance learning are unaware or cavalier about it, but, as the World Bank states with reference to its own distance-education programs: "Overlying these [other issues of delivery] is the issue of cultural imperialism—the risk that materials originating elsewhere, particularly when they go from industrial to developing countries, will be seen as an attempt to impose a stronger, alien culture."[3] Ultimately, hybridity offers a potential way out of a kind of educational colonialism, but not without some costs.

Postcolonial studies as a field of inquiry is generally dated from Edward
Said's *Orientalism*, which traced, read, and interpreted the Western idea of the
Orient and its wide-ranging effects on the lived experiences of both Westerners and the peoples designated "Oriental" from the Middle East to Asia, and
which exposed the "*positional* superiority" by which the West dominated the
East through representation, and also the positive influences of each culture
on the others.[4] Postcolonial studies itself is a broad field, arguably drawing on
the bulk of the world's literatures, cultures, and traditions, particularly as
they emerged from European colonialism in the twentieth century, but also
necessarily dealing with the long period of European world expansion from
roughly the fifteenth century to the present day.[5] As such, it is concerned
with "the historic struggle against European colonialism and the emergence
of new political and cultural actors on the world stage."[6] The concept of the
hybrid is a key element of postcolonial studies owing to its use by the theorist Homi K. Bhabha and others. Bhabha, in *The Location of Culture*, posits a
"third space," a term borrowed from Fredric Jameson, in which the colonizer
and colonized interact with and change each other, producing a "hybrid" that
carries the potential of resistance to the colonial. Postcolonial theorists Bill
Ashcroft, Gareth Griffiths, and Helen Tippen write that hybridity "commonly
refers to the creation of new transcultural forms within the contact zone produced by colonization." They connect hybridity both with the polyvocality
celebrated by the Russian cultural theorist Mikhail Bakhtin in *The Dialogic
Imagination* and with the work of "Homi K. Bhabha, whose analysis of colo-
nizer/colonized relations stresses their interedependence and the mutual
construction of their subjectivities," making note of the "empowering" qualities offered by the concept as articulated by Bhabha.[7] Hybridity, writes David
Theo Goldberg, "is taken as conceptually catching the in-between, as the
product if not the very expression of mixture, of the antipure, of Becoming in
the face of Being's stasis."[8] Ashcroft and his colleagues write approvingly of
the postcolonial theorist Robert Young's careful efforts to acknowledge the
racialized history of "hybridity" and thus delimit its use, while still reading it
as opening potential for resistance to hegemony. But they also note that the
term has occasionally been used in a way that "replicat[es] assimilationist
policies" and runs roughshod over difference. Further, they write that "the
assertion of a shared post-colonial condition such as hybridity has been seen
as part of the tendency of discourse analysis to de-historicize and de-locate
cultures from their temporal, spatial, geographical and linguistic contexts,"

surely something to be guarded against.[9] Still, while hybridity, as I argue, offers a way out of the binary relations potentially represented by global distance education, it is necessary to note that its history is not untroubled. The critiques of critical race theorist David Theo Goldberg and of Robert Young acknowledge the racialized history of the term "hybrid." Goldberg summarizes: "The combining of racial hybridism with colonialism in the nineteenth century was a 'social-scientific' way of managing these related concerns: keeping the Other from polluting and diluting the Same" while also "benefiting from the material and libidinal pleasure exploitation of colonized Others made possible."[10] But, as Gayatri Spivak's concept of strategic essentialism demonstrates, even historical conditions of oppression can be turned into tools of resistance. According to literary critic Jaina Sanga, hybridity "implies a syncretic view of the world in which the notion of the fixity or essentiality of identity is continually contested. The concept of hybridity dismantles the sense of anything being 'pure' or 'essential,' and stresses instead, the notion of heterogeneity, difference, an inevitable hodge-podge." Sanga, following Bhabha, emphasizes that hybridity occurs in both directions, rather than the one-way street of colonial interaction.[11] Accepting this idea in principle helps frame thinking about the hybrid course, which fluctuates between virtuality and presence, between distributed and centralized venues and activities, making possible changes to the teacher/institution, as well as to the student, while the simple fixity of traditional (i.e., lecture) courses tends toward the imposition of knowledge/information only in a hierarchy from teacher to student.

Higher education's engagement with "hybridity," absent explicit acknowledgment of this racialized history, shares space with another term, "emergence" or "emerging." References to "emergence" or "emerging" technologies signify "patterns, structures, or properties [in complex systems] that do not seem adequately explained by referring only to the system's pre-existing components and their interaction."[12] The concept of emergence is used to discuss the creation of life or lifelike forms in computer intelligence or other complex systems.[13] "Emergence" suggests the creation of something that is greater than the sum of its parts—in other words, the unpredictable synergistic results of hybridization. In common usage, per the *Merriam-Webster Collegiate Dictionary*, "hybridity" refers to "an offspring of two animals or plants of different races, breeds, varieties, species, or genera"; "a person whose background is a blend of two diverse cultures or traditions"; "something heterogeneous in origin or composition"; or, interestingly, "something (as a power plant, vehicle, or electronic circuit) that has two different types of components performing essentially the same function." The first definition comes from biology and botany, the second has currency in cultural studies, while the third resonates with the situation of contemporary higher education. In all distance models of education, teachers and students share more and more of the same responsibilities and rights, becoming teacher-students and student-teachers, or an emergent system that creates a third space and a third, possibly homogenized, people to occupy it.

In any systemic change, those participating have to accommodate to new practices and outcomes. In that respect, the rise of professional curriculum designers and instructional technology specialists, and their participation in the creation and delivery of higher education, has created in distance education a different culture with respect to education. In this culture, the mechanics of teaching and learning receive significantly more attention than in the still-prevalent older system of courses designed and delivered by faculty trained as researchers but not as teachers. Attention to matters of teaching and learning is normally given short shrift in the research-intensive university setting. This fact gains a new exigency in the context of the export of U.S. attitudes, ideas, even doxa—and export conducted to such a great extent through a higher-education system that receives much less attention as a shaper of consumer and political attitudes than it might well invite. As education professor Nelly Stromquist writes: "Globalization is promoting the homogenization of cultural values and forms of expressions. . . . Several observers fear that globalization has been successful in introducing uniformity of thought inclined toward consumerism and individualism, a process greatly assisted by the use of global media and the increasing concentration of decisions on programming by a few media firms."[14] In education, this process is assisted by the one-way transmission of higher-education courses from the United States to the world, and the prominence of U.S. higher-education institutions in distance-education ventures such as the Global University Alliance, a consortium of U.S. and Australian universities trying to make inroads in the large Asian market; the World Bank Global Distance Education.Net, a clearinghouse of distance-learning information for World Bank clients; and the World Bank–affiliated Global Development Learning Network, a consortium of distance-learning providers and associated parties. The list of institutions participating or exploring participation in global distance-learning ventures is long and changes daily, even though the long-term prognosis for distance-education programs is unclear, judging by the experience of Temple University, Columbia University, and New York University, all of which started large distance-learning ventures that quickly tanked. But the very real financial pressures on U.S. universities, the large potential market of international students who cannot travel to the United States, and the potentially powerful political advantages to be gained by distributing education throughout the world are clear, creating an exigency for the people who run higher-education institutions: Distance education is a means of opening a world market for U.S. educational ventures. As Stromquist notes, this development may have negative consequences, too. Modular distance learning transmitted from the United States to everywhere else could raise the market value of U.S. academics by possibly restricting world employment in higher education in favor of those who create and deliver courses from the United States. It is not a very great leap to surmise that there will be a concomitant flattening or lessening of non-U.S. perspectives, histories, and cultures. The Nigerian artist and postcolonial theorist Olu Oguibe notes that the "desire to locate and consume that is facilitated by the Network exposes [non-Western] populations to the unscrupulous machinations of traders desperate to satiate a growing demand." Oguibe uses the capitalized "Network" to refer to the whole range of global electronic communications, but especially the Internet. He further claims: "By default, [the Network] readily locates or fabricates voices within who assume the authority to speak for the Other since, quite often, parties and individuals are not in short supply who would ride on the event to appoint and delegate themselves as representatives of the absent."[15]

The power to speak not only to but also for the Other attracts people to the Network. But—owing to its divorce of the discourse and places of education from their otherwise necessary attachment to the places occupied by our literal, human bodies—on another level, distance education appeals to U.S. universities perhaps because of a belief that U.S. university students do not wish to be members of an actual intellectual community. I mean this in the sense that these universities may be cynically exploiting what the writer Erik Davis says about Americans: "The American self is a gnostic self, because it believes, on a deep and abiding level, that authenticity arises from independence, an independence that is at once natural, sovereign, and solitary."[16] Similarly, in creating and administering on-line educational ventures, there is at times a quite astonishing dip into condescension and caricature, as when we read in the *Chronicle of Higher Education* about the "technological savvy demonstrated by many Asian universities" participating in a new distance-learning consortium.[17] What's more, in addition to state-sponsored initiatives affiliated with higher-education institutions, private educational initiatives affiliated with universities around the world largely focus on "instrumental fields linked to economic globalization" rather than on the broad range of liberal education associated with free inquiry and participatory democracy.[18] Such a focus is a means of masking a belief in certain arguable propositions, such as the transparency of teaching and learning, which any reasonable person might surmise to be as difficult, complex, and interpretable as any other human behavior, never mind one that is both culturally and economically positioned to irrevocably shape the lives of individual humans.

The Internet and, in particular, the World Wide Web are bringing together long-separated elements of academic and other worlds—teachers with students, classes with people in the community, the private with the public, and the pedagogical with the scholarly. Consider, for example, the formerly private apparatus and results of instruction—syllabi, assignments, papers, comments, discussions—which have become quite public in the form of Web publications, and consider the ways the Web appears to be pushing both students and teachers simultaneously into homogeneity via a shared, public, published space that rotates their relationship from a traditionally vertical to a more contemporary horizontal axis. In the long run, this mashing together and reformulating of traditional relationships in the modern iteration of the ancient university will require concepts of hybridity and emergence that are both useful for their explanatory power and open to critique, with particular attention to asymmetries of power.

Asymmetries of power occupy contemporary social theory through and through, but they have also been for a long time a central concern in popular culture, which, though situated squarely in the present, occasionally looks to the future, as when cyberpunk and its immediate predecessors imagined a cyberspace that in its turn went from science-fiction metaphor to the real description of the virtual world of the Internet. Thus, before returning to the postcolonial engagement with the concept of hybridity, let me walk through some other takes on it. One approach to hybridity with specific reference to human-computer interaction might be the perspective offered by science-fiction literature and film. Science fiction as we know it can be fairly dated to Mary Shelley's *Frankenstein: or, the Modern Prometheus*, a novel which in no uncertain terms engages the consequences of hybridity on multiple levels: the mixing of ancient with modern belief systems, the creation of hybrid humans, the responsibility of the superior power toward its hybrid creations.[19] The disciplined scholarly study of science fiction provides a lens through which Western culture examines the influence, position, and insights of scientific inquiry. Biology and chemistry, which in Shelley's day had replaced alchemy and folklore, raised the question of the limits of the scientist's power. Today's emerging technologies, in many cases hybrids themselves by bringing together biology, chemistry, physics, and engineering, continue to raise such questions, to such an extent that, while theorists in the humanities explore the range of the posthuman, scientists in the field raise the possibility that the hybridized posthuman future is literally on the horizon. Thus Ray Kurzweil, a respected computer scientist and inventor, predicts that in twenty-five years we will see "self-replicating nano-engineered entities," and that human-machine hybrids will create "a utopia . . . in which humans [gain] near immortality by becoming one with robotic technology."[20] Bill Joy, a computer scientist at the head of Sun Microsystems, argues in response that the consequences of Kurzweil's vision are rather a dystopia in which self-replicating and conscious machines will literally have no need for human progenitors.[21] That is, Joy does not claim Kurzweil is incorrect but, rather, points out that Kurzweil naively sees hope where there is none. This is of course the ground of *The Terminator* and of *BladeRunner*, not to mention its source, Philip K. Dick's "Do Androids Dream of Electric Sheep?" in which human-machine hybridity, carried to its logical extreme, results in evolutionary competition.

Finding examples that address cyborgism, global technologization, and informationalization in science fiction written by practicing scientists, such as Arthur C. Clarke's "Dial F for Frankenstein," is particularly easy. Clarke, remember, is not just the creative mind behind *2001: A Space Odyssey* but is also the inventor of the global satellite network which sends your television, voice, and Internet signals here, there, and everywhere. No, it is not that the theme is new. But what strikes the explorer of fringe ideas in science is that a respected academic mathematician such as Vernor Vinge predicts with a straight face something he calls "the singularity," the spontaneous development of superhuman intelligence. Vinge offers four scenarios: one in which individual computers may attain the status of consciousness, and three in which human-computer hybridity, coupled with biological and technological advances, may cause emergence of something neither human nor machine but a third kind of being.[22] Vinge's singularity suggests an alteration in the body that houses consciousness, a transformation like that represented in folklore in such common hybrid or transfigural images as the werewolf, reflecting cultural anxieties about otherness. But contemporary representations of literal hybridity—such as the silliness of the "uplift" subgenre, which descends from H. G. Wells's *The Island of Dr. Moreau* (that quintessential example of human-animal hybridity)—have much less cachet than do the combinatory possibilities of human and machine, commonly referred to as cyborgs and widely explored in both popular fiction and film and in cultural theory, most notably following the work of science historian and cultural critic Donna Haraway and Alluquere Rosanne Stone, the cyberspace and body theorist. It is becoming commonplace to view the connected human as a hybrid consciousness participating in a global network.

Let me give a brief example, using the already-cited definition from engineering, "something (as a power plant, vehicle, or electronic circuit) that has two different types of components performing essentially the same function." P2P networks, such as Gnutella, which hosts the popular Morpheus file-sharing program, create conditions under which these two components do in fact perform essentially the same function. Imagine that I want to find, say, scenes from the quintessential text of hybridity, Rudyard Kipling's *Kim*. So I launch Morpheus, which connects me to the Gnutella network through at least four servers anywhere in the world. In this case, though, "server" is not necessarily a traditional computer that exists only to "serve" or give out files to end-users, but many of the other computers connected to the Gnutella service. I enter my search terms, "kim kipling," and seek files. If I find some, then I can download them into my computer. Once downloaded, those files become available for downloading from my computer to others on the network. Thus, if I and a child in Kuala Lumpur or International Falls or Mexico City are looking for the same files, we will become different components performing essentially the same function. This will be true even if our access and hardware differ significantly. In this sense, everyone becomes the same on the network—that shift of axes from vertical to horizontal.

But this is probably a bit of false consciousness when applied to the specific site of education. Teachers retain their power on-line as surely as people retain their gender, and as surely as people retain their first-world or third-world status.[23] Try as I might, I cannot deny that I have a broadband connection to the Internet at home and work all day every day, that this connection grants me access to a research university's proprietary information sources, as well as to an astonishing range of newspapers and other media outlets, and, ultimately, access to means of publishing my words or other artifacts representing my ideas. It is difficult under these conditions to imagine that such different components as a first-world university professor and a third-world Internet surfer are "performing essentially the same function."

If, however, that is the reading that the rhetoric of distance learning asks me to accept, it is worth following out a bit. Let me mildly expand, then, the analogy with postcolonial studies. The university in this reading is a country or civilization or state with a colonial program, which accords with the long historical and scholarly tradition acknowledging the socialization functions of the university. The university is arguably a utopian space, in the sense that it expresses a particular kind of what the political scientist Lyman Tower Sargent calls "social dreaming . . . that concern[s] the ways in which groups of people arrange their lives and which usually envision a radically different society than the one in which the dreamers live."[24] The social dream of the university expresses a necessary tension between stasis and action, or between a desire to replicate the past (through inscription of the sum of knowledge in the body of the student) while also improving the future (through progressive transformation of each generation). Such an interpretation of the utopianist impulse at the university is a cognate of the generative or productive reading of intercultural or transcultural hybridity: the conflicting desire to reproduce the home state in the colony while also producing an improvement in the colony-state. That neither species of utopian hope and desire achieves its end in a transparent or uncomplicated way is also worth noting. Any educational system is a concrete expression of critical theorist Ernst Bloch's principle of hope, or of utopian desire, which he argued was not a species of wishful thinking but an impetus of human action in the world. It is an expression of a social dream to make real the possible improvements in lived experience that people can imagine. If education is an expression or form of utopianism, then distance education must too be a form or expression of utopianism—but what kind? It is a transcendental utopianism that relies on a gnostic error—that we can transcend our bodies and their situatedness in time and place in order to learn. But one can never do so, and to make such a claim is to fall into gnosis, but a peculiar, sham kind of gnosis, one that presumes that because the body is not present in the classroom, the body is not present. It shifts the time, place, and other material conditions from the symbolically powerful centralized space of the bricks-and-mortar university into the imagined space of virtuality. Hybridity offers at least a partial way out of the gnostic error by keeping the body in play.

If the university is a state engaged in a colonizing enterprise, then the site of education is a colonial site which also forms a "contact zone," canonically defined as "social spaces where disparate cultures meet, clash and grapple with each other, often in highly asymmetrical relations of dominance and subordination—like colonialism, slavery, or their aftermaths as they are lived out across the globe today."[25] Whatever the forces from outside acting upon it—enrollment pressures, standardized testing, financial difficulties, increasing penetration by digital computing of all aspects of life—the contemporary trajectory of the university is to create and maintain far-flung outposts across town or across the world, as well as to create and maintain virtual outposts in cyberspace. It is a trajectory that leads to contact zones in which students in the process of being colonized live in simulacra of university culture, representations of university culture, not terribly unlike a Disneyfied Main Street U.S.A., with its careful façade masking an empty expanse. It is in this space that the colonial supplicant for entrance into full citizenship increasingly encounters the university. And it is in this space that a concept of hybridity holds some possibility for intercultural sensitivity and for enculturation to the university project: if the bricks-and-mortar university is one example of a centralized power, and the distance-education or "clicks" university is another, then the bricks-and-clicks hybrid, which necessarily combines both presence and virtuality, is a hybridized and decentralized space for both transmission and critique of global university—and other—culture.

To give the trajectory of emerging technologies in higher education a true and full contrapuntal reading in the sense employed by literary and cultural critic Edward Said in *Culture and Imperialism*, one which "take[s] account of both processes, that of imperialism and that of resistance to it," to reveal not just the facts of the text but the material and social conditions in which it is situated and that make it possible, would require a long digression; that digression would lead to the space already occupied by such works as the sociologist Herbert Schiller's *Information Inequality*, which lays out the vertical hierarchy of economic and social class as it relates to access to basic information in an information-dependent society such as our own.[26] Such a reading would expose the tradeoffs universities make in their attempt to participate fully in the rapidly changing world of emerging information technologies—tradeoffs between attention to the local issues and physical spaces of the university located in a particular place and nation, versus attention to the distributed but still embodied consciousnesses participating in the distance-learning experience and the significant amount of attention they demand, as numberless accounts by on-line teachers attest.

It is not that universities are rushing blindly or inappropriately to embrace these technologies, which are woven throughout the fabric of contemporary life in and out of the university. Trying to move away from them would be like trying to capture smoke and put it back on the fire: foolish and impossible. But the material conditions which underlie the development of hybrid models can be contextualized within the current university push to encourage on-line transmission of course-related information, development of completely on-line and hybrid course models which assume persistent, high-speed Internet connections—at the expense of the student user—and the increasing conduct of university business via e-mail and common scheduling software. In that context, diversion of scarce university resources—not just financial but intellectual and physical—to emerging technologies can be seen as not only a push to reduce seat time and thus reduce pressure on a cramped physical environment but also a push to open access only for those who can afford to maintain a separate, persistent Internet connection in addition to paying for tuition, books, and parking. We do not need Schiller's analysis to determine that the corollary effect is to create a new vertical division of classes within the classes: freshman haves and freshman have-nots.

In discussion of bricks-and-mortar, distance-education, and hybrid models, the focus is often on the frame or structure that organizes teaching and learning, presuming that there is a transparency of roles and effects within the frame. But that is like focusing on the bureaucracy of government and ignoring the lived experience of governors and governed. The space of hybridity in digital education is a mediated third space, neither brick nor click. It preserves important elements, such as physical presence, nonverbal communication, symbolic public buildings and places, and synchronic interaction in a centralized space characterized largely by one-way transmission and reception of knowledge. At the same time that it does so—and thus preserves, for good or ill, existing hierarchies and relationships—it also distributes power and responsibility diachronically and geographically via the dispersion of time on task throughout the week or other unit of instructional time. Where classroom-based education can easily serve the colonizing functions of education, hybridity, by mediating distance with presence, opens the possibility of resistance to those functions. It opens the possibility of global connection fully contextualized with local culture, preserving the autonomy and character of a region while maintaining access to global markets, ideas, and technologies. It awaits further elaboration, but in this sense, a global network of hybrid educational centers would look a lot like anarchism, formally defined.

Let me close by reemphasizing a point made earlier: Hybrid forms of online education reinscribe the body in a discourse that is largely conducted in terms of gnostic transcendence. This is terribly important for the fates of cultures and knowledges whose histories diverge from the Western narrative. The philosopher Michael Heim writes:

> Computers may at first liberate societies through increased communication and may even foment revolutions [he refers to the role of computers at Tiananmen Square]. . . . They have, however, another side, a dark side.
>
> The darker side hides a sinister melding of human and machine. The cyborg, or cybernetic organism, implies that the conscious mind steers—the meaning of the Greek *kybernetes*—our organic life. Organic life energy ceases to initiate our mental gestures. Can we ever be fully present when we live through a surrogate body standing in for us? The stand-in self lacks the vulnerability and fragility of our primary identity. The stand-in self can never fully represent us. The more we mistake the cyberbodies for ourselves, the more the machine twists ourselves into the prostheses we are wearing.

This dark side helps "technology [to] increasingly eliminat[e] human interdependence," according to Heim.[27] This accords with the conclusion drawn by the philosopher Hubert Dreyfus in his *On the Internet*, another attempt to bring the tools of analytic philosophy to bear on technology in modern society:

> In sum, as long as we continue to affirm our bodies, the Net can be useful to us in spite of its tendency to offer the worst of a series of

asymmetric trade-offs: economy over efficiency in education, the virtual over the real in our relation to things and people, and anonymity over commitment in our lives. But, in using it, we have to remember that our culture has already fallen twice for the Platonic/Christian temptation to try to get rid of our vulnerable bodies, and has ended in nihilism. This time around, we must resist this temptation and affirm our bodies, not in spite of their finitude and vulnerability, but because, without our bodies, as Nietzsche saw, we would be literally nothing. As Nietzsche has Zarathustra say: "I want to speak to the despisers of the body. I would not have them learn and teach differently, but merely say farewell to their own bodies—and thus become silent."[28]

Dreyfus correctly points out that much of the discourse about the Internet depends on a metaphor of transcendence. The urge is to leave "meat" behind, as cyberpunk writers have it, and enter a zone where the mind is free to play without the concerns of the flesh inhibiting it. But even in cyberpunk the urge is a device for thinking through the problem of the body in modern life, not a literal representation of actual dissolution of corporeality in favor of a disembodied consciousness. Over against such binaries, hybridity—which Bhabha says takes the postcolonial subject into a "third space," the space of potential resistance to the disabling binary of the colonial relationship—offers a solution to what is essentially a mind-body problem, where the alternatives are a gnostic belief that illumination will bring transcendence and release from materiality, or mere physicality, where neither mind nor idea can resist the tethers of the body. Bloch once said in a joint interview with the philosopher Theodor Adorno that "utopia . . . is not something like nonsense or absolute fancy; rather it is not *yet* in the sense of a possibility; *that* it could be there if we could only do something for it."[29] A globally connected, culturally sensitive, and *physically* distributed hybridity, an admixture of both the locally present and digitally delivered in a global educational system that crosses geographical boundaries without trampling cultural identities, renders *possible* the utopianist or hopeful model of the university in which the balance between preservation and change tilts toward progress.

NOTES

1 Jeffrey R. Young, "'Hybrid' Teaching Seeks to End the Divide between Traditional and Online Instruction," *Chronicle of Higher Education* 48, 28 (28 April 2003): A33. Also available at http://chronicle.com/weekly/v48/i28/28a03301.htm (accessed 22 November 2003).

2 Andrew Herman and Thomas Swiss, eds., *The World Wide Web and Contemporary Cultural Theory* (New York: Routledge, 2000), 3.

3 World Bank, *Policy and Programs*. August 2000 (accessed 1 February 2003), http://www1.worldbank.org/disted/Policy/policy.html; World Bank, "Global Policy—Cross-Cultural Issues," August 2000, http://www1.worldbank.org/disted/Policy/Global/cultural.html.

4 Edward Said, *Orientalism* (New York: Random House, 1979).

5 Henry Schwarz and Sangeeta Ray, eds., *A Companion to Postcolonial Studies* (New York: Blackwell, 2000), 1–2.

6 Ibid., 1.

7 Bill Ashcroft, Gareth Griffiths, and Helen Tippen, *Key Concepts in Post-Colonial Studies* (New York: Routledge, 1998), 118.

8 David Theo Goldberg, "Heterogeneity and Hybridity," in *Companion to Postcolonial Studies*, ed. Schwarz and Ray, 72.

9 Ashcroft, Griffiths, and Tippen, *Key Concepts*, 119.

10 Goldberg, "Heterogeneity," 72–86, 83.

11 Jaina Sanga, *Salman Rushdie's Postcolonial Metaphors: Migration, Translation, Hybridity, Blasphemy, and Globalization.* (Westport, Conn.: Greenwood, 2001), 76–77.

12 "Why Emergence?" *Emergence: A Journal of Complexity Issues in Organization and Management*, 2003 (accessed 23 November 2003 at <http://emergence.org/Why_Emergence.htm>).

13 Mitchel Resnick and Brian Silverman, "Exploring Emergence," 4 February 1996, MIT, at http://el.www.media.mit.edu/groups/el/projects/emergence/ (accessed 23 November 2003).

14 Nelly Stromquist, *Education in a Globalized World: The Connectivity of Economic Power, Technology, and Knowledge* (Lanham, Md.: Rowman and Littlefield, 2002), 81.

15 Olu Oguibe, "Connectivity and the Fate of the Unconnected," in *Relocating Postcolonialism*, ed. David Theo Goldberg and Ato Quayson (Ames: Iowa State UP; Malden, Mass.: Basil Blackwell, 2002), 179, 175.

16 Erik Davis, *Techgnosis: Myth, Magic, and Mysticism in the Age of Information* (New York: Three Rivers, 1998), 102.

17 David Cohen, "Pacific Rim Colleges Consider Prospects for a Virtual University," *Chronicle of Higher Education,* May 10, 2002, http://chronicle.com/daily/2002/04/2002042401u.htm (accessed August 20, 2002).

18 Stromquist, *Education*, 121.

19 Brian Aldiss and David Wingrove, *Trillion-Year Spree: The History of Science Fiction* (New York: Avon, 1986), 25.

20 Ray Kurzweil, "The Law of Accelerating Returns," March 7, 2001, http://www.kurzweilai.net/meme/frame.html?main=/articles/art0134.html (accessed August 20, 2002).

21 Bill Joy, "Why the Future Doesn't Need Us," *Wired* 8, 4 (April 2000), http://www.wired.com/wired/archive/8.04/joy_pr.html (accessed August 20, 2002).

22 Vernor Vinge, "Vernor Vinge on the Singularity," 1993, http://kuoi.asui.uidaho.edu/~kamikaze/documents/vinge.html (accessed August 8, 1998); "The Coming

Technological Singularity," 1993, http://www-rohan.sdsu.edu/faculty/vinge/misc/singularity.html (accessed August 20, 2002).

23 See Susan C. Herring, "Gender and Democracy in Computer-Mediated Communication," *Electronic Journal of* Communication 3, 2 (1993), http://www.cios.org/www/ejc/v3n293.htm (reprinted in *Computerization and Controversy*, ed. R. Kling [New York: Academic Press, 1996], 476–489), and Herring, "Gender Differences in Computer-Mediated Communication: Bringing Familiar Baggage to the New Frontier," http://www.cpsr.org/cpsr/gender/herring.txt (8 Nov 1995); Susan Romano, "The Egalitarian Narrative: Whose Story? Which Yardstick?" *Computers and Composition* 10, 3 (1993): 5–28.

24 Lyman Tower Sargent, "The Three Faces of Utopianism Revisited," *Utopian Studies* 5, 1 (1994): 3.

25 Mary Louise Pratt, *Imperial Eyes: Travel Writing and Transculturation* (New York: Routledge, 1992), 4.

26 Edward Said, *Culture and Imperialism* (New York: Knopf, 1993), 66; Herbert I. Schiller, *Information Inequality: The Deepening Social Crisis in America* (New York: Routledge, 1996).

27 Michael Heim, *The Metaphysics of Virtual Reality* (New York: Oxford, 1993), 99–100, 99.

28 Hubert L. Dreyfus, *On the Internet* (New York: Routledge, 2001), 106–107.

29 Ernst Bloch, *The Utopian Function of Art and Literature: Selected Essays*, trans. Jack Zipes and Frank Mecklenburg (Cambridge: MIT P, 1988), 3.

@HENRYPARKESMOTEL.COM

STEVE JONES

Firewall

Henry Parkes Motel. Google turns up 434 matches to those words. At the top of the list, http://www.ennew.com.au/henryparkes.htm, the Web site of Ennew Allsopp, "not just Property Valuers but Property Experts." The company's origins go "as far back as 1979." In "Internet years" one might say that is a lifetime, but in regard to the real estate industry one must wonder whether that is at all a long time. One of the company's founders, Owen Allsopp, its director, "has specialised almost exclusively in Compulsory Land Acquisition work." What has happened to this hotel that Ennew Allsopp is touting it?

The Web site provides a photograph of the hotel. There, among the "Residential Valuations," "Commercial, Retail and Industrial Valuations," "Rural Valuations," is the category "Hotels and Motels and RSL's," and beneath it a photograph of Henry Parkes Motel—Tenterfield. Click on the photograph and go to http://www.ennew.com.au/henryparkes.htm.

Meaghan Morris's eminent essay "At Henry Parkes Motel" uses the image of Henry Parkes Motel, of being a visitor, a traveler, and of tourism generally, to critique the conventional dualism of home/travel, ordinary/extraordinary. In the essay, Morris is able to weave notions of mobility, place, time, and text to critique patriarchal notions of tourism and travel as an escape from the home and the everyday. In her essay the motel serves both as a home (away from home) and as a space of confinement, but not as a fixed space. It is, rather, a space of temporariness and temporality, one that serves as a metaphor for explaining travel as an everyday occurrence rather than as a practice disconnected from everyday realities and that connects to other spaces through which one passes, in which one lives.

Morris notes that the experience of "[t]he motel can be used to frame and displace," and in the case of the Ennew Allsopp Web advertisement it is used to exemplify a type of property, along with the Alstonville Hotel, Bay Royal Apartments Byron Bay, Max Hotel Moree, and Ballina RSL.[1] Of the several properties in the category, Henry Parkes Motel is the only one not modern, indeed the one least modern, and the only one without an image of an automobile in the photo. Yet it appears first in the category, its pink stucco structure drawing one's gaze toward it irresistibly, while on the rest of the page of look-alike concrete and glass buildings there is little on which the eye might linger.

As with the rest of the properties pictured, there is no text beyond a property name. There is no written history, no marker, no inscription, no "Legend of Parkes" like the one Morris found. Unlike Morris's journey, here the virtual trip to Henry Parkes Motel begins not "with a view on the run from the road," but rather with a site/sight given by a search engine.[2] As Morris's "'populist' approach" to theorizing tourism is meant to re-view Henry Parkes Motel and renew theoretical approaches, another popular practice can be retheorized and placed alongside the activity that "motels work to foster," namely the practice of Web surfing for/as tourism.

The opposition between home and travel that Morris insightfully theorizes in her essay must now be joined with theorizing about the Internet. As do other technologies of transportation and communication, the Internet has had consequences for travel and for the home. The parallels and intersections between home, travel, tourism and the Internet are rich and deep and cannot be adequately addressed in a single essay. Nevertheless this will be an attempt to draw some of their broad strokes, to interrogate notions of territory and ownership, and metaphors of space, that now intersect with on-line and off-line mobilities.

Home Pages

In Internet parlance, home is the home page, about which there is nothing particularly or necessarily domestic. Indeed the term is misleading, for "home" as it refers to domestic space denotes a private space (albeit one on which public space has been encroaching via the media, and via announcement of the "TIPS" program that may make informants of service employees in the U.S., government and private, who enter the home). But in Web terms a home page is public—in fact the notion of a private home page is somewhat of an oxymoron. The practice of going to one's own home page on a regular basis for any reason other than assessing changes one has made, or wishes to make, is probably somewhat narcissistic—home pages are made for others.

Put another way, there is nothing domestic about a home page. The term originated from computer jargon, from the notion of a "home" or "root" directory in which one stores files and finds paths to other files. The shift to a home *page* came when Tim Berners-Lee and others developed HTML (Hypertext Markup Language) to publish documents, "pages," on the Internet. They used the term "home page" unproblematically and without definition as early as 1992 in the seminal paper "World-Wide Web: The Information Universe." The notion of a home page as the root directory of a hypertext document seemed natural to those steeped in computer programming, as is clear from this passage in the paper in which the connection to a directory is explicit: "A menu becomes a page of hypertext, with each element linked to a different destination. The same is true of a directory, whether part of a hierarchical or cross-linked system."[3] Interestingly, the notion of a "cover page" that Berners-Lee and his colleagues coined, a page that provides indexing information for a home page or Web site, never caught on. Perhaps the metaphors of ownership, security, and domesticity that "home" engages ultimately captured the popular imagination.

In its original Web usage, the home page was considered a place to which one comes back, and to which one comes back from travel with, one might say, mementos. Note in the following description by Berners-Lee and his colleagues the "comfort" of the browser and home page ("the consistent user interface"), the invocation of space and distance ("a further index"), and, most important, the placement of "a new link" after search of "a further index," like the placing of a souvenir in a curio cabinet in the home:

> Enthusiastic users of the browsing software particularly appreciated the consistent user interface for all types of data. Reading news articles as hypertext was a good example: the same user interface is provided, and references between articles, and between articles and the news groups in which they are published, are all consistently represented as links.
>
> It became evident that both hypertext links and text search are important parts of the model. A typical information hunt will start from a default hypertext page by following links to an index. A search of that index may return the required data, or some more links may be followed. Sometimes a further index may be found, and that searched, and so on. When the user of a hypertext editor has found what he wants (no

matter how remote), he can make a new link to it from his home page so that he can find it again later almost instantly. This is generally preferable to making a copy which may soon be out of date.[4]

The home page in this formulation is a place that you come back to repeatedly, that you design and decorate, that you go out from and return to, but, crucially, it is not a place in which you spend very much time. It is more akin to a tourist information center you operate for yourself than it is to a home. But this is not the formulation that has come to dominate the Web. Rather than a place for one's souvenirs, a jumping-off point for further travel, the home page has become a billboard.

Banner/Ad

Using Lawrence Grossberg's insightful analysis of billboards, Morris notes that "billboards are dominated (unlike the motel) by the operationality of space and the modality of the tour, by 'going' rather than 'seeing,' they enable in turn the making of maps, the citing and sighting of places." Home pages are more akin to billboards in this regard (as well as in others, when it comes to banner ads and e-commerce). No one "surfs" billboards, and home pages, like billboards, "are neither authentic nor inauthentic; their function cannot be predefined, nor are they distributed according to some logic of the 'proper' organization of space or the 'proper' use of place."[5]

Home pages—indeed the Web, by the nature of its hyperlinked structure—are akin to billboards, acting as markers, literally. Some are scanned, some glanced at, while others command more attention and engagement (Burma Shave as mobile hypertext). Unlike billboards home pages are not a boundary, they do not "take up space," nor do they "block out the landscape," and they do not denote any space other than that of the Web. As Berners-Lee and his colleagues suggest, the construction of a home page is in a sense the construction of a hypertextual map.

The nature of this map, however, ought to be questioned. It is clearly not a linear map, one that can be printed in two dimensions and read like a conventional road map. Nevertheless, most of the time it is conceived of as a literal map—one follows hyperlinks from page to page in search of information. But the home page itself can be considered a "mattering map," particularly insofar as home pages can be analyzed as texts:

> These mattering maps are like investment portfolios: there are not only
> different and changing investments, but different forms, as well as dif-

ferent intensities or degrees of investment. There are not only different places marked out (practices, pleasures, meanings, fantasies, desires, relations, and so on) but different purposes which these investments can play, and different moods in which they can operate. Mattering maps define different forms, quantities and places of energy. They tell us how to use and how to generate energy, how to navigate our way into and through various moods, and how to live within emotional and ideological histories.[6]

On the Internet, some maps are made deliberately by users, as is the case of home pages or even of lists of "bookmarks" or "favorites." But others are made inadvertently, or one might even say maliciously, as is the case with "cookies" and cache files that track a browser's movement through the Web. Consider the myriad issues concerning privacy and surveillance of Internet use—then consider the manner in which mattering maps are constructed "for" Internet users based on Internet maps drawn from cookie or cache data. In the case of the hapless employee whose cookie file shows visits to pornographic Web sites he did not visit but that are the result of "pop-up" advertisements, those maps may matter most of all. What counts in such a case is not where do you want to go today, but where your browser was taken for a ride.

Surf/Browser

Morris writes that "'motels in fact demolish sense-regimes of place, locale, and history.'"[7] The Web demolishes these, too, then attempts to piece them back together via the hyperlink, although the piecing together is "hyper"— the assemblage is subject to the rearticulation of linking pieces almost haphazardly. It is as if Humpty Dumpty were, in fact, put back together again, but each of the king's horses and each of the king's men, if they were at all successful, put him back together differently—and never quite in the shape of an egg.

On the Web the "piecing back together" is typically called "surfing," and it involves moving from Web site to Web site in an ongoing process of interpretation that has, underlying it, the sense that there must be something more, some more information, somewhere on-line. Perhaps the most meaningful word with which to describe the Web is "meanwhile": In the time during which a page or image loads, or during which one looks at a Web site, there is ever the sense that something else is happening but a mouse click away.

It is interesting that we have continued to use the term "surfing" to denote what a person who uses the Web does. The term's origin owes more to its prior use in the practice of "channel surfing" while watching television than to any unique attribute of Internet use. In both television and Web parlance, surfing (or the equally applied and inaccurate "Web browsing"— "hopping" would be a more accurate term) denotes the experience of riding a wave, a practice on the one hand requiring a great deal of control and quick reflexes on the part of the surfer, but on the other hand a practice to a great degree out of the surfer's control. The best one can do is choose a wave to ride, and then ride it. This is not an inaccurate description of using the Web. Moving from link to link does have parallels to moving from one wave to another, although it is more accurate to say that what is being invoked by the surfing metaphor is not the temporal thrill, inevitability, or the challenge of choosing a wave and riding it through to its end. Instead the surfing metaphor is being invoked to connote what appears to be the speed, zig-zag motion, smoothness of surfing on water (and, perhaps, the notion of "thinking on one's feet" that is nowhere better illustrated than on a surfboard). The surfing metaphor when employed in the context of the Web fails to transfer its meaning as a practice that puts the body at risk. There is no "impact zone" (the area where a breaking wave lands and exerts downward force) in Web surfing.

The surfing metaphor, furthermore, disconnects use of the Web (and television) from travel metaphors that are otherwise commonplace (e.g., "going on-line" or "going on the Internet").

Click

The Web surfer most closely resembles the "nomadic subject" about whom Lawrence Grossberg writes:

> The nomadic subject exists within its nomadic wandering through the ever-changing places and spaces, vectors and apparatuses of everyday life (including, but not limited to, those of signification and ideology). Coherent subjectivity is always possible, even necessary, and always effective, even if it is also always fleeting. This subject's shape and effectivity are never guaranteed; its agency depends in part on where it is located, how it occupies its places within specific apparatuses, and how it moves within and between them. . . . Nomadic subjects are like "commuters" moving between different sites of daily life, who are always

mobile but for whom the particular mobilities and stabilities are never entirely directed nor guaranteed. Like commuters, they are constantly shaped by their travels, by the roads they traverse; but as they struggle to adjust their shape they also reorganize their vehicles, they construct new billboards, they open up new roads. And, like commuters, they take many different kinds of trips, beginning from different starting points, punctuated by different interruptions and detours, and arriving at different stopping points.[8]

Though he did not intend to specify or narrow the description to Web browsing, the preceding passage from Grossberg provides many connections to it (not the least of which is, of course, the lately forgotten metaphor of the "information superhighway"). The nomadic experience of browsing the Web is akin to finding "that the strange is always and already familiar" and remakes us as cultural critics who "construct a record, always partly imaginary, that re-marks the densities and distances within which our travels are constituted."[9] Indeed, one can claim that travel and Web surfing are critical practices, at least insofar as they involve observation, interpretation, and decision. But these acts, while present in the practice of Web surfing, come with less immediacy to the Web surfer than to the traveler. That is not to say that there is an "authenticity" to travel that is lacking on the Internet. Rather, the *consequences* of decisions during travel are generally greater than those of decisions made on-line. While a tourist, there is rarely the opportunity to press the "Back" button and return to one's previous location. (One wonders why the "Esc," or "Escape," key is not automatically mapped to the "Back" function in most browsers.)

Port Scan

Seeking travel information on-line is a moderately popular Internet activity in the United States, judging from results generated by the Pew Internet and American Life Project. About 7 percent of Internet users look for travel information on the Internet. Among broadband Internet users, however, a much higher number, 23 percent, reported that they use the Internet for travel information. And while only about 2 percent of all users buy travel on-line, 14 percent of broadband users report buying travel on-line.[10]

Perhaps these findings at least somewhat support Morris's refutation of van den Abbeele's claim that "a tourist does research for his trip not merely to avoid discomfort in strange places, but to prepare himself, like an assiduous art student, . . . for *grasping* the eventual authentic 'sight.'"[11] The disparity between broadband and dial-up users may be evidence of broadband's utility for travel research and evidence of its utility as an "always-on" information medium. But their disparity also parallels disparities of travel—speed, money, richness of experience, are factors that influence travel and Internet use, even though these media are entirely different. To dial up itself requires preparation, and waiting. In some cases, such as those where there is only one telephone line in the home, or when all dial-in access lines are busy, the on-line journey may need to be put off for a time. Broadband access promises an on-line journey, and a rapid one at that, all the time, but at greater cost than dial-up's coach-class travel.

Movement is not all that is needed for travel. At some point a traveler needs shelter and respite. James Clifford noted the textual use of the hotel as a place that signifies a shelter for travelers and a marker of history and culture.[12] Morris noted the strategic placement of hotels in relation to space and transportation:

> The installation of any one motel can easily be seen as strategic. There is not only rhetorical competition with neighbors ("address" projected in space), but a conative effort at stopping the traffic over days as well as moments, to slow transients into tourists and divert energy to places (the motel and its vicinity). The aim of a specialist motel like the *Henry Parkes* is an elaboration on this—an attempt from a small-town highway spot to alter urban maps of significance.[13]

But in cyberspace, on the Web journey, there are no hotels or motels in that first sense—there are only Web pages that serve as markers and demand movement elsewhere. One may linger at a page, even bookmark the page, but every instance of its viewing at another time is a return and again requires travel. The closest one comes to, say, a Grand Hotel on-line is what is referred to as a "portal," a site that aggregates (and in some cases personalizes) information. But a portal is less like a hotel and more like the signpost with dozens of road signs pointing in different directions ("Chicago, 280 miles; Tokyo, 2800 miles; Budapest, 1765 miles").

Where Do You Go to Want Today?

What makes the Web's notion of a home page interesting in light of Morris's essay is her critique of patriarchal assumptions about travel (as an escape from home, *domus*) and the home's configuration as a place of feminized captivity. The Web home page can be thought of, at least insofar as computer use and Web-page creation continue to be dominated by men, as a place that *excludes* the feminine.

One result of "the relative dearth of women in cyberspace" is "a great deal of 'computer cross-dressing,'" according to Lisa Nakamura. As a place of "identity tourism," of people who take on personas on a moment's notice (gender, race, ethnicity, even species can be changed, communicated, negotiated), the Web is clearly a place where colonial narrative is reproduced along with its tourism offshoots. What makes cybertourism different from its off-line counterpart is that it "allow[s] identity tourists to simultaneously claim two positions, that of the tourist and that of the native; they can be both inside and outside."[14]

What is unclear is what they are inside and outside of, and who is inside and who is outside, the tourist or the native. With what may one judge either position? There is a distinct need for landmarks, but on the Web there are no landmarks, only bookmarks. The importance of landmarks for assessing one's own and others' positions is pointed out by Massumi:

> The way landmarks function in the actual course of orientation is very different from reading a map. They are what you habitually head for or away from. . . . Landmarks are like magnetic poles that vectorize the space of orientation. A landmark is a minimal visual cue functioning to polarize movement's relation to itself in a way that allows us habitually to flow with preferential heading. The vectorial structuring effected by landmarks gives the space of orientation a *qualitative* dimension, in tropistic preference.[15]

I routinely shift-click on links so that a new browser window opens with a new link, leaving the window that had the link in the first place to reside behind the new window. It is my landmark, the point of departure and, if need be, of instant return. Even when not on-line I have many such landmarks now, though few are made of real estate as such: Global Positioning System (GPS) devices, which have now shrunk to a size that allows them to be incorporated into mobile phones and PDAs, tell me with remarkable precision my location. I know where my spaces are, too—multiple webcams at home and at work show me where I have been and where I will be, at home, at work. The Weather Channel, local news, webcams, a plethora of media, show me what it is like outside, be it a few yards or continents away.

My mother travels in Europe—I watch webcams of places she is visiting. When she e-mails that the weather is nice, I already know that it is.

Ping (There)

To travel to the Henry Parkes Motel on the spur of the moment in any way but via the Web is, at least for those outside Australia, impracticable. And the Web does little to convey one there. The motel itself does not have a home page. And the pictures and words that one finds pale by comparison to the motel's description by Morris.

But even if the motel had a home page, would the pictures, text, audio, and video get one "there"? As Jerzy Kosinski pointed out in his archly titled "Being There," at least in the realm of attention, one who watches television is "there" rather than "here." One might make the same claim for the viewing of a Web page, perhaps for Internet use generally (after all, to access the Internet requires a screen, as does television).

The Web is particularly a medium of "there" and not "here," as hyperlinking (hyper, indeed) entices us to move from every here to another there. What is there to absorb one's interest beyond the opportunity to click on a link? Television is a dynamic visual medium, while the Web acquires movement only through a user's actions. While parts of a Web page may move, as is the case with animation, or may play video or audio files, the page itself is an additional screen within the screen, a reinscription of the inscribed space of the Internet and computer. Yet on the Web I can "ping" another computer, send it an electronic sonar signal so to speak, to verify its existence. On television I can only assume television sets and broadcasters are out there.[16] (I'd like to teach the world to ping.)

404 Not Found

Past the first couple of Google results and on to the third, but it proves a disappointment—http://www.countryhaven.com.au/npm.html. North Parkes Motel is near Henry Parkes Museum but there is no mention of Henry Parkes Motel. The North Parkes Motel is a "home away from home" and "Parkes newest motel." The image of it at http://www.northparkes.com is little more than a thumbnail, and it is a building virtually indistinguishable from any other brick building.

Click on the "back" button to return to Google. Next result: http://www.wilmap.com.au/parkes.html and a history of Parkes. I learn that Parkes "was originally called 'Currajong,' but was renamed after an early Governor of the state, Sir Henry Parkes, who visited the gold diggings in 1873. Sir Henry Parkes was born in 1815 near Coventry, England, Parkes' Sister City. . . . The main street name was later changed to Clarinda St. in honour of his wife." There is a Hamilton's Henry Parkes Motor Inn listed on the page, but without a hyperlink. What of Tenterfield's Henry Parkes Motel? Is Hamilton's another Henry Parkes Motel? How has Henry Parkes, as symbol, traveled, and why has his name been affixed to two motels?

There must be more pictures of Henry Parkes Motel on the World Wide Web than the one at Ennew Allsopp's Web site, but traveling through Google results link by link is akin to stopping every few miles while driving, asking for directions, and being given different ones each time.

Rather than cast a wide net I attempt the opposite. I type www.henry-parkesmotel.com into the browser's URL window. The browser responds "www.henryparkesmotel.com does not exist. Please check the name and try again." In hope of the motel's holding an Australian top-level domain I try www.henryparkesmotel.com.au but the browser again tells me the domain name does not exist. Had there been a domain name I might have attempted a port scan, a common means of detecting what Internet services a computer provides, and a common means by which hackers learn what connections might be exploited on a computer.

Instead I refine the Google search, hoping to narrow my choices. This time I try "Henry Parkes Motel," the quotation marks designating to the search engine that I want results returned only where those three words appear one next to the other in succession. There are forty-four results. Surely this is a manageable number.

Manageable perhaps, but the first two are again links to Ennew Allsopp. The third link's synopsis reads:

SpacePlaceandLandscape . . .
Nov. 20: Tourism, Pilgrimage, Migration, Exile, Diaspora. Dean McCannell, from The Tourist Meaghan Morris, "At Henry Parkes Motel," John Durham Peters, "Exile . . . home.uchicago.edu/~wjtm/SpacePlace-andLandscape.html-9k

It is an irresistible summary and even if it were not the next logical link I cannot help but be curious about what it might say in regard to "The Tourist Meaghan Morris." The site is a course syllabus at the University of Chicago, the summary itself created by Google.

Why not simply register henryparkesmotel.com myself? Why not, indeed? Moments later, I am @henryparkesmotel.com.

NOTES

1 Meaghan Morris, *Too Soon Too Late: History in Popular Culture* (Bloomington: Indiana UP, 1998), 32.

2 Ibid., 33.

3 T. Berners-Lee, R. Cailliau, J. Groff, and B. Pollermann, "World-Wide Web: The Information Universe," 1992, 3, http://www.w3.org/History/1992/ENRAP/Article_9202.

4 Ibid., 8.

5 Morris, *Too Soon*, 313. And see Lawrence Grossberg, *Bringing It All Back Home* (Durham, N.C.: Duke UP, 1997).

6 Lawrence Grossberg, "Is There a Fan in the House?" in *The Adoring Audience: Fan Culture and Popular Media*, ed. Lisa Lewis (London: Routledge, 1992), 50–61.

7 Morris, *Too Soon*, 33.

8 Grossberg, *Bringing*, 314.

9 Ibid., 312, 315.

10 Lee Rainie, *Tracking Online Life* (Washington, D.C.: Pew Internet and American Life Project, 2000), http://www.pewinternet.org/reports/toc.asp?Report=11

11 Morris, *Too Soon*, 41.

12 James Clifford, *Routes: Travel and Translation in the Late Twentieth Century* (Cambridge: Harvard UP, 1997).

13 Morris, *Too Soon*, 37.

14 Lisa Nakamura, *Cybertypes* (London: Routledge, 2002), 43, 57.

15 Brian Massumi, *Parables for the Virtual* (Durham, N.C.: Duke UP, 2002), 180–181.

16 From "The Jargon File" (http://www.dpmms.cam.ac.uk/~gjm11/jargon/jargP.html):

> *ping* [from the submariners' term for a sonar pulse] 1. n. Slang term for a small network message (ICMP ECHO) sent by a computer to check for the presence and alertness of another. The UNIX command 'ping(8)' can be used to do this manually (note that 'ping(8)''s author denies the widespread folk etymology that the name was ever intended as acronym 'Packet INternet Groper'). Occasionally used as a phone greeting. See ACK, also ENQ. 2. vt. To verify the presence of. 3. vt. To get the attention of. 4. vt. To send a message to all members of a mailing list requesting an ACK (in order to verify that everybody's addresses are reachable). "We haven't heard much of anything from Geoff, but he did respond with an ACK both times I pinged jargon-friends." 5. n. A quantum packet of happiness. People who are very happy tend to exude pings; furthermore, one can intentionally create pings and aim them at a needy party (e.g., a depressed person). This sense of ping may appear as an exclamation; "Ping!" (I'm happy; I am emitting a quantum of happiness; I have been struck by a quantum of happiness). The form "pingfulness", which is used to describe people who exude pings, also occurs. (In the standard abuse of language, "pingfulness" can also be used as an exclamation, in which case it's a much stronger exclamation than just "ping"!) Oppose blargh.

Is Television a Global Medium?

A Historical View

Jérôme Bourdon

In recent years, much writing on television has suggested that television is the global medium par excellence, having imposed the same culture of images, the same news, the same media events, or even the same "Western culture" on huge populations worldwide.[1] Historians striving to write "global history" have noted that television and communication technologies at large seem central to explaining "why ours is a global age."[2] Those who claim that television is predominantly a global medium have focused on direct global diffusion as a major factor in the history of television: This is one of the bases of the powerful "mythology about globalization" that has shaped much comment on television, but less, as I will argue, its actual history.[3] On the other hand, with few exceptions, television history is always written in a strictly national framework—this despite the fact that television history has been blooming for the last ten years, especially in Europe (e.g., in Spain, Italy, or France).[4] Most authors pay little attention to global trends and influences and put forward the tight relation between television as a mass medium and national culture and politics.

The aim of this essay is to propose analytical tools which will enable researchers to connect the national and the global and thus to reconcile these two views of television in an integrated global history. To achieve this aim, I will have to amend both the global view that exaggerates the global potential of television and the national view that ignores it. My focus will be on interactions between nations. There have been numerous international interactions during the whole history of television that have been neglected by top-down globalizing views and by isolationist national historical writing.

A Typology of International Interactions

Interactions between nations have been a key part of television history from the very beginning. Those interactions can be classified into three categories: policy, technology, and programming. First: policy. National governments that established television stations had to adopt a legal framework: The flow of policy models inherited from former colonial masters, imposed by powerful neighbors, or, more rarely, negotiated within democratic states is the "infrastructure" of television history, since it has direct implications for all other aspects of broadcasting. Second: technology. Technology transfer is closely related to policy transfer. Supported by their governments, Western (and, later, Japanese) corporations have massively exported transmission and production equipment to other countries. Third: programming. This is the form of interaction most debated. Direct sales of programs, mostly fiction, have been the major focus of researchers, who have neglected flows in other genres such as news stories, as well as exchanges of formats, ideas, and scheduling strategies.[5]

My perspective on the history of television starts with policy and ends with program circulation and diffusion. Globalization, taking international relations as a key part of the process, does not mean the demise of the nation-state, but its transformation and reevaluation. I claim that television is a global medium precisely because it has always been a national one and will remain so in the foreseeable future. However, "the nation" is neither a stable nor a homogeneous notion.

The emphasis on national policy does not contradict the view that television is a global medium. The expansion of the nation as the form of collective identification and organization is an integral part of globalization, a view long held by anthropologists and historians with an eye to long-term evolutions. Anne-Marie Thiesse rightly wrote about the "cosmopolitism of the national."[6] Nationalism is an aspect of the globalization of culture: the political and cultural form called the nation-state has become the dominant form of organization and identification for human collectivities. Nations-states have adopted increasingly similar shapes. Immanuel Wallerstein has noted that "over time, the particular nation-states have come to resemble each other more and more in their cultural forms. . . . It is almost as though the more intense the nationalist fervor in the world, the more identical seem the expressions of this nationalism."[7] Television has been an important instrument of this cultural convergence between nations, and thus of the transformation of the nation-state into a new global entity, no less a nation but less a state.

Television, the Nation, and Models of Media Policy

It is customary to classify national media systems according to normative theories, following Fred Siebert, whose four theories (authoritarian, libertarian, social responsibility, and soviet) have been refined by Denis McQuail into six: authoritarian, free press, social responsibility (public service), soviet, development, and democratic participant.[8] This kind of typology suffers from two major interrelated faults. First, it originates in political philosophy and neglects economics. Freedom from state control is equated with freedom of enterprise, democracy with capitalism. It leaves no room for a free market/unfree media situation, that is, for situations where television stations are free to earn advertising revenues as long as they comply with restrictions of press freedom. These have been far from infrequent, especially in the U.S. sphere of influence. Second, although McQuail partly corrected this, as the sovereign Western nation was the taken-for-granted framework of Siebert's typology, the way "theories" circulate between nations has been neglected, especially in situations of clear inequality between nations.

As far as international relations are concerned, the critical division is between two models: commercial advertising-financed television, whose management is in the hand of private owners, and public-national television, whose management is in the hand of ministers, civil servants, or public service employees, and whose revenues are mostly public (license fees or taxes). The relation between degree of political freedom and each model has been an evolving one. However, beyond the question of the democratic dimension of each model, both have a direct influence on the way the nation has been and is being shaped as a political and cultural form. The models reflect different views of the nation. The interaction between the models is key to the global history of television.

Public-National Television as the Early Dominant Model

Until the eighties, most television stations in the world were public-national stations. The major exception was the commercial U.S. model, which was imitated in the U.S. sphere of influence. I include western European, Soviet, and third-world stations in the same category of "public-national." Of course, a crucial difference among them was (and still is) the amount of political freedom enjoyed by broadcasters, especially by journalists, a range that varied from the totalitarian Soviet Union or China through semi-authoritarian Gaullist France to the more independent public service broadcasters in Scandinavia or the United Kingdom.

Why then group them together? Historically, third-world broadcasting stations have been modeled after those of their former colonial masters (mostly France and the United Kingdom, but also the Netherlands for Indonesia). In former British colonies, television was founded mostly by corporations modeled after the BBC. There also was some involvement of commercial interests (e.g., British commercial ITV's company Rediffusion in Nigeria.) At any rate, commercial losses and/or government interference quickly left room for direct state intervention and for "the control of broadcasting by the ruling group, often military, in each country."[9] In former French colonies, where broadcasting depended directly on the Ministry of Information, the road to governmental control was better paved.

However, the resemblances among western European, Communist, and third-world countries can be explained not only by direct historical links between countries, but also by the needs of emergent states in the former colonial world. All the stations have had much in common as far as the relation between television and nation is concerned. All states shared a basic tenet: Television is a public medium that has a part to play in representing and building the nation.

The national missions of public television can be divided into three types: symbolic, political, and educational. First, television has been a symbol; a state television was considered part of being a full-fledged nation. Second, television has had a political mission, namely, it was a means to integrate mostly recent or emerging political bodies around their leaders. Third, television has had the mission of educating people, especially as citizens of new nations, and of making available to them a national culture, if not a national language.

Television as a Symbol of the Nation

When I say that television was considered a symbol of "the nation," I do not wish to discuss "the nation" as a concept of the social sciences. I ask what "nationals" are considered to be part of the definition of their specific nation. In particular, what do rulers consider necessary to have the status of a full-fledged independent nation, beyond the minimal requirements of international law—a population, a territory, a state? Undoubtedly, after radio, and maybe even more than radio, setting up a national television station has been part of the definition of a modern nation.

How did a television station become a national symbol? First, let us note how pervasive this belief is, since many historians have stated that the development of television has "lagged behind" in their countries, which implies that television is a "natural thing" for a modern nation to possess. Unless one considers the United States and the United Kingdom as universal models, it is hard to explain why French or Australian researchers readily claim that television came "late" to their countries: late absolutely, not "later" than in other countries.[10]

Only the fact that television was perceived as a symbol of true national sovereignty can explain the sense of urgency both rulers and historians have had about the development of television. At a global level, "the medium was the message," that is, starting television was a way of sending a message of national "completeness" to other nations. Television was the best, most visible symbol of modernity for newly independent states, and also for Communist countries, where industrialization and technological progress (in competition with the West) were an integral part of state ideology. Finally, television nicely fit into the global ideology of development through modernization supported by international organizations in the fifties and the sixties.

The desirability of television was so high that even the poorest of countries invested in it. The former colonial powers, sometimes supplanted or replaced by noncolonial industrial powers (in the United States, Germany, and later Japan), were active exporters of broadcasting technologies in the field of production and transmission, sometimes through aid-tied equipment offers. However, third-world states contributed their share, even in Africa, which is quite remarkable considering their low levels of development. African states made tremendous efforts to start television right after independence. As early as 1965, thirteen African states had set up television stations, twenty in 1980, and thirty-seven in 1990.[11] The country that resisted the longest—and has only recently launched a national station—is Tanzania, which tried to promote an original, non-Western ideology of development and also picked an African language, Swahili, as its first national language.

Once a national public station had been set up, many countries did not seem to care whether viewers could purchase the television sets needed to receive the message broadcast by huge and costly networks of transmitters. In India, public broadcaster Doordashan has long boasted of being one of the largest broadcasting organizations in the world, "reaching ninety-five percent of the country's 850 million people."[12] However, transmitter coverage is not the same as number of households equipped to receive broadcasts, which, in 2000, was below 40 percent.[13] In most of black Africa, the gap between potential coverage and actual reception remains huge. This relative indifference to actual reception can be derided as a waste of energy. It can be explained by the fact that television was first of all a symbol for other states to see, not a means of communication—a place which foreign heads of state could visit, not programs for all citizens to view.

Television and National Integration

Television, however, was also a tool for integrating and building the nation. Radio, especially during World War II, demonstrated the power of electronic communications. The image added a sense of extra power and immediate seduction. Television could become a reservoir of visual symbols of the nation. It could also materialize the links between the center of power and the periphery by allowing direct one-way communication between new rulers and their national populations.

The sense that television was a tool for integrating citizens into a common culture was felt most strongly where foreign broadcasts could be received. The threat of overspill, perceived as damaging to sovereignty, has played a key part in the global history of television. The presence of U.S. Army stations and the resulting fear of foreign entertainment penetration accelerated the development of television in countries as diverse as the Philippines, Iceland, and South Korea.[14] Where television exposed minorities to a similar yet "foreign" culture, governments hastened either to set up new transmitters (as France did in its eastern part, from fear of German television stations) or to launch national television they had so far been reluctant to start, as Israel did in 1968, partly because of the success of Arabic-language broadcasts among its Arab minority and Sephardic Jews from the Middle East, or as Pakistan did in 1964 because of the fear of broadcasts from India.[15] Where this overspill included advertisements, as was the case in Canada for U.S.

broadcasts, the fear concerned not only national sovereignty and identity but also loss of advertising revenue, especially when advertising was restricted in the country "targeted" by the overspill.

Beyond the prevention of foreign influences, "nation building" could be interpreted in a more specific manner. In many countries, such as South Korea and Italy, television has been perceived as having contributed to the development or consolidation of the national language.[16] In China, although major cities developed their own stations in regional dialects in the late fifties, the national network, CCT (Central China Television), was established in the midseventies "to unify the country" through, among other things, "use of the official dialect, puonyantin Mandarin, which is promoted as the national language."[17] In general, broadcasting contributed to the promotion of large, nation-based linguistic communities and to the global rarefaction of languages.[18] Only in poor countries of extreme linguistic heterogeneity could broadcasting not be used to encourage the formation of a national lingua franca. This was especially the case in Africa, where big and relatively rich Nigeria is one of the few countries in which television started along regional lines until the government created a national network broadcasting in English, which has never become a dominant national station.[19]

Public-national television everywhere assigned national missions to its programs. It is easily forgotten that the classic trilogy of public service missions—inform, educate, and entertain—was framed nationally. Public service television had to inform viewers about the nation (especially about its leaders and politicians) and to educate them about the national culture. Much of its entertainment, game shows, and variety shows emphasized national trivia and national artists and festivals, while its fictional programs emphasized national authors.[20] There is an implied paternalism in stressing the national values of broadcasting for the third world, but everywhere, not only in the third world, national-public television was used for nation building and nation maintenance.

This link between television and national culture affected all genres, including the first media events, often considered the most global genre. In the early days of each national television, media events played a crucial part in publicizing the new medium, boosting sales of receivers. These events were also charged with symbolic national significance. Speeches by major politicians, military parades (Israel 1968), and royal and imperial marriages

(Spain 1956, Japan 1961) have all been major media events. Few had success outside their countries, a major exception being the 1953 British coronation, which was eagerly viewed, although not by many, in France and Germany. The major events that had international implications were sports competitions, especially the Olympic Games. Again, their national signification should not be overlooked, especially for host countries, which regarded the Olympics as an occasion to connect with the rest of the world (e.g., for a remote "Western" nation like Australia with the Melbourne Olympics of 1956, the year television started) and also to gain legitimacy in the global arena.

The U.S. Exception: The Paradox of Commercial Imperialism

Until the eighties, most television stations in the world were public stations. The major exception was the United States and its area of influence. Compared to that of other countries, television history in the United States is exceptional for two reasons: It is a commercial system, and, no less important, it is a relatively stable system, based on technical and legal rules which early on allowed the creation of three extremely profitable networks (CBS and NBC, with ABC emerging as a serious competitor in the early sixties), a factor that has influenced the whole history of world television.

In this powerful, self-contained national system, the relation between national culture and television was quite specific. There was no worry about foreign influences. There was no sense that the state had a part to play in using television to promote national identity (the comparison with neighboring Canada, where broadcasting is central to debate over national identity, is striking). However, commercial motives did push the networks into promoting and consolidating a national U.S. culture. Particularly, they nationalized regional and local musical and theatrical repertoire, simply because this appeared the best way to create and exploit a market.[21]

Where and how was commercial television exported from the United States? Public-national television was dominant in western Europe, the former Western colonial empires in Asia and Africa, and in the Communist world(s). By contrast, "the North American pattern has tended to find its way into Latin America and into such parts of the Pacific and South East Asia as were not under the direct influence of one of the European powers."[22] However, it did not find its way "naturally." From the very start, U.S. television organizations lobbied to promote commercial television wherever they could, by direct participation (especially in Latin America), by proposing management counsel, by coproducing (especially to circumvent quotas), and by exporting their programs. In 1950, "representatives of seventeen [U.S.] firms met and agreed to form the Television Program Export Association (TPEA)," which systematically promoted exports.[23] Their efforts had considerable consequences: Where commercial television was introduced, it was extremely difficult for states to wrest control out of the hands of private businesses.

In the Latin American "backyard" of the United States, the influence was most direct. Southern governments and corporations were in no position to resist U.S. influence. As Silvio Waisbord points out: "Once rates of television penetration reached a point of saturation in the United States in the late 1950s, the 'Big Three' vigorously courted the untapped markets southward."[24] Overall, the rare "early nationalist policies" developed in some countries (Mexico, Peru, Uruguay) quickly had to yield to commercialism.[25] In the rest of the third world, when commercial broadcasting was possible, the U.S. networks were also active. According to Herman and McChesney: "By 1965, ABC had financial stakes in fifty-four stations in twenty-four countries in Latin America, Africa and Asia."[26] The U.S. pattern was partly exported to Thailand, the Philippines, and, to a lesser extent, Iran. The most important Asian country, because of its regional influence, was Japan, where a public license fee funded NHK in 1953, the same year private broadcaster NTV debuted. This early competition explains why entertainment was considered a major mission of television.[27] Japan, also the target of direct lobbying by U.S. producers, was open to U.S. television imports.[28] Japan's commercial system, in turn, had some influence in Asia; for example, Japanese television companies had a direct stake in the TTV (Taiwan Television Company), which transmitted its first signal in 1962.[29]

In Anglo-Saxon countries, the long history of cultural relations with the United States had a direct impact on the televisual landscape. In the United Kingdom, ITV's commercial network started alongside the BBC in 1955. This gave a decisive impetus to U.S. imports in a country that so far had been considered extremely reluctant to buy U.S. products. Australia had a dual system from its televisual beginning in 1956, although, compared to the United Kingdom's, Australia's regulatory body was weaker and the balance of power tilted in favor of the commercial broadcaster. In the 1990s, this imbalance would prevail in most European countries.

Entertainment: The Early Americanization

In the late fifties and early sixties, U.S. sales and export of entertainment programs abroad prompted some negative critical reactions, especially where their presence was massive: in Australia, in the United Kingdom, in Japan, and of course in Latin America. Where they were contained to a modest proportion, especially on western European public television, they were not a major source of worry. Because entertainment was not considered central, because it did not receive the attention of television critics and prestigious professionals, the early expansion of U.S. entertainment was not always perceived by public service professionals, especially among the sometimes complacent European monopolies, but also in some parts of the third world.[30] Long before the great *Dallas* debate of the eighties, however, some U.S. heroes had become global heroes, or at least were well known in major countries on almost all continents, with the exception of Communist countries. Such was the case with *Rin Tin Tin*, *Perry Mason*, and, most "innocently," famous Disney cartoon characters for children. As early as 1958, as Karen Seagrave explains: "Over 100 different American television programs were running every week in 543 nations ranging from a height of ninety-three half-hours series aired by Australian stations down to just three per week in France."[31] Exports' gross receipts were around 10 percent of the total gross for U.S. programs.

Another reason for the early relative acceptance of, or at least indifference to, U.S. programs is that formats were exported and sometimes hybridized and thus domesticated for audiences and politicians, who saw only what appeared to be a purely national product. Again, the early history of Latin American television gives us a flavor of what would happen later around the world. The most well known and successful U.S. hybrid was the telenovela. Latin American telenovelas were inspired by the soap operas on radio and television, even though they very early evolved into something distinctive, as has been often documented.[32] There are other early stories of hybridization and format adaptation that continued a process initiated by the print press in the nineteenth century. In particular, in the fifties and sixties, game shows and variety shows were borrowed and adapted by some European public services, which expanded game shows into lengthy evening shows. If format trade has recently become one of the hot topics of the international television industry, format adaptations as such are nothing new.[33]

Deregulation: Weaknesses of Public Television

Why the world rallied to commercial television in the eighties is a question beyond the scope of this essay. I will here emphasize only the specifically tele-visual factors that led to global deregulation and the way this affected the relation between the national and the global levels in television history. Political criticism leveled at public television because of its total or partial lack of independence has been a major factor of deregulation, especially in dictatorial regimes but also in France and Italy, where a single party had long dominated the country. Openly (when possible) or stealthily, public-national television came under criticism for being undemocratic, manipulated during elections, and censored or self-censored, ignoring or blackening the opposi-tion and supporting the powers-that-be.

A second weakness of public-national television has been its willingness to compromise with commercial forces. Financing has almost always con-sisted of both public resources (government budget or license fee) and advertising revenue. In the third world, the license fee was out of the ques-tion for economic and practical reasons. Instead, television was supported sometimes by international aid (mostly at the time of setting up a station); mostly by direct government financing, sometimes fed by a tax on the sale of receivers; and finally, almost everywhere the market was big enough, by some amount of advertising. In 1977, out of seventy-nine third-world countries, only five operated a system supported by the government or a license fee with no advertising revenues.[34] In western Europe, between 1956 (Germany) and 1968 (France), all major state broadcasters started broadcast-ing advertisements, with the exception of the BBC (which had a commercial broadcaster as competitor) and Scandinavian stations that were modeled after it.

Finally, after years of reluctance, public-national television often yielded to the seduction of U.S. or Americanized entertainment. This was especially striking in the Soviet bloc. As television became the medium of the majority of the audience in the seventies, the first research on television consumption made the tastes of the audience "visible."[35] State-controlled stations started resorting to U.S. series, and U.S. television stars provided, if not a global cul-ture, at least some global drama. The world of television was made aware of the magnitude of U.S. exports by the famous 1974 UNESCO report, aptly en-titled *Television Traffic: A One-way Street?*[36] In 1979 and 1980, miniseries such as *Holocaust* and *Roots* proved that commercial U.S. television could tackle controversial subjects. In their wake, the success of *Dallas* prompted a debate among European broadcasters who felt they had to produce similar success-ful prime-time fiction. With unequal success, France, Germany, and Romania broadcast homemade series as their national responses to *Dallas*.[37]

Overall, political subservience and resort to advertising and to U.S. imports stimulated negative critics of public television. Paradoxically, much of the criticism leveled at public television regarding the poverty of the mass culture it delivered to its viewers recalls the scathing attacks launched on U.S. networks in the early sixties, summed up in 1961 by new FCC head Newton Minow's famous phrase, "the vast wasteland."[38] Some twenty years later, in the world of public-national television, the "vast wasteland" of commercial television seemed to carry promises of freedom and industrial dynamism. Except in countries that had an early experience of commercial television (mostly in Latin America), deregulation and commercial television came to be seen, in large parts of the world, as a way to solve what was perceived to be the continuous crisis of television, and as a path to freedom.

Globalization Mythologies as a Trojan Horse of Deregulation

Deregulation had also been prepared for by the globalizing discourse of the seventies and eighties: Through cable and satellite, it was widely believed, a cultural invasion would take place from the sky, and numerous new channels would be available to viewers. This invasion might be viewed positively or negatively, but it was always presented as somehow inescapable, "a unidirec-tional process or a fait accompli," which carried "ideological baggage whereby globalization becomes the new dynamic, the motor of world change."[39] The success of CNN in covering certain major events in the late eighties and early nineties (especially the Gulf War) was the occasion of a new discourse of instant global news being shared worldwide, often repro-duced in academic works.[40]

The idea that a metanational global culture was in the making was so strong that it stimulated powerful media groups into launching new transna-tional channels. The growth of the European Union and the coming of a united European market prompted the launch of Sky Channel (1982), MTV Europe (1987), and Euronews (1990). In other markets the idea of global or "pan" satellite systems gained ground, such as the ASCO system for Arabic audiences (1985). The story of those systems is mostly one of failure and return to home base (in 1990, Sky Channel absorbed its domestic rival

BritishSatelliteBroadcasting to form BritishSkyBroadcasting) or of "domestication"; they were used as the basis for building national-themed cable channels. They remain relatively successful only where there is no national competitor.[41] In general, their profits still come predominantly from the home base, and they have to fight hard when competition grows (witness the competition between Fox News and CNN in the United States today). Satellite and cable channels might not have built a new global culture, but they have served the interests of transnational private media corporations, as they helped persuade national governments that private broadcasting was inevitable and should be developed nationally, to counter "invasions" from the sky.

In the eighties and nineties, together with the continuous expansion of television, especially in Asia, the commercial model took precedence over the public-national model. The process started in western Europe, where new broadcasting laws were passed in most countries between 1982 and 1990. After the fall of the Berlin Wall, the Soviet world introduced private television alongside the former state stations. Finally, and more slowly, the third world followed suit, and private stations were created in Southeast Asia and Africa.

To a large extent, global television history of the eighties and nineties repeated the history of television on the American continent in the fifties. Commercial lobbying at the national level became global commercial lobbying. This became apparent in the direct relations between new media moguls and heads of state; for example, Rupert Murdoch visited India in 1984, a year before François Mitterrand met Robert Maxwell and Silvio Berlusconi to negotiate the deregulation of French television.[42] Such lobbying went beyond such relations: A major lobbying force behind the growth of commercial television has also been the increasingly concentrated advertising agencies, which played a key part in promoting the liberal communication policy of the European Union.[43]

Demise or Metamorphosis of the National? Marketing and Identity

What globalization mythologies, the crises of public television, and global commercial lobbying have brought about is not global television, but mostly the proliferation of new commercial stations, both more national and less national than their former monopolist public counterparts. This result is both a cause and a symptom of a change in the definition of the nation, but it is too early to claim there has been a "demise of the national," as has been written about international coproductions.[44]

Commercial stations are less national than public-national stations, because the state had much less control over them and cannot use them so easily for its pedagogical/national aims. In that sense, it is right to talk of the erosion of the nation-state. Public television stations, despite some variable amount of political and professional independence, were all shaped directly by governmental decisions and sometimes controlled by governments. For commercial television stations, decisions are made by private managers under the intense pressure of competition. These managers are often controlled by foreign, that is, transnational interests, which promote U.S. fare because this is what history has made available as popular global fare. That is, the nation-state symbolized by public-national television has given way to a new relation between the state, on the one hand, and commercial interests, both global and national, on the other, using the nation as marketing space.

The main transformation commercial stations may have fostered is not globalization but regionalization: Commercial stations have looked for new ways of creating communities of audiences around their schedule. Autonomous regions but also rich urban areas have seen the growth of new commercial regional and local stations. The state has sometimes accepted the creation of regional public stations (financed by regional subsidies and advertising). In very diverse situations, some audiences now enjoy both the national stations and increasingly powerful regional stations (again, in very different nations, such as Spain, China, or Nigeria).

In most cases, commercial television has clearly chosen the nation as the right marketing space. After the failure of global or transnational channels in most parts of the world, the nation has turned out to be the right space for popular programs formatted and scheduled as national programs, with a national content or at least in the national language. National spaces have turned out to be the strongest spaces of culture and identity, and therefore the best marketing spaces.

This being said, the national imperative is not the same for public and private stations. Public-national stations had a duty to produce as much original fare as possible, extolling the national heritage. Commercial stations produce original programs when the market is rich enough, because they know this is what succeeds best. They also produce such programs after an initial period, when, much to the chagrin of the state, "wall-to-wall Dallas" is the strategy for quickly drawing audiences.[45] After a few years, they try to produce local fare when this is economically viable. However, they represent the nation in a different way from public-national stations. The dominant figures are celebrities of wealth, fashion, and music, instant heroes of game and reality shows, and, if there is enough money, local actors playing contemporary characters in national soaps, crime series, and sitcoms. Surprisingly enough, as far as news is concerned, this leads commercial television to be more national than was public-national television, which often felt it had a duty to inform the nation about the world beyond its borders. Comparative surveys between public and commercial stations' news coverage regularly show that commercial stations' newscasts are more national than those of public stations.[46] Indeed, since the fifties, international coverage has diminished in the European media.[47]

Format Circulation and New Forms of Public Address

All this being said, television is also a more global medium, mostly because it is formatted in increasingly similar ways in different national contexts. This process takes place at two levels. First, format circulation. In the eighties, and even more in the nineties, formats were increasingly traded as such, that is to say, rigorously copied and not loosely adapted as they were in the fifties and the sixties. This global circulation started with game shows and continued with fiction, while the global circulation of reality shows has grown in the 1990s and the 2000s.[48]

Second, schedules are now built along the same lines, if not with the same content. On public-national stations, the schedule was less rigid and less regular, except for specific programs like the news. Advertisements might have been present, but only in certain time slots and—mostly—not as program interruptions. Previews and promotions were not needed. In prime time, the same evening of the week was not necessarily devoted to the same series, or even to the same genre. Some famous programs reoccurred only every month or were suspended for a few years and then came back: This "courteous" model, as it has been dubbed, has been the policy of most European public service channels for years.[49]

The commercial, competitive model of television provided viewers with a different sense of time. The day became rigidly divided according to slots— "prime time," "daytime," "access." The words became international professional parlance. Time slots were also rigidly associated with genres and programming strategies. In daytime, and more crucially in access prime time, "horizontal programming" (or "stripping") became the rule: The same program, for instance, a game show or sitcom, was to be found at the same time of the day, every day. Viewers, in this context, are rarely submitted to schedule changes. On the other hand, their pleasure is constantly disrupted by advertisements and promos that invite them to do something besides viewing a specific program: to view more television, or to buy specific products.

Diasporic Viewing: Nations without Territories?

Thus, with television and through television, the nation has been deeply transformed. Commercial television is less busy building the nation than formatting it to the needs of the market. This is not the only transformation the nation has experienced. Through increased population movements worldwide, and the globalization of national channels through the media, typically satellite television, national communities are also deterritorialized, or at least they are less attached to their territories than they used to be.[50] This process is crucially related to the availability of national channels worldwide, which are no longer strictly national but connected to wider "geolinguistic regions" or to diasporas who variously combine the culture of an increasingly imaginary homeland with the culture of their land of residence, as many scholars have explored in a variety of contexts.[51] The best example of such a diaspora is the Hispano Americans, 26 million out of a U.S. population of 265 million, with a complex media system that includes several Hispanic television channels. However, most diasporas still rely on channels which have a clear national identity (like Spain's TVE international, or the various Arabic channels). Small diasporas who cannot enjoy a television channel have also developed a strong video culture, such as Croats in Australia during the Balkans war.[52]

Again, we are entitled to say that "global television" is not less national, but differently national. Diasporas are sometimes called "postnational," but they still have some relation to nations, both of origin and of residence. They are multinational diasporas, whose television menu is made up of channels that, paradoxically, do not (cannot?) take into account this multinational character. As Silvio Waisbord has observed about Latin American television, television, a supposedly global medium, has ignored the multicultural character of many nations. "It is still predominantly centralist, often propagating images of middle-class lives and delivering news about big cities to a national audience"; it often "opts for tested formula, crass commercialism, racial, gender and sexual stereotypes, and crude sensationalism." Far from being the ultimate global medium, he explains, television has been "an arena for the representation and interpretation of nationhood in a globalized era."[53]

Television thus has become the major locus of a new crisis in culture—not the disconnection between increased technological knowledge and resources and the incapacity to use them for the collective well-being of humankind (to the contrary), which has been several times diagnosed in very different ways from Simmel to Freud to Arendt, but the disconnection between levels of collective conscience and levels of collective action. Commercial television pictures a world of nations, giving much value to national language, national knowledge (including trivia), national politicians and celebrities—with the international addition of U.S. stars. However, major decisions are taken at other, nonnational levels, the level of multinational corporations and organizations (not necessarily coordinated). Thus, and much beyond the usual debate on the objectivity of news, television has become a deeply alienating medium: internationally patterned and controlled, but staging mostly culturally self-sufficient national communities in a world of postnational, diasporic, multicultural, uncertain communities and individuals.

NOTES

1 See Chris Barker, *Global Television: An Introduction* (Oxford: Blackwell, 1996); Stuart Hall, "Old and New Identities, Old and New Ethnicities," in Anthony D. King, ed., *Culture, Globalization, and the World-System: Contemporary Conditions for the Representation of Identity* (Minneapolis: U of Minnesota P, 1997), 27; Ingrid Volkmer, *News in the Global Sphere: A Study of CNN and Its Impact on Global Communication* (Luton, U.K.: U of Luton P, 1999); Daniel Dayan and Elihu Katz, *Media Events: The Live Broadcasting of History* (Cambridge: Harvard UP, 1992); Anthony Smith, introduction to *Television: An International History*, ed. Anthony Smith (Oxford: Oxford UP, 1998), 1.

2 Raymond Grew, "On the Prospect of Global History," in *Conceptualizing Global History*, ed. Ralph Buultjens and Bruce Mazlish (Boulder, Colo., and San Francisco: Westview P, 1993), 233.

3 Marjorie Ferguson, "The Mythology about Globalization," *European Journal of Communication* 7 (1992): 69–93.

4 Manuel Palacio, *Historia de la television en Espana* (Barcelona: Gedisa Editorial, 2000); Aldo Grasso, *Storia della televisione italiana*, 2d ed. (Milan: Garzanti, 2000); Jérôme Bourdon, *Haute fidélité: Pouvoir et Télévision, 1935–1994* (Paris: Seuil, 1994).

5 Akiba Cohen, Mark Levy, Michael Curevitch, and Itzhak Roeh, eds., *Global News-rooms, Local Audiences: A Study of the Eurovision News Exchange* (London: John Libbey, 1996); Albert Moran, *Copycat Television: Globalization, Program Format, and Cultural Identity* (Luton, U.K.: U of Luton P, 1998). Jérôme Bourdon, "Genres télévisuels et emprunts culturels. L'américanisation précoce des télévisions européennes," *Réseaux* 14 (2000): 209–236.This is new territory for research. See, for Europe, Jérôme Bourdon and Régine Chaniac, "L'Europe au prime time," *Mediaspouvoirs* 20 (1990): 145–152.

6 Anne-Marie Thiesse, *La création des identités nationales. Europe XVIIIèmes-XXèmes siècles* (Paris: Seuil, 1999), 108.

7 Immanuel Wallerstein, "The National and the Universal: Can There Be Such a Thing as a World Culture?" in *Culture, Globalization, and the World-System: Contemporary Conditions for the Representation of Identity*, ed. Anthony D. King (Minneapolis: U of Minnesota P, 1997), 93.

8 Fred S. Siebert, Theodore Peterson, and Wilbur Schramm, eds., *Four Theories of the Press: The Authoritarian, Libertarian, Social Responsibility, and Soviet Communist Concepts of What the Press Should Be and Do* (Urbana: U of Illinois P, 1956); Denis McQuail, *Mass Communication Theory* (London: Sage, 1994), 84–100.

9 Elihu Katz and George Wedell, *Broadcasting in the Third World: Promise and Performance* (London: Sage, 1978), 84.

10 Pierre Albert and André-Jean Tudesq, *Histoire de la radio-télévision* (Paris: Presses universitaires de France, 1981), 14; Elisabeth Jacka and Lesley Johnson, "Australia," in *Television*, ed. Smith, 208.

11 Figures quoted in André-Jean Tudesq, *L'Afrique Noire et sa television* (Paris: Anthropos, 1992), passim.

12 Doordashan Web site, 1998.

13 Marc Balnaves, James Donald, and Stephanie Hemelryk Donald, eds., *The Global Media Atlas* (London: British Film Institute, 2001), 47.

14 Kerry Segrave, *American Television Abroad: Hollywood's Attempt to Dominate World Television* (Jefferson, N.C., and London: McFarland, 1998), 92.

15 Dan Caspi and Yehiel Limor, *The In/Outsiders: The Media in Israel* (Cresskill, N.J.: Hampton P, 1999); Dietrich Berwanger, "The Third World," in *Television*, ed. Smith, 189–190.

16 Grasso, *Storia della televisione in Italia*, 22.

17 James Lull, *China Turned On: Television, Reform, and Resistance* (London: Routledge, 1991), 22.

18 Abram de Swaan, "Notes on the Emerging Global Language System: Regional, National, and Supranational," *Media, Culture, and Society* 13 (1991): 309–324.

19 Tudesq, *L'Afrique Noire et sa télévision*, 28.

20 Adriano Belloto and Luigi Belloto, *Sipario! Volume Terzo. Teatro e televisione: modelli europei a confronto* (Roma: RAI-VPQT, 1996).

21 J. Fred MacDonald, *One Nation under Television: The Rise and Decline of Network TV* (New York: Pantheon Books, 1990).

22 Katz and Wedell, *Broadcasting in the Third World*, 101.

23 Segrave, *American Television Abroad*, 18, 28.

24 Silvio Waisbord, "Latin America," in *Television*, ed. Smith, 255.

25 Elisabeth Fox, *Latin American Broadcasting: From Tango to Telenovela* (Luton, U.K.: U of Luton P, 1997).

26 Edward S. Herman and R. W. McChesney, *The Global Media: The New Missionaries of Corporate Capitalism* (London: Cassell, 1997), 21.

27 Hidoteshi Kato, "Japan," in *Television*, ed. Smith, 173.

28 Segrave, *American Television Abroad*, 44.

29 Chin Chuan Lee, *Media Imperialism Reconsidered: The Homogenizing of Television Culture* (London: Sage, 1980), 149.

30 Bourdon, *Genres télévisuels et emprunts culturels*; Katz and Wedell, *Broadcasting in the Third World*, 36.

31 Segrave, *American Television Abroad*, 20.

32 Ana M. Lopez, "Our Welcome Guests: Telenovelas in Latin America," in *To Be Continued . . . Soap Operas around the World*, ed. Robert C. Allen (London: Routledge, 1995).

33 "Full Monte: Format Focus Keeps Numbers Up at Mart," *Variety*, February 26, 2001.

34 Katz and Wedell, *Broadcasting in the Third World*, 51.

35 Ellen Mickiewicz, *Split Signals: Television and Politics in the Soviet Union* (Oxford: Oxford UP, 1988), quoted in Tristan Mattelart, *Le Cheval de Troie Audiovisuel: Le rideau de fer à l'épreuve des télévisions transfrontalières* (Grenoble: Presses Universitaires de Grenoble, 1995), 158.

36 Karle Nordenstreng and Tapio Varis, *Television Traffic: A One-way Street?* (Paris: UNESCO, 1974)

37 Alessandro Silj, *East of Dallas: The European Challenge to American Television* (London: British Film Institute, 1988); Mattelart, *Le Cheval de Troie audiovisuel*, 192.

38 Jérôme Bourdon and Jean-Michel Frodon, *L'œil critique : Le journaliste critique de télévision* (Brussels: de Boecke; Paris: Institut National de l'Audiovisuel, 2002); MacDonald, *One Nation under Television*, 157.

39 Ferguson, "The Mythology about Globalization," 73.

40 Volkmer, *News in the Global Sphere*.

41 Jérôme Bourdon, "Une communauté inimaginable: L'Europe et ses politiques de l'image," *Mots: Les langages du politique* 67 (2001): 150–167.

42 S. D. MacDowell, "Globalization and Policy Choice: Television and Audiovisual Services Policies in India," *Media, Culture, and Society* 19: 151–172 ; Bourdon, *Haute fidélité*, 267.

43 Peter Humphreys, *Mass Media and Media Policy in Western Europe* (Manchester, U.K.: Manchester UP, 1996).

44 Sharon Strover, "Recent Trends in Coproductions: The Demise of the National," in *Democracy and Communication in the New Europe: Change and Continuity in East and West*, ed. Farrel Corcoran and Paschal Preston (Creskill, N.J.: Hampton P, 1995), 97–123.

45 Chris Dunkley, *Television Today and Tomorrow: Wall-to-Wall Dallas* (London: Penguin, 1985).

46 Jérôme Bourdon, "A History of European Television News: From Television to Journalism, and Back?" *Communication: The European Journal of Communication Research* 25 (2000): 61–83.

47 Jostein Gripsrud et al., "Comparative Historical Research on News in Europe," panel at the European Science Foundation Conference on European Media, Cultural Identities, Cultural Politics, Copenhaguen, April 18–21, 2002.

48 "Worldwide Webs Wake Up to Reality," *Variety*, June 3, 1991. "Two-Way Transatlantic: Euro Coin and Creativity Make Sizable Inroads into US Market," *Variety*, September 25, 2000.

49 Bourdon and Chaniac, "L'Europe au prime time."

50 Arjun Appadurai, *Modernity at Large: Cultural Dimensions of Globalization* (Minneapolis: U of Minnesota P, 1996).

51 John Sinclair, *Latin American Television: A Global View* (Oxford: Oxford UP, 1999); Asu Aksoy and Kevin Robins, "Thinking across Spaces: Transnational Television from Turkey," *European Journal of Cultural Studies* 3 (2000): 343–365.

52 Dana Kolar-Panov, *Video, War, and the Diasporic Imagination* (London: Routledge, 1997).

53 Waisbord, "Latin America," 263.

THE LAND GRAB FOR BANDWIDTH

DIGITAL CONVERSION IN AN ERA OF CONSOLIDATION

SUSAN OHMER

A key feature of the history of television technology has been the simultaneous global development of the medium in various countries throughout the world. In the 1920s and 1930s, experiments in transmitting images over long distances occurred in France, Germany, Japan, the Soviet Union, England, and the United States, using both mechanical and electronic means, and relying on financing from either corporate or government sources. Both the material bases of the medium and the way these experiments were financed reflected the industrial and governmental structures that shaped broadcasting in each country.[1]

Nearly one hundred years later, at the beginning of the twenty-first century, many industrialized nations are developing a form of television technology that represents the most significant change in the medium's format since its inception. Though scholars credit Japan with launching the earliest experiments in high-definition television (HDTV), most of western Europe and the United States have committed themselves to making this technology the industry standard.[2] Just as in the earliest days of the medium, the introduction of HDTV in each country has been marked by a notable variety of formats and institutional and governmental interventions.

This essay identifies and analyzes key factors influencing the introduction of HDTV in the United States in the early twenty-first century. High-definition television takes advantage of new digital technologies to increase the amount of data that is transmitted to our sets. What those sets will look like, what kind of material they will transmit, and who will transmit that material are some areas of contestation. This technology is emerging in an industrial environment that increasingly favors large media conglomerates and in which the Federal Communication Commission (FCC), the government entity that regulates broadcast media, intercedes in debates about the form and structure of technology. The availability of additional bandwidth in HDTV has launched a struggle among various industry groups, in particular, the networks and local stations, for control over this broadcast landscape. The massive technological changes HDTV brings about are felt from the levels of production through transmission, and require substantial financial investment, which has also altered the relationships among these entities.

All of these institutional, economic, and technological factors work together to shape the look and function of HDTV, yet trade papers and financial publications often discuss them in separate contexts. In such an active and constantly shifting environment, where multiple forces intersect to produce dramatic changes, it is vital to understand how these forces interact. This essay aims to break down the artificial barriers that often divide issues of technology and institutional dynamics in public discourse, in order to uncover the links among them and to make clear their profound importance for our understanding of media.

Hearing Voices: The Struggle over Ownership

HDTV is emerging in the United States during a period of rapid deregulation of media industries. Though it is not surprising that a Republican administration under President George Bush and a Federal Communications Commission chaired by Michael Powell strongly support this trend, it actually began in the latter part of the Clinton presidency. In 1996 Congress passed the Telecommunications Act, the most significant piece of legislation to affect communication in the United States since the 1930s. The act changed limits on ownership that had been in effect since the industry's origins. One provision removed the cap on the number of television stations a network could own, as long as it reached no more than 35 percent of the national population. Any stations that were jointly owned with another network did not count toward the cap. Broadcast licenses were granted for eight years instead of the previous three, and the FCC was required to grant licenses for HDTV to broadcasters who were already established in the field. Though a network could own only one television station in a market, it could own a cable system in the same market as its local station. Finally, the act permitted the larger networks such as CBS or NBC to own smaller ones, such as UPN or the WB. Though one purpose of the Telecommunications Act was to promote competition among the players in the industry, it also tended to solidify the power of the existing "Big Four" networks (ABC, CBS, NBC, and Fox) and to promote the consolidation of smaller stations and cable systems into larger media entities.[3]

Over the next few years, media companies constantly pushed the boundaries of the act. Though the Telecommunications Act specified that companies could own only one television station in a market, in August 1999 the FCC ruled that companies could own two under certain circumstances.[4] A duopoly could occur if at least eight "independently owned and operating full power commercial and noncommercial television stations would remain in that market after the combination," what became known as the "eight voices" test.[5] The ruling spurred several large purchases. In May 2000, Viacom and CBS merged, bringing UPN and CBS and the local stations each company owned under the same corporate umbrella, and in August 2000, Fox bought ten stations owned by Chris-Craft for $5.4 billion, giving it duopolies in four major markets: New York, Los Angeles, Phoenix, and Salt Lake City.[6]

Media conglomerates were quick to figure out how the easing of ownership limits could work in conjunction with the new lenience toward duopolies. If a company owned two local stations in the same market, both did not count toward the ownership cap, since the areas they reach usually overlap. Media companies began to swap with each other to gain duopolies and stay within the cap. The combined Fox and Chris-Craft reached 48 percent of the U.S. market, significantly more than the 35 percent allowed by the FCC cap, but by swapping stations with Viacom, it remained under the FCC's radar. In August 2001, Fox swapped station KBHK in San Francisco for Viacom's stations WDCA in Washington, D.C. and KEXH in Houston. No money traded hands, and the deal gave each company a duopoly in each city. By July 2002, Fox had duopolies in nine markets, including Chicago, Dallas, and Orlando.[7]

Duopolies offer several advantages to their owners besides the obvious one of increased control of the airwaves. Running two stations in one market can be done with fewer people, and owners can reduce the competition for advertising dollars by reducing the number of choices that advertisers have.

Duopolies also enable their owners to negotiate lower prices with program suppliers, thus placing more power in the hands of television distributors and weakening the clout of content producers.[8] Duopolies can show the same syndicated programming at different times, and can use their schedules to experiment with time periods and programming sequences.[9] Yet this consolidation of operations almost always results in layoffs, and the increased emphasis on cost cutting usually hurts news programming, which is expensive to present.[10] Advertisers complained that networks that owned two stations in a market tried to force them to pay higher rates for the combined audience of each station.[11] The end result of the new leniency toward duopolies has been to promote network consolidation and to accelerate the switching of local stations among network owners. As of January 2002, there were seventy-five duopolies in the U.S. market.[12]

Though the advantage of the duopolies for the networks is obvious, many local stations also supported this system. The Association of Local Television Stations (ALTS) argued that stations in small markets could also benefit from mergers, because consolidating operations would allow them to combine forces to pay for new digital technologies and to compete with the wider programming choices of the networks.[13] After the first ruling allowing duopolies in larger markets, the National Association of Broadcasters (NAB), whose governing board is made up primarily of station managers, also lobbied for the rule to be relaxed, on the grounds that mergers could save weaker stations from shutting down.[14] In April 2002 the U.S. Court of Appeals for the District of Columbia ordered the FCC to reconsider its limits on duopolies in smaller markets, on the grounds that even in smaller markets, the public enjoys the multiple perspectives provided by many of the cable and satellite programs that are available to larger markets.[15] In January 2003 both the NAB and station groups such as LIN Television and Sinclair Broadcasting lobbied the FCC to allow triopolies, even in smaller markets where there would be fewer than eight voices, as a way to keep struggling stations alive.[16] The financial pressures on small stations, and the cost of converting to digital, are propelling groups whose interests do not always coincide, such as networks and local stations, to support consolidation. In this debate, few voices are heard to support the public's need for a diversity of perspectives.

In February 2002 the appeals court announced several other rulings that opened the door to further consolidation. The court struck down prohibitions against cable systems' owning television stations in the same market. Cable companies argued that the need for diverse voices has been met by direct broadcast satellite, whose subscribers had quadrupled in the previous five years, from 4.4 million to 17.6 million. This ruling means that AOL, for example, which had been barred from acquiring broadcast stations because of its ownership of Time Warner Cable, is now free to acquire stations or station groups that are already affiliated with the WB network, such as Tribune Broadcasting.[17] At the same time, the court ordered the FCC to reconsider the fundamental premise of its 35 percent cap on television station ownership. In scathing language, it ruled that this limit was "arbitrary and capricious and contrary to law," and ordered the FCC to collect empirical evidence to support the number, or rethink it. The case was brought to the courts by CBS, Fox, and NBC, who argued that this limit made sense during the time when there were only a handful of networks, but in the current environment, it infringed their First Amendment rights to free speech.[18] Though the court rejected their argument that limits on ownership were unconstitutional, it asked the FCC to justify them. Media analyst Tom Wolzien noted that the decisions broke down the walls that separated various groups in the industry. Anticipating even more mergers, he exulted: "Gentlemen, start your engines."[19]

The increased leniency toward consolidation in the cable industry also permitted the merger of two competitors, Comcast and the cable unit of AT&T, in December 2002, creating the largest cable company in the United States. The merger meant that three companies—AT&T Comcast, AOL Time Warner, and Charter Communications—controlled 65 percent of the U.S. cable market. The companies argued that consolidation enabled them to negotiate better prices for programs from content suppliers such as Walt Disney and Viacom and to compete with satellite companies in the same market. Smaller, independent cable operators who serve mainly rural areas argued that the mergers hurt them, because they could not afford to pay more for programming and upgrade their systems at the same time. Many blame consolidation for the 31.9 percent rise in cable subscription prices from 1996 to 2001.[20] Faced with fewer programming choices and outdated equipment, many rural customers are deserting their cable systems for satellite providers.[21]

In fall 2002 the FCC announced that it would delay any further changes and defer its reconsideration of the ownership caps. The commission decided to conduct several studies to assess the results of its decisions and to provide the empirical evidence that the appeals court had demanded.[22] Studies that the FCC has released so far suggest that increased concentration of ownership has not diminished the variety of news voices and has improved local station finances.[23] Though many others in the industry attacked the reports, most believe that the FCC will use them as the basis for further easing restraints.[24]

A key issue in each of these decisions is what constitutes a local voice. Both the FCC and the appeals court have argued that in judging whether or not there are enough diverse voices in a community, one must look beyond any one medium to consider the entire number of media available. It doesn't matter if one company owns multiple stations and a cable system in the same community, the argument goes, if people can get their news through the Internet, or from newspapers. The court said that, as the FCC reviews the ownership cap, it should consider not only what constitutes a "voice," but also how many voices are needed to assure diversity in a market.[25] Networks have urged a "technology-neutral" approach that measures diversity across a range of media, including nonbroadcast forms such as magazines and newspapers.[26] Others argue that new television voices have little chance of success in an environment in which a few media companies dominate.[27] As one Senator asked the FCC commissioners who appeared before him, "When you talk about more voices, are you talking about more voices by one ventriloquist?"[28]

Also during fall 2002, the FCC announced that it would streamline the process by which it reviews regulations. The 1996 Telecommunications Act requires the FCC to review all media-ownership rules every two years and to eliminate any that are not necessary to protect the public interest. In September 2002 the FCC announced that it would consolidate this rule review into a single biennial review and request public comments.[29] The commission held several hearings to which content producers and station owners were invited to add to its pool of voices.[30] At the beginning of January 2003, journalists reported that the FCC was poised to issue the most significant range of regulatory changes since the Telecommunications Act, including a reevaluation of rules in place since the 1940s. Most expected the commission to announce sweeping changes in the direction of easing ownership caps and regulation.[31]

A Dumb Pipe? Control at the Local Level

Regulatory and legal changes at the national level have profound consequences at the local level as well. Historically, local television has been an
important site of innovation in U.S. broadcasting, particularly in the areas of
children's programming and sports.[32] Local television is also the first place
many people turn for information about their immediate environment: for
weather, school closings, news about layoffs, or the latest developments in
city or state government. Local television functions as a key voice within a
community, as a public representation of itself and its interests. Structural
changes at the national level, due to increased consolidation and an easing
of ownership caps, have realigned the interests of many local stations. Networks have absorbed some as affiliates, while others have become part of station groups. Through these combinations local stations become part of a
larger economic and industrial framework that has often put them at odds
with their commitment to local needs.

Even before the struggle over ownership caps, the traditional relationship
between networks and their affiliated local stations had been changing. Historically, networks have provided high-quality entertainment programming,
sports, and national news to local stations that agreed to run this programming during most of the day. By doing so, local stations make their markets
accessible to the networks for advertising. Networks compensate affiliates for
clearing their programs with cash payments that may cost several thousand
dollars an hour during prime time, and by offering short periods of time for
local advertising.[33] Altogether, NBC, CBS, ABC, and Fox pay affiliates between
$150 and $200 million dollars annually in exchange for airtime in their markets, time which allows them to advertise to a national audience.[34]

Networks have long tried to reduce the amount of compensation they pay
to affiliates, and in the 1990s, they succeeded. Beginning in 1990, Fox and ABC
argued that the high cost of sports programming, for instance, and its proven
popularity with viewers, meant that local stations should pay them to cover
part of the cost. Networks threatened to drop their affiliations with stations
that would not comply—a move made easier by their ability to purchase more
stations. Since television stations and cable systems can also combine forces,
some networks began using local cable systems to air programming that their
affiliates refused to pay for.[35] Networks even eliminated the annual conferences through which they wooed affiliates to sign up programs, arguing that

all-expense-paid trips to Hawaii did not create the most "productive" environment for discussions.[36]

In March 2001 the tensions between the networks and their affiliates broke into the open when the National Affiliated Stations Alliance (NASA), a coalition representing six hundred local television affiliates, filed "A Petition for Inquiry of Network Practices" with the FCC. The organization asked the commission to investigate the "strong-arm" tactics the networks were using against them, alleging that the networks were interfering with their rights to exercise control over their assets and programming.[37] Affiliates said the networks hindered their ability to run local programs that serve the needs of their communities. "We are partners with the networks, but we cannot stand by and let them control our local stations. We know what works best for our local communities, and by law those decisions cannot be made in Hollywood or New York," the organization's chair told the FCC.[38]

Affiliates charged that networks were demanding more clearance for network-originated programming, often insisting that up to 90 percent of the network's schedule be carried by affiliates, even to the exclusion of locally originated programs. If local stations didn't accept network programs, they risked losing their affiliation. Some stations complained that they had been prevented from airing broadcasts of local high school and college sports or public affairs programs. It was also more difficult for communities to refuse programming that might be considered "racy" by local community standards, such as *Temptation Island* or the XFL football league.[39] According to one representative, the networks had gone from allowing one hour a week of prime-time preemption to permitting only four to five hours a year.[40]

The affiliates also complained that networks were trying to hinder their ability to sell local stations to whomever they choose. When NBC wanted to buy KRON in San Francisco, for example, it sent a letter to the investment bankers who were handling a deal saying that it would renegotiate its affiliation with anyone else who bought the station, a tactic that would reduce the station's value to investors.[41] The networks used the leverage they held as program providers to disrupt local stations' efforts to become stronger financially.

The petition and general ill will between networks and affiliates affected all levels of the television industry during 2001. The tensions became apparent within the National Association of Broadcasters, the professional organization that includes networks, affiliates, and independent-station owners among its members. Both the networks and local stations wanted the NAB to take a stand on the issue of the 35 percent ownership cap. The station alliance pushed the NAB to support a cap, while the networks wanted it to oppose ownership limits. Fox, NBC, and CBS pulled out of the organization over this dispute, and ABC threatened to do so as well. The debate prompted NAB president Eddie Fritts to call for a full organization meeting to discuss how the NAB could continue to function in this increasingly tense environment.[42]

The affiliates group filed its petition less than one week after the appeals court lifted the ownership caps on cable systems, at a time when many thought the ownership caps on local television stations would probably fall as well. If the FCC were to lift ownership caps, it would fuel efforts by media conglomerates such as Viacom or News Corp. to take over large stations groups, such as Sinclair Broadcast group of Baltimore, with sixty-one stations, Hearst-Argyle of New York, or Paxson Communications of West Palm Beach. Instead of having to cherry-pick individual stations or acquire smaller station groups, media conglomerates could go after groups that own fifty or sixty stations.[43] Conversely, large station groups could become even larger, as they attempt to stave off being acquired by buying more stations themselves. Thus local television stations, most of which are already part of large groups, would be swallowed up by even larger corporations if the ownership cap is increased or eliminated.

The prospect of an easing or even a removal of the cap has divided groups that represent local stations. Companies that own groups of stations, such as Paxson and Sinclair, have said that they welcome deregulation, because it will make them more attractive to investors and able to expand into other markets.[44] Network affiliates, however, have objected to the idea of lifting the ownership cap on the grounds that this will spur the networks to gobble up stations and convert more of them into affiliates, thus weakening the bargaining power of each. Network affiliates have an incentive to broadcast all network programming, and without some sort of cap, NASA argues, viewers will lose local stations that cover local and regional events.[45] NASA and the NAB argue that the court has not invalidated the cap, only asked for a justification of the 35 percent figure.[46]

Local stations argue that what is at stake is a fundamental principle of the U.S. communications industry. According to Andy Fisher of the Cox stations, a former chair of the station alliance:

What's at stake here is a social issue. And the social issue is something that the government will have to decide. The social issue is whether or not the historic ability of local stations and a broad variety of companies of all sizes—small, medium and large—are going to be permitted to make independent decisions that deal with a very narrow margin of time, or whether the networks have the right to say in their contractual negotiations that we have basically ownership of certain chunks of your day over which you will have virtually no control and from which you can never deviate.

According to Fisher, station owners feel that what the networks want is "a dumb pipe," a relationship in which they exert total control over affiliates.[47]

Industry insiders expect that many of the changes that began in the early 1990s will continue into the twenty-first century. In 2003, NBC executives estimated that the networks' compensation payments to affiliates would drop to one quarter of their 1999 level by 2006, and by 2010, when the next cycle of affiliate renewals starts, many believe that compensation will no longer exist.[48] This will hit smaller stations especially hard, as compensation payments represent the only profits some of them earn.[49] At the same time, affiliates are being asked to shoulder a larger percentage of the networks' cost for expensive programming such as sports. Under the terms of a 1999 agreement, ABC affiliates chipped in $45 million each year to subsidize *Monday Night Football* and gave back ten commercial spots during the network's Saturday-morning programs. Networks are demanding that affiliates pay more of the cost of the programs they receive at the same time that affiliates face massive financial burdens in converting to digital.

The extent to which networks can "repurpose" programming on local cable systems or other local stations has also become a common item in affiliate negotiations.[50] By the end of 2002, each of the major networks had acquired cable outlets in the same markets as some of its local stations. Some networks began experimenting with using local cable systems, rather than television stations, as affiliates and reran programming on them. NBC bought Bravo as an outlet for its shows; ABC "repurposed" programs on the ABC Family channel; and Fox "cross-pollinated" shows on its FX cable channel. Reruns of primetime programs on other cable channels have become commonplace, as illustrated by NBC's repeats of *Law and Order: Special Victims Unit* and *Criminal Intent* on the USA Network and the multiple screenings of *The Weakest Link* on cable.[51] In 1999 the WB cobbled together a cable affiliate system, the

WeB, to air programs in small markets where there are not enough unaffiliated stations to carry its signal. Other networks eye this model as a way of extending their systems and of forcing their existing affiliates to share the cost of programming.[52] The increased consolidation in the cable industry, and the networks' strategic alliances with cable companies, are putting increased pressure on local broadcast stations to give in to network demands for more control.

The Cost of Conversion

The trend toward consolidation and deregulation that characterizes U.S. media industries in the early twenty-first century affects the conversion to digital technologies that is taking place at the same time. To understand how this complex environment of competing interests shapes the emerging structure of HDTV, it is helpful to know what characteristics of this new technology affect networks and local stations. In essence, high-definition television separates the continuous signals of conventional analog television into discrete units that can be transmitted in compressed form. This is done through two steps that may be thought of as synchronic and diachronic. First, in a process called sampling, the analog signal is measured at regular intervals, where its distinguishing features are selected. Sampling reduces the size of the data stream by eliminating redundancies to create a new, more condensed synchronic form. At each point in the sampling, the complexity or depth of the signal is captured through a process called quantization, what we might call the diachronic element in digital television. In this step a crucial decision is how dense to make each point along the signal, how many pixels are necessary to capture the distinctive visual qualities of each moment.

Both processes, sampling and quantization, focus on distinctive elements and eliminate redundant ones, making the signal more compressed than in analog. Once a signal has been sampled and quantized, it is encoded into a binary form that can be transmitted rapidly. That digital signals are transmitted as binary code also means that they can be manipulated in various ways to rearrange the visual elements, unlike analog signals, whose contents cannot be manipulated. Such dense signals cannot be transmitted over ordinary broadcast or cable equipment, but require fiber-optic lines or other large "pipes" that can accommodate the massive amount of information they contain.[53]

Digital television changes the language and technology of broadcasting from the familiar one of film and video to the less familiar realm of information technology. Stations must now think of equipment in terms of platforms, servers, and software packages, rather than video or tape decks.[54] Cameras use disks instead of tape, and prime-time shows become files that can be stored on computer drives.[55] All of this complex equipment uses more electricity, so stations have had to upgrade or replace much of their electrical wiring. These changes in equipment often lead to changes in the design of workspace itself, toward more open arrangements around computer areas rather than small, individual rooms.[56] Large scale postproduction suites are replaced by "graphic bullpens" in which activities that were formerly separate, like video and sound editing, can be done together.[57] The enhanced visual quality of the high- definition image also makes every object in front of the camera more visible, forcing stations to improve the look of many production elements such as sets, clothing, makeup, and props.[58]

In order to transmit these new digital signals, stations must invest in new towers, transmitters, antennas, and switchers. The total cost of converting just one television station to digital is estimated to run between three and six million dollars, and if a station chooses to upgrade equipment used in production as well as transmission, such as the trucks and satellites needed for local news, that cost can double or triple.[59] The amount of money that television stations and networks are spending to convert to digital is comparable to what film studios spent when converting to synchronized sound in the late 1920s.

The speed at which stations convert to digital technology is governed by FCC mandates. In 1996 the FCC ruled that all television stations had to be digital by 2006. To implement this decision, the commission established a set of deadlines. ABC, NBC, CBS, and Fox affiliates in the ten largest markets were required to convert by May 1999, and the remaining network affiliates by November 1999. All other commercial stations, including those in smaller markets, were expected to be digital-ready by May 1, 2002, and public television stations by May 2003.[60] These staggered deadlines reflect the FCC's recognition that stations of different sizes and profitability may need more time to absorb the cost of the change. It quickly became apparent that for many local stations, the transition would not be rapid or easy. One week before the May 2002 deadline by which all commercial stations were expected to be digital, only 297 out of 1,400 stations were broadcasting digital signals, and more than half had filed for extensions.[61] Small stations in particular felt the brunt of the change: Only 14 percent of the stations in smaller markets had begun digital broadcasts by the deadline.

Networks and stations both experience financial hardships from this conversion, but for different reasons. Networks who took advantage of the looser ownership cap to buy more stations are faced simultaneously with the need to pay for their acquisitions and to digitize the facilities they've acquired. They must also pay to convert their owned and operated affiliates, and to digitize the production technology they use to create programming. Many television stations operate as part of chains, and the owners of these chains must also meet the expense of multiple conversions. Networks and station groups must also pay to redesign sets, wiring, and workspaces at more than one facility.

The impact of digital conversion on individual stations depends on the size of their market and their profitability. Stations in larger markets pay for many of the same things that stations in smaller markets pay for, but they have a greater revenue stream to cover the expense. In larger markets, the cost of conversion might be 11 percent of a station's yearly revenues, but in smaller markets, the cost could amount to two or three times more than its annual revenues. In some markets, the cost of conversion is more than a station's total value. Since most viewers do not have high-definition TVs, advertisers won't pay a higher premium for digital broadcasts, so stations do not have many ways to recoup these costs. Some station owners estimated that it would take all of their profits for several years to cover the conversion.[62] And if networks do away with compensation payments to local stations, that will eliminate a key source of their revenue.[63] Many local stations failed to meet the FCC deadline on purpose, because they were not able to cover the cost of these new technologies. And some wondered why they should even bother, if most of their audience couldn't receive the signals anyway.[64]

The FCC schedule itself also caused problems for both networks and stations. Having one deadline for hundreds of stations meant that everyone was ordering equipment and transmitters at the same time, and calling upon the services of a small corps of engineers and consultants. Stations that waited until the deadline approached to order equipment sometimes found it was not available. When the equipment was finally installed, some cities complained about the look and location of transmission towers. And they had unexpected other consequences. One station in Dallas found that its new digital transmitter interfered with heart monitors in a local hospital, leading the FCC to require stations to notify hospitals in their communities when they were going to begin digital transmissions.[65] Given the cost and complexity of the equipment, some local stations decided to share facilities and equipment with other stations in their area, further increasing consolidation at the local level.[66]

The cost of converting to digital is changing the financial structure of television as well. Some media companies borrowed money to pay for the conversion, which meant they took on additional debt and committed themselves to long-term payments. Others sold off assets to finance the cost of digital equipment. The move to digital is one force propelling television stations to divest themselves of their radio holdings, for example. With the conversion to digital absorbing so much of a station's costs, other aspects suffered. A station might not be able to put as many news trucks or satellite hookups in the field, for example, reducing its capacity to follow local stories.[67] The expensive technology of digital television has caused reverberations through many other areas of the industry.

The Land Grab for Bandwidth

The conversion to digital technology has made much more spectrum space available to the television industry. When the FCC decided to promote digital technology, it allocated $70 billion worth of additional spectrum space for its development. To help the transition go more smoothly, the commission allowed stations to keep the space through which they transmit analog signals, so that they could develop digital transmissions without compromising their existing programming. This allowed stations to simultaneously broadcast both kinds of signals, thus introducing additional space into the television arena. At the same time, networks and local stations have gained the increased bandwidth provided by digital technology, which enables much denser streams of data to be transmitted. How networks and stations will use all this space has become the subject of fierce debate. What one news producer described as the "land grab" for bandwidth is intensifying the already heightened strain between local stations and national networks for control over programming.[68] In addition to being programmers, television stations today must also become "bandwidth managers."[69]

One way to use the new digital capacity is to devote it to high definition. Since networks have historically produced the big-budget, star-studded spectacles of television, they have been the first to use digital technology to broadcast programs such as sports and special features in high definition. The earliest network broadcasts in HDTV included astronaut John Glenn's return to space in 1998, ABC's *Wonderful World of Disney*, *The Tonight Show with Jay Leno*, and CBS's *Chicago Hope*.[70] At first, networks broadcast only selected programs in high definition, but by December 2002 CBS and ABC were broadcasting most of their prime-time comedies and dramas in the new digital format, as well as the Super Bowl, the NCAA Men's Final Four, the U.S. Open tennis tournament, and the Stanley Cup finals.[71] In 2003 several networks announced that they would broadcast major awards shows in high definition: the Grammy Awards on CBS, and the Oscars on ABC.[72] The first all-high-definition channel, HDNet, debuted in spring 2002, founded by Mark Cuban, the billionaire owner of the NBA Dallas Mavericks. HDNet offers a sports-oriented network to subscribers of DirecTV on which all the programming is in high-definition. Cuban has also partnered with NBC to broadcast the Salt Lake City Olympics in high definition, and with Fox Sports to share broadcasts of Major League Baseball and the National Hockey League.[73]

But high-definition television is only one way to use digital technology. The amount of space required to broadcast one high-definition program can also be used to transmit three or four programs in standard definition. What is now Channel 16 might become Channels 16.1, 16.2, and 16.3, for example. This use of digital capacity, called "multicasting," would allow networks to air many of the programs in their schedules in the space now occupied by just one analog channel. Multicasting programs would enable them to reach many different kinds of audiences at the same time and not have to rely on their affiliates or local cable stations to carry their programs.

Cable networks already provide a model for how broadcast networks can implement multiple channels under the same network brand. The Discovery channel has launched six digital channels, including Discovery Science and Civilization, that use programs from its existing analog channels, Animal Planet, the Learning Channel, and the Travel Channel. Similarly, Nickelodeon is developing a digital spin-off in conjunction with the Children's Television Workshop that will make use of three thousand hours of *Sesame Street*. Each additional channel can generate subscription fees to cable systems or networks.[74] Both companies illustrate the value of having a recognizable "brand" in the new digital world, and the usefulness of libraries of programs. Networks could begin to sell packages of features in the way that cable systems do now, and the larger library a network has, the more ways it can be packaged.[75]

Such a model favors media conglomerates such as Time Warner, who could put CNN on one channel and air Warner Bros. films on another. Programming that is now diachronic will become synchronic: Instead of dividing programming across time slots, networks can air shows simultaneously. Networks can use the additional space for round-the-clock news and weather, or to air classic films from their libraries. Or the bandwidth could carry the same program, but in staggered time periods, much as HBO does today. This use of bandwidth, termed "multiplexing," would give viewers the opportunity to watch programs at times best suited to their schedules. As networks gain more means of distribution through acquiring more owned and operated stations or through digital transmissions, some are asking why they would even need affiliates.

Another possibility digital technology affords is multichannel-casting. With this mode of transmission, viewers can choose among multiple versions of the same event. One could watch a football program, for example, and select the camera angle and degree of zoom one preferred for each play.[76] This technology is already available in Britain through BskyB, which allows viewers who have the appropriate set-top device to split the screen into eight images and select among them. One can choose among different news items on Sky News, or switch among the weather, a sports feature, and Hollywood gossip, on screens displayed side by side.[77] As of April 2002, Sky was Britain's largest television provider, and each of its customers had digital TV.[78]

To guarantee access to the additional spectrum space that digital affords, networks are insisting that affiliates sign over a portion of their additional digital spectrum as part of the affiliation agreement. If you want our programming, the logic goes, you have to give us some of your additional space. In some cases the network may not have a clear strategy for using this extra bandwidth. NBC is thought to lack a coherent strategy for using its digital resources, whereas CBS and Fox are producing more programming in HDTV and have plans for the future development of their share of the digital spectrum.[79] Local stations, then, may be hamstrung in their ability to make use of this extra capacity because of their network affiliation.

Local stations point out that, under law, broadcast licenses are granted to them, not to network organizations, so they should control the bandwidth assigned to them. Since most cannot afford to originate their own high-definition programming, they are exploring other uses for the additional bandwidth that digital technology makes available. Using the extra channel capacity to air multiple broadcasts in standard definition is an attractive option for local stations, as it makes more room available for programs of local interest. Or a station might mix formats, multicasting local programs in standard definition by day, and airing network programs in HDTV by night.[80] Local stations argue that they need to preserve control of their extra bandwidth as a way to preserve the voices of the local communities they serve.

Many local stations are exploring another use for digital technology, datacasting. In this model, televisions function in much the same way personal computers do, by streaming data, such as stock market quotes, sports scores, or weather reports, into our living rooms. Information that is now available on station Web sites might be streamed onto our sets. Companies that include both television stations and newspapers under one corporate umbrella view datacasting as a way to maximize the use of data in each medium.[81] Using spectrum space in this way would also open up additional sources of revenue for local stations from businesses that want to use this additional space to transmit games, email, and other interactive services such as shopping into our homes.[82]

Various models have developed to use datacasting. Several station groups banded together to establish iBlast, a company set up to deliver data and music to home sets.[83] I-blast trolls for unused bandwidth during television broadcasts, finding excess capacity that varies according to daypart. I-blast and other companies will pay to use this transmission capacity, in much the same way that internet service providers pay to use excess telephone capacity.[84] In April 2000 Geocast Network Systems demonstrated software that would enable stations to deliver customized news and entertainment, as well as targeted advertisers, to viewers in the same way that desktop computers do. One year later, however, Geocast shut down, suggesting that some delivery systems might be ahead of their time. Station groups also band together to aggregate spectrum space in order to offer packages of datacasting services that can be used for long-distance education, military programs, or business-to-business communication.[85]

Of course, networks are also planning their own datacasting services to make use of the digital space that affiliates sign over to them. Yet the datacasting agreements some stations have arranged can mean that they have no bandwidth left to transmit the network's datacasting services. I-blast is a particular concern because it uses more spectrum space than other options and can interfere with network high-definition signals. Affiliates anticipate that when they renegotiate their contracts with the networks, the agreements will specify how many of the network's high-definition programs or datacasting services they must carry. Networks, on the other hand, say they want to maintain a cordial relationship with their affiliates, as local stations provide access to the national market. As one network executive said, "We want them to work with us and we don't want them to go off the reservation."[86]

Adding Our Voices

The tug-of-war for control over bandwidth promises to have profound, long-term implications for the television industry and for us as viewers. For both networks and stations, digital technologies have necessitated massive changes in production and distribution that are altering the material bases on which they operate. These changes have caused the industry to develop new strategies for financing and marketing television. How networks, stations, and cable and satellite systems interact with each other and rethink their own identities are also affected by the conversion to digital. The extra spaces that digital technologies introduce are creating new frontiers for television, where forces compete to grab as many resources as possible.

The increased bandwidth that digital technology provides is supposed to enhance diversity in programming, not diminish it. But in an era of consolidation, the opportunity for distinctive independent voices diminishes. The technology that was supposed to provide more room for alternative forms of representation may, ironically, serve as an additional venue for the same homogeneous products we see on-screen today. Though some speak warmly of the possibility for increased public access that extra bandwidth affords, if we remain oblivious to these debates, it will not be available for our use.

There is very little public awareness of the nature and significance of the transition to digital television. Most likely this indifference is due to the fact that, as of 2002, less than 100,000 homes had HDTV sets, and most people have yet to see a program broadcast in this format. Just as in the 1940s, there is not enough critical mass in programming to propel people to buy HDTV sets, and the prices of sets, though now under $2,500, are still out of reach for most viewers. Stations are transmitting digital signals that reach more than three-quarters of U.S. households, but most of us don't receive them. Many people buy digital TVs just to watch their DVDs.[87]

When digital technology is discussed in the press, it is often framed in terms of HDTV and its unique visual format, rather than as a struggle for control over the digital spectrum. But there is more involved in the transition to digital than just new gadgets. The changes affecting television today are worth knowing about, and we can participate in them by educating ourselves about their implications. The history of media provides many examples of other struggles that can help us understand where we find ourselves today. We have the ability to add our voices to this debate, and perhaps redirect its outcome.

NOTES

I would like to thank my colleague Gary Sieber, of WNDU-TV, for suggesting the title of this essay.

1 A history of television that places the medium in a global context is Anthony Smith, ed., *Television: An International History* (New York: Oxford UP, 1995).

2 Michel Dupagne and Peter B. Seel, *High-Definition Television: A Global Perspective* (Ames: Iowa State UP, 1998), provides a good overview of the global context in which HDTV has developed.

3 For a detailed and insightful analysis of the Telecommunications Act, see Patricia Aufderheide, *Communications Policy and the Public Interest: The Telecommunications Act of 1996* (New York: Guilford Press, 1999).

4 John M. Higgins and Steve McClellan, "Everything's in Play," *Broadcasting and Cable*, February 25, 2002, 18.

5 "FCC Action" page on the Web site of the Association of Independent Video and Filmmakers, http://www.aivf.org.

6 Joe Schlosser, "Two Nets One Basket," *Broadcasting and Cable*, December 17, 2001, 16–17; J. Bednarski, "A Screed against Greed," *Broadcasting and Cable*, January 1, 2000, 32.

7 Bill McConnell and Susanne Ault, "Fox TV's Strategy: Two by Two," *Broadcasting and Cable*, July 30, 2001; Dan Trigoboff, "Fox Swaps for a Pair of Duops," *Broadcasting and Cable*, August 13, 2001, Steve McClellan, "Fox Duops in Chicago," *Broadcasting and Cable* 1 July 2002, all at http://www.broadcastingcable.com. Joe Flint, "Viacom, News Corp. Set Swaps of TV Stations in Three Markets," *Wall Street Journal*, August 9, 2001.

8 Flint, "Viacom, News Corp. Set Swaps."

9 Susanne Ault, "Duops Do Deals," *Broadcasting and Cable*, August 20, 2001, http://www.broadcastingcable.com

10 Bednarski, "A Screed against Greed," 32.

11 Susanne Ault, "Duopolies Test Market Muscle," *Broadcasting and Cable*, September 10, 2001, http://www.broadcastingcable.com.

12 Bill McConnell, "Duopolies: The Pair Necessities," *Broadcasting and Cable*, January 21, 2002, 58.

13 Ibid.; McConnell, "Review, Relax, Relieve," *Broadcasting and Cable*, February 5, 2001, Perry A. Sook, "Voice Rule Gotta Go," *Broadcasting and Cable*, March 4, 2002, http://www.broadcastingcable.com.

14 McConnell, "Duopolies," 58; ibid., "Powell Likes Duop," *Broadcasting and Cable*, May 14, 2001, 10–11; ibid., "NAB Unveils Duop Plan," *Broadcasting and Cable*, January 6, 2003, http://www.broadcastingcable.com.

15 Mark Wigfield, "FCC Ordered by Court to Revisit Broadcast-Ownership Restrictions," *Wall Street Journal*, April 3, 2002.

16 Bill McConnell, "TV Owners Urge Duopoly Leniency," *Broadcasting and Cable*, January 3, 2003, http://www.broadcastingcable.com.

17 Yochi J. Dreazen and Joe Flint, "Court Rejects Curbs on Media Ownership," *Wall Street Journal*, February 20, 2002.

18 Ibid. See also Pamela McClintock, "Feds Bottle Caps," *Variety*, September 9, 2001, http://www.variety.com

19 Higgins and McClellan, "Everything's in Play," 18.

20 Deborah Solomon and Robert Frank, "Broad Bands: Comcast Deal Cements Rise of an Oligopoly in the Cable Business," *Wall Street Journal*, December 21, 2002, http://www.wsj.com.

21 Jennifer Lee, "Small Cable Operators Worry about Life after Big Mergers," *New York Times*, December 26, 2001, http://www.nytimes.com.

22 Bill McConnell, "Reg Review Is Spring-Loaded," *Broadcasting and Cable*, August 15, 2002, http://www.broadcastingcable.com.

23 Pamela McClintock, "FCC Is Owning Up," *Variety*, October 1, 2002, http://www.variety.com.

24 Stephen Labaton, "F.C.C. Weighs a Sharp Easing of Size Limits on Big Media," *New York Times*, September 7, 2002, http://www.nytimes.com; McClintock, "FCC Is Owning Up."

25 Mark Wigfield, "FCC Ordered by Court to Revisit Broadcast-Ownership Restrictions," *Wall Street Journal*, April 3, 2002; Bill McConnell, "Judges Attack Eight-Voice Duopoly Rule," *Broadcasting and Cable*, April 3, 2002, http://www.broadcastingcable.com.

26 McConnell, "NAB Unveils Duop Plan."

27 Jim Rutenberg, "Fewer Media Owners, More Media Choices," *New York Times*, December 2, 2002, http://www.nytimes.com.

28 Senator Byron Dorgan (D-North Dakota), quoted in Elizabeth Olson, "F.C.C. Chief Dismisses Talk of Extensive Rule Changes," *New York Times*, January 15, 2003, http://www.nytimes.com.

29 "FCC to Hold Public Hearing on Broadcast Ownership Rules," press release, Federal Communications Commission, Washington, D.C., January 23, 2003, http://www.fcc.gov.

30 Jill Goldsmith, "Dizzy Data Has FCC in a Cap Tizzy," *Variety*, January 16, 2003, http://www.variety.com.

31 Lynette Holloway, "The Balance of Media Power Is Poised to Change," *New York Times*, December 30, 2002, http://www.nytimes.com; Pamela McClintock, "The Year in Regulation," *Variety*, January 19, 2003, http://www.variety.com; Stephen Labaton, "Dream Nears Reality: Ease Up at the F.C.C.," *New York Times*, February

2, 2003, http://www.nytimes.com; Mark Wigfield, "FCC Could Sweep Out Key Telecom Rules in 2003," *Wall Street Journal*, January 6, 2002, http://www.wsj.com.

32 Michael D. Murray and Donald G. Godfrey, eds., *Television in America: Local Station History from across the Nation* (Ames: Iowa State UP, 1997), xxiii–xxv.

33 James Walker and Douglas Ferguson, *The Broadcast Television Industry* (Boston: Allyn and Bacon, 1998), 85–86.

34 Joe Flint, "How the Top Networks Are Turning the Tables on Their Affiliates," *Wall Street Journal*, June 15, 2000, A1, A8.

35 Ibid., A1.

36 Steve McClellan, "NBC: The Party's Over," *Broadcasting and Cable*, February 2, 2001, 10.

37 "Local U.S. TV Stations Seek FCC Investigation of Major Networks," March 9, 2001, http://www.cnet.com; Steve McClellan, "It's War!" *Broadcasting and Cable*, March 12, 2001, 6–10, http://www.broadcastingcable.com.

38 Alan Frank, quoted in Pamela McClintock, "Affils Fightin' Mad," *Variety*, March 7, 2001, http://www.variety.com.

39 Joe Flint, "Local TV Stations Ask FCC to Investigate Big Networks," *Wall Street Journal*, March 9, 2001, http://www.wsj.com.

40 "It's Come to This," *Broadcasting and Cable*, April 9, 2001, 19.

41 Ibid, 18–22.

42 Steve McClellan, "Network, Affils Fight On," *Broadcasting and Cable*, April 2, 2001, 5–6; Paige Albiniak, "Nets vs. Affils: Another Round," *Broadcasting and Cable*, April 9, 2001, 8–9; and Yochi J. Dreazen, "CBS, Infinity Leave Trade Group NAB over Ownership Cap," *Wall Street Journal*, April 5, 2001, http://www.wsj.com.

43 Robert Frank and Joe Flint, "Broadcasters Are Poised for Consolidation," *Wall Street Journal*, February 21, 2002; Aaron Barnhart, "Court Ruling Could Bring Changes to Local Television Stations," *Kansas City Star*, February 22, 2002, http://www.KansasCity.com.

44 Bill McConnell and Steve McClellan, "Duopportunity Knocks," *Broadcasting and Cable*, April 8, 2002; Bill McConnell, "TV Owners Urge Duopoly Leniency," *Broadcasting and Cable*, January 3, 2003, both http://www.broadcastingcable.com.

45 Alan Frank, "Keep Cap on Number of TV Stations for One Owner," *USA Today*, February 2, 2002, http://www.usatoday.com.

46 "NAB, NASA: FCC Has Cap Power," *Broadcasting and Cable*, April 2, 2002, http://www.broadcastingcable.com.

47 "It's Come to This," 20.

48 Steve McClellan, "Peace, Love, and Affiliates," *Broadcasting and Cable*, March 11, 2002, http://www.broadcastingcable.com.

49 Steve McClellan, "Small Towns, Big Problems," *Broadcasting and Cable*, August 6, 2001, 20.

50 Michael Schneider and Craig Offman, "ABC, Affils Kick Around NFL Deal," *Variety*, July 10, 2002, http://www.variety.com.

51 Meredith Amdur, "NBC's Cable Vision," *Variety*, November 4, 2002, http://www.variety.com.

52 John M. Higgins, "Frustration Put Cable in Equation," *Broadcasting and Cable*, January 18, 1999, 24.

53 My discussion here draws on the following sources: Joan Van Tassel, *Digital TV over Broadband: Harvesting Bandwidth* (Boston: Focal Press/Butterworth-Heinemann, 2001), 44–53; Don West, "The Medium That Couldn't Kill," in "The Dawn of Digital Television," special supplement to *Broadcasting and Cable,* November 1998; Chris Forrester, *The Business of Digital Television* (Boston: Focal Press/Butterworth-Heinemann, 2000), 50–61.

54 Ken Kerschbaumer, "Taking Digital Further," *Broadcasting and Cable,* March 11, 2002, http://www.broadcastingcable.com.

55 Margot Suydam, "The All-Digital TV Network," *Broadcasting and Cable,* January 11, 1998, 86.

56 Alan Waldman, "Digital Garden of Eden," *Broadcasting and Cable*, April 25, 2001, 24.

57 Karen Anderson, "Your New Digital Home," *Broadcasting and Cable,* January 11, 1999, 72.

58 Van Tassel, *Digital TV over Broadband,* 126.

59 Glen Dickson, "The High Cost of Pioneering in DTV," in "The Dawn of Digital Television," supplement to *Broadcasting and Cable,* November 1998, S36–S39.

60 Jim Rutenberg, "A Digital Divide Threatens Public TV," *New York Times,* April 15, 2001, http://www.nytimes.com; Tim Cuprisin, "Few Stations Will Meet Their Digital Deadlines," *Milwaukee Journal Sentinel,* April 24, 2002, http://www.jsonline.com; "DTV Primer: DTV Roll-Out Schedule," http://www.pbs.org/digitaltv/dtvtech/rollout.htm.

61 Cuprisin, "Few Stations."

62 David Lieberman, "Small TV Stations Reel under Order to Go Digital," *USAToday,* July 17, 2002, B1, B2.

63 McClellan, "Small Towns, Big Problems," 20.

64 Michael Grotticelli, Ken Kerschbaumer, and Bill McConnell, "Trying Times for DTV," *Broadcasting and Cable,* April 25, 2001, 6; Lieberman, "Small TV Stations Reel," B1.

65 Andrew Bowser, "The DTV Waiting Game," *Broadcasting and Cable,* September 4, 2000, 42–50; ibid., "Leading the Charge from South Bend," *Broadcasting and Cable,* April 8, 1998, 20; Karen Anderson, "Fighting the Towers-To-Be," *Broadcasting and Cable,* April 5, 1998, 46–49; Andrew Bowser, "Digital in the Heart of Texas," *Broadcasting and Cable,* July 20, 1998, 32.

66 Bowser, "The DTV Waiting Game," 42–50.

67 Lieberman, "Small TV Stations Reel," B1.

68 Gary Sieber, WNDU-TV, conversation with the author, June 16, 2001, Notre Dame, Ind.

69 Van Tassel, *Digital TV over Broadband,* 106–107.

70 Paige Albiniak, "HDTV: Launched and Counting," *Broadcasting and Cable,* November 2, 1998, 6–8.

71 Glen Dickson and Paige Albiniak, "Where's the HDTV?" *Broadcasting and Cable,* October 12, 1998, 10–14; Bill McConnell, "CBS Threatens to Stop HDTV," *Broadcasting and Cable,* December 12, 2002, http://www.broadcastingcable.com.

72 Phil Gallo, "Grammys Tuned for HDTV," *Variety,* January 14, 2003, http://www.variety.com; David Bloom, "Oscars Get Close with High Definition," *Variety,* January 9, 2003, http://www.variety.com; Eric A. Taub, "The Big Picture on Digital TV: It's Still Fuzzy," *New York Times,* September 12, 2002, http://www.nytimes.com.

73 "Mark Cuban's HDTV View," *Business Week,* December 16, 2002, http://www.businessweek.com; Elliot Spagat, "Dallas Mavericks Owner Makes a Big Bet on Digital Television," *Wall Street Journal,* March 7, 2002, http://www.wsj.com.

74 Donna Petrozzello, "Bite-Size Branding in Digital Age," *Broadcasting and Cable,* May 4, 1998, 88–92.

75 "What's So Great about Digital?" *Broadcasting and Cable,* May 4, 1998, 30–36; Steve McClellan, "Multicasting's in the CBS Mix," *Broadcasting and Cable,* October 13, 1997, 6, 10; Joe Flint and Bruce Orwall, "'ABC Family' Cable Channel Will Replay Network Fare, Plus Some Original Shows," *Wall Street Journal,* July 24, 2001, http://www.wsj.com.

76 The analysis here draws on the discussion in Van Tassel, *Digital TV over Broadband,* 106–107.

77 Sophie Pedder, "Entertain Me," *Economist,* April 11, 2002, http://www.economist.com.

78 Christine Chen, "I Want My iTV," *Fortune,* April 1, 2002, 124.

79 Employee of WNDU-TV, conversation with the author, June 16, 2001, Notre Dame, Ind.

80 This analysis draws on Michael Mirabito and Barbara L. Morgenstern, *The New Communications Technologies: Applications, Policy, and Impact,* 4th ed. (Boston: Focal Press/Butterworth-Heinemann, 2001), 159–162, and Ian Baldwin, "Test Tubes," *Kiplinger's,* July 2000, 97.

81 "Editorial Independence," *Broadcasting and Cable,* April 10, 2000, http://www.broadcastingcable.com.

82 Ronald Grover, "Stealing a March on the Networks," *Business Week,* November 13, 2000, 92–96.

83 Ibid.

84 Michael Grotticelli, "Wither iBlast?" *Broadcasting and Cable,* May 7, 2001, http://www.broadcastingcable.com.

85 Ken Kerschbaumer, "Datacasting: Sowing the Seeds," *Broadcasting and Cable,* August 6, 2001, http://www.broadcastingcable.com; Glen Dickson, "Datacasting for Dollars," *Broadcasting and Cable,* April 24, 2000, http://www.broadcastingcable.com.

86 Ken Kerschbaumer, "Battle Brews for Spectrum," *Broadcasting and Cable,* April 3, 2000, 10.

87 Spagat, "Dallas Mavericks Owner."

POSTHUMAN LAW

INFORMATION POLICY
AND THE MACHINIC WORLD

SANDRA BRAMAN

It is an unspoken assumption that the law is made by humans for humans.
That assumption no longer holds: The information, communication, and culture that are the subject of information law and policy increasingly flow
between machines, or between machines and humans. Machinic rather than
social values play ever-more-important roles in the decision-making calcu-
lus. Information policy making for human society is being supplemented,
supplanted, and superceded by machinic decision making. With the implan-
tation of technologies in the human body—it is now possible to connect computer chips directly to the neural cells of the brain—the legal distinction
between the human and machinic may well fall altogether. This would be a
logical next step in the progression from viewing information and communication technologies as:

barriers to experience,[1]
shaping experience,[2]
experience itself,[3]
to seeing technology as the reality being experienced.[4]

These transformations are profound enough that we may begin to refer to
the emergence of posthuman law.

This is of course not the first time the content and practice of the law
have mutated in response to new conditions. Technological developments
such as the railroad and electricity; the shift from an agrarian to an industrial

economy; the social changes wrought by urbanization, the rise of the middle class, populism, and successive waves of immigration; the geographic expansion of the West; and changing relations with other countries have all brought U.S. law into new areas of activity and stimulated the development of new types of policy tools.[5] Ideological and theoretical developments have generated political and economic conflict that resulted in legal change.[6] Information-related issues have been among the stimuli for changes in the law since the beginning,[7] though it is only in recent decades that they have come to dominate.

The growing importance of posthuman law in the sense that technologies increasingly provide the goals, the subject, and the tools of policy making is one characteristic of the emergent global information policy regime. Three factors are contributing to the development of this regime: First, technological innovation and globalization of the firms, content, and audiences of the media of information, communication, and culture. Second, the intertwining of regulation of the information infrastructure with that of other types of activities that exist within and are reliant upon that infrastructure, what is referred to in Europe as the *filière électronique*. And third, decisions made by the private sector and in public-private policy networks that are often global rather than international in nature today have as much or more structural effect than decisions made by nation-states and via the nation-state-based system of international law. Some key aspects of the emergent global information policy regime did not exist in legacy law and are therefore not visible using traditional types of analytical tools. This can be a dangerous situation from the perspective of participatory decision making regarding the most fundamental elements of our communicative existence; the argument being put forward here therefore has not only theoretical interest but critical political implications. The phenomenon being described is worldwide but presents its most sophisticated case in the U.S. example. The U.S. example is also important to understanding the global information policy regime because it continues to be highly influential in shaping that regime.

This article examines technologies as the subject of information policy, as determinant of the values that inform information policy, and as policy makers. The word "technologies" as used here refers to both technologies and to meta-technologies—that is, to the technologies limited in the range of inputs, outputs, and processing steps that characterized the industrial era as

well as to the meta-technologies of unlimited inputs, outputs, and processing steps that characterize the information society.[8] The assemblage presented by the often-intertwined types of technologies is described as
"machinic."

Technologies as the Subject of Information Policy

The notion of the information society is based on Engels's law—the quantitative increase in the number of information technologies upon which we are
dependent and the number of ways in which we are dependent upon them
has yielded a qualitative change in the nature of society. As human dependence upon the information infrastructure grows, the network and other
information technologies are increasingly included within the social universe to which policy applies. Already, policy is being made that changes law
as it was designed for the human in order to take care of the needs of the
machinic. The U.S. Telecommunications Act of 1996 provides a vivid example
by distinguishing between the social and the machinic: Universal service
obligations require access to the network for *individuals*, while universal
access obligations require access for *telecommunications networks*. In popular,
and often policy, discourse the difference between the two is often elided.

Regulation that mandates the interconnection of telecommunications
networks, which first appeared in the U.S. following the positive experience
with the utility and value added when the telegraph, telephone, and radio
systems were nationalized during World War I, was one of the first types of
policy directed at the network itself. Today, there are policies explicitly
directed at technologies in the areas of surveillance, encryption, copyright
protection, and censorship (filtering). This raises questions about the types
of policy tools used when technology is the policy subject, the relationship
and differences between the human and the machinic as policy subjects, and
problems raised by technology as a policy subject.

POLICY TOOLS FOR THE REGULATION OF TECHNOLOGY

Policy specialists have been discussing the regulatory implications of computer code since the mid-1990s,[9] and the topic reached public discourse after
it was popularized by legal scholar Lawrence Lessig.[10] Manipulations of code
for regulatory purposes can take place at four different levels of the infrastructure: At the root server level of the domain name system, at the application layer of the TCP/IP protocol that defines the Internet, on individual

users' hard drives, and in the design of digital products that may be sold or distributed off-line or online.[11]

Code is not the only means by which technologies are subjected to regulation, however. Technical standard setting in the private sector, government procurement practices, public statutory and regulatory law, and decision making by emergent regulatory entities such as ICANN all direct policy tools at digital technologies. Specific policy tools include requiring adaptations to technologies, antitrust law, differentially taxing different types of technologies and/or their production, and promoting the development of certain types of technologies through government procurement practices, funding for research and development (R&D), or simply looking the other way when innovations are put into place that are destructive (as when copyright protection mechanisms destroy hardware and prevent the use of services). Constitutional law, too, regulates technologies, for the question of whether or not information processing is a form of speech and/or information gathering necessary for the exercise of First Amendment rights and therefore deserving of constitutional protections is still being debated.[12]

Analysis of technologies as a regulatory subject is complex because of the mix of public, private, and "networked" (combined public and private) policy settings in which decision making takes place. Nor is all pertinent regulation the result of centralized decision making; notably, much of the technical development of the Internet with social effect was deliberately decentralized.[13]

SOCIETY VS. TECHNOLOGY AS THE POLICY SUBJECT

There is a spectrum of motivations for directing policy at technologies as the regulatory subject. As a result, there are differences in the degree to which such regulation should be considered social policy as well—and in whether the effects on social policy are direct or indirect. At one extreme, the use of a technological intervention to achieve a social goal is explicit, as in the requirement that packet-switched telecommunications networks be adapted to enable surveillance for law enforcement purposes as it was in U.S. law in the Communications Assistance for Law Enforcement Act of 1994 (CALEA). At the other extreme, decisions are put in place that present themselves as required solely for technical reasons with only technical impact, as exemplified by Internet protocols up to and through the domain name system. That technical decisions in fact have direct tremendous social, political, cultural, and economic impact is now widely understood,[14] however, and first steps towards developing methods for taking such decisions into account in the conduct of information policy analysis are beginning to appear.[15]

The heavy center of this spectrum is filled with policies that appear to be justified for social or economic reasons but that are so oriented around technological issues that they have the effect of permitting the "needs" of technological systems to dominate decision making for the social world. This is the case, for example, when federal law preempts state law regarding cable television content because doing so was necessary for the growth of the national cable system, an argument upheld by the U.S. Supreme Court in *Capital Cities v Crisp*,[16] as if the rights of the network itself were specified in the Constitution. Creating exemptions to antitrust law for the purposes of research and development for very high speed integrated chips (VHSIC) in the early 1980s is another example. While the strengthening of foreign competition in this area provided a social justification for this change in the law, the feature of this technology that required a loosening of antitrust, or competition, law was the requirement to collaborate in the use of intellectual property rights held by multiple firms. This was not new—multiple patents, often with different owners, have been involved in the production of individual information and communication technologies since the late nineteenth century. Numerous times in the past corporations have merged or combined efforts in various ways in order to share the necessary intellectual property rights, and numerous times antitrust law has been used to tear those combinations apart. By the early 1980s, however—a century after the tension between antitrust law and the need to share access to intellectual property rights first became clear—the weight of the argument finally shifted in favor of serving technological rather than social goals.

The notion of "standing" before the law—the right to pursue redress for perceived injustice within the legal system—has steadily broadened over the past couple of hundred years within the social and natural domains. The boundaries of the social domain to which policy applies have expanded in the U.S. through redefinition of the population to be considered for the political purposes of the census to include women, children, immigrants, and those who had been slaves; the franchise—the right to vote—was expanded through a process that took most of the twentieth century; and expansion of the public sphere, the site for public discourse about political matters, is still under way. The legal status of the natural world before the law has been raised by those concerned about environmental matters in recent decades, manifesting itself in the concept of environmental security as a form of national security,[17] and in the U.S. Supreme Court consideration of the granting of legal rights to natural environments such as forests.[18] It is likely that consideration of the "rights" of the technologies upon which we are dependent will become more explicit over the next few years. Analysis of the liability issues raised by the decisions made and actions taken by intelligent agents will inevitably raise the salience of this type of question on the policy agenda.

PROBLEMS RAISED BY TECHNOLOGY AS THE POLICY SUBJECT

There are both implementation and conceptual problems when regulating technologies as a policy subject. At the implementation level, code-based changes can be countered by other code that bypasses, breaks through, or otherwise circumvents the effects of policy. Alternative technological systems can have the same effect, as in the growing use of a domain name system that falls completely outside the purview of ICANN. Anticircumvention rules may be built into the law, as they were in the 1996 WIPO Treaty and the 1998 U.S. Digital Millennium Copyright Act, but both court challenges and practice are likely to undermine these provisions at the level of implementation. There is a danger that too much regulation will drive users away. And regulation directed at one type of technology may have unintended effects on other technologies or practices, as when copyright protection schemes for software wind up disabling hardware.

Conceptually, technologies and humans as agents are different in ways that problematize the extension of legal principles to the machinic world. Whether it is a question of freedom for political speech or antitrust, the goal of information policy is to constrain or encourage the actions of agents in order to minimize or maximize particular types of effects. Causality within the world of policy has been understood as direct—meaning discernible, affected by relatively few intervening variables, and occurring via single or very few causal steps. Agents were identifiable, whether in the individual person or the organizational persons created by the legal fiction of incorporation. In the contemporary environment, however, technological agents are not recognized by the law as fictive or real persons and yet there is clearly implied agency in the identification of technology as a policy subject. This is a conceptual problem that has not yet been adequately resolved within the law. The historical analogue of creation of the fictive person of a corporation with legal status under the law suggests the possible creation of a second category of fictive person with legal status for technologies and/or technological systems.

Machinic Values in Information Policy

One of the unique features of information policy is the multiplicity of values that inform decision-making processes. This is exacerbated by the dispersal of policy making across multiple venues, each with a different portfolio entailing its own value hierarchy, modes of argument, and operational definitions. Technology can be considered among these values in both an abstract and a concrete sense. Conceptually, technology is a manifestation of the value of "technique," defined by philosopher of technology Jacques Ellul as a predetermined means of achieving a predetermined end.[19] On the ground, technology informs information policy making as a value when machinic analytical techniques are relied upon exclusively for the data inputs upon which decisions are made.

Attitudes toward the desirability of this type of influence on policy making have gone back and forth. There have been repeated rounds of experimentation with such approaches or their actual incorporation within the law, only to be questioned in the courts or rejected by practitioners.[20] The Regulatory Reform Act of 1982 (which amended the Administrative Procedure Act), for example, required agencies to perform cost-benefit analysis when proposing and promulgating regulations,[21] though the U.S. Supreme Court has several times considered the appropriateness of such techniques in particular situations worthy of constitutional consideration.[22] Both justification for accepting a role for machinic values in information policy and arguments against doing so are several.

JUSTIFICATIONS

A philosophical basis for the use of computerized approaches to legal decision making can be found in the probabilistic thinking that lies at the heart of all rules and in utilitarian principles for governance.[23] "Winning" in such a situation is defined as maximizing benefits of a policy. Thus the "efficiency" claim holds only in the sense betrayed by cost-benefit analysis.

The use of inference strategies to support legal decision making does have a long history in the distinction between material and procedural law. The utility principle of governance, in accordance with which governments would try through careful calculation to achieve the greatest happiness for the greatest number, offers an alternative justification for using technologically derived inputs into policy making. The subtlety of such approaches has improved; even game theory today is sensitive to ways in which small changes in information at the disposal of actors can affect both the existence and character of equilibria achieved.[24] The concept of an algorithm as it is used in computing is broader than that of a mathematical formula, referring to the basic design for how data is to be organized and manipulated in a program in order to establish certain results.[25] In distributed computing systems, the interactions and results look ever more organic.

Other advantages can appear when it is possible to use expert systems to make the tacit knowledge of individuals available to others and when the factors being analyzed are quantifiable. Historically, such techniques came to dominate policy making under the rubric of operations research during World War II when the amount of information to be managed exploded and personnel with training in systems analysis became involved in government. Clearly computerization makes it easier to compare the possible consequences of alternative policy approaches or to explore possible implications further out than ordinary human vision can necessarily see.[26] There are times when such techniques are required to dissolve the ambiguity of other types of data, as when the military uses the sophisticated software of MASINT (Measurement and Signatures Intelligence) known as "exploitation algorithms" for this purpose.[27]

The ease of use of computerized approaches to decision-making support for policy making may be the most overwhelming advantage. Indeed, precisely for this reason analytical techniques that can be so treated tend to be favored over those that may be more representative of the diversity of interests and values that should be incorporated into the decision-making process.[28] On its own, however, this is hardly a strong justification. Such approaches have been most acceptable when they provide inputs into decision making, assessing alternative policy choices or assisting in the development of legal arguments. Even under such circumstances, though, governments often appear more interested in minimizing cost than in maximizing benefits, responding to the results of such analyses only with conflict avoidance.[29]

WEAKNESSES

While it can be argued that computers "rationalize" policy, however, there are different types of decision-making rationality: Logistic rationality (control maximized at the top at the expense and degradation of those below), tactical rationality (certainty maximized at the top at the expense and degradation of trust and morale below), and strategic rationality (unilateral gains maximized at the top at the expense of negotiation and cooperation).[30] What is required to maximize one form of rationality may well not serve another.

Other weaknesses of basic policy on machinic values are myriad. Inappropriate values may be established in this way.[31] Such approaches rely on quantifying variables that are not validly quantifiable.[32] They cannot cope with modifications in underlying assumptions.[33] They may be vulnerable to similarly motivated methods of avoiding detection of a lack of compliance[34] or to manipulation of decision-making processes.[35] Issues of morale disappear, differences between simulation and reality blur, situations are idealized in such a way that possible sources of friction are not visible, and it is assumed that all actors think alike. They are prone to data error at every level, can erase distinctions among different phases of decision-making processes, and treat as discrete events matters that are highly interrelated.[36] They are incapable of taking into account differences in the ways the information they provide will be cognitively processed by those who use it,[37] the politics of the situations in which it will be used,[38] or, so far, the realities of networked as opposed to hierarchical environments. The use of computer models by an administrative agency reduces the discretion of agency officials and the courts and precludes in-depth analysis.

Because most attorneys have no training in either research methods or the formal economic, political, and sociological presuppositions of particular types of computer analysis, their actual uses of information provided by models are restricted to three possibilities: They may deny computer models any value, they may believe anything a computer model says, or they may examine those using models on moral grounds such as corruption or bias. What they won't be able to do is engage in meaningful dialogue with the model builders concerning the basic assumptions that guide the construction of social reality.[39] Excessive reliance upon computers for policy inputs could even displace human experts, as it has in other social sectors.[40]

Reliance upon computers introduces vulnerabilities, such as the possibility that development of an electronic database to handle the massive amounts of information generated through discovery in a major case may bring a trial to a halt if there is a glitch. Competitive use of computerized supports for policy making can change the balance of power when those who are more technologically sophisticated gain the advantage.[41] And though in the U.S. judges and regulators are required to explain each of their decisions as a critical requirement of fairness, computerized decisions are not supported by rationales.[42]

A last class of problems in using computerized inputs into decision making is its potential for changing the very nature of the policy process. The impact of computer systems on legal research,[43] discovery processes, court planning,[44] development of legal arguments,[45] administering government services,[46] and enabling alternative dispute resolution[47] have received a fair amount of attention in public, professional, and scholarly literatures. Software to serve such purposes continues to be developed.[48] There has been far less attention, however, to the impact of computerization on the nature and outcomes of policy-making and legal processes, the relationship between government and society, and the vulnerabilities introduced. Often computers will propose things that humans will not, as when computers cross the nuclear threshold in war games while humans will not. Such technologies can blur the distinctions between different types of decision-making responsibility, such as that between advisors and the executive, and on the other hand treat as if they are discrete questions that cannot be fully understood other than as part of interrelated processes. And there are implications for the relative power of political institutions as they take up such approaches at different speeds and with varying degrees of sophistication. Ultimately, computerization of legal decision making profoundly affects the nature of the law at the constitutional level without the political discussion that should precede radical changes in the nature of the legal system.

Technologies as Policy Makers

As economic historian Alfred Chandler, Jr., argued in his seminal work *The Visible Hand*, decision-making power began to be transferred to machines as early as the 1870s.[49] In that book Chandler talks about the impact of automation but the argument is even more important with computerization. The transfer is fundamental to the nature of the law because its effects include the migration of logical structures and decision-making procedures from the human mind through notation and representation systems to the environment itself.

Use of computational aids to decision making actually began with the appearance of modern war games—distinguished from games of war such as chess by their linkage of conflict modeling with representations of the environment in which conflict was taking place—early in the nineteenth century.[50] A shift in attention from conflict to the rules of conflict, development of quantitative approaches to the analysis of conflict, and the steady increase in computing speed[51] provided the basis for a real takeoff in the use of computerized approaches to decision making during World War II. When directed at conflict, this was known as game theory, while in other contexts it developed as operations research. In 1959 Dr. Lucien Mehl first presented the idea of constructing a "Law Machine" that would provide legal decisions within highly specialized fields of law when armed with legal concepts, logical functions, and facts.[52] By the 1960s a new style of writing in judicial opinions appeared that mimicked or tried to develop formulaic approaches through use of such terms as "tests," "prongs," "requirements," "standards," and "hurdles."[53] The types of problems addressed via computerization significantly expanded with efforts to model cooperation as well as competition in the 1970s.[54]

By the 1980s the use of computers in communication policy making began to be explicitly discussed[55] and they were actually used to allocate spectrum globally. Analyses of courts[56] and of litigation[57] as computerizable systems began to appear, the computerized form of intelligence work known as MASINT (Measurement and Signatures Intelligence, referring to statistical analysis of a number of types of sensory information) came into use, and the first widely known use of artificial intelligence (AI) in administration appeared with the logic programming used to implement the British Nationality Act.

Computerized decision making has infiltrated policy-making processes in three ways: It *supplements* human decision making when it provides aids to humans for specific decision-making tasks. It *supplants* human decision making when it appears that the decisions are human but in fact are made by machines. And it *supersedes* humans when effective decision making—even for the social world—is undertaken by autonomously evolving nonhuman electronic intelligences.

SUPPLEMENTING HUMAN DECISION MAKING

The process Chandler was talking about in his analysis of the late nineteenth century was replacement of humans by machines for specific narrowly defined tasks such as coordinating train schedules or multistep manufacturing processes. Examples of the replacement of human decision making with computers in the contemporary legal environment include profiling, sentencing, and, in the area of communications policy, spectrum allocation.

Profiling entails developing a statistical portrait on the basis of a few identifying features and differentially treating those individuals who fit the parameters thus defined. This statistical portrait replaces the legal judgment of individuals with the responsibility of examining the facts of a case in the same way that statistical fragments have replaced holistic approaches to the human body in medicine: Both the medical subject and the legal subject have been shattered into pieces amenable to computerized decision making.

The first profile was developed to identify drug couriers in 1974 and, despite what many felt to be inconsistencies and absurdities in the results, was rapidly taken up by the police and courts to both trigger investigations of particular individuals and to justify arrest.[58] Because early U.S. court cases established that mere conformity to some or all of the characteristics of a drug courier didn't amount to probable cause, judges took the position that partial conformity to a profile reaches the lower barrier of reasonable suspicion. When the U.S. Supreme Court examined the practice, it was awarded high accolades for innovativeness and for the expertise, training, and organization required to use it.[59]

In an interesting example of interactions between the use of a specific decision-making tool and changes in the very nature of the decision-making processes themselves, the earliest drug courier profiles relied heavily on evidence used in courts for the data upon which the profiles were based. Computerized databases offered a technological boost, however, that changed the way in which profiles were shaped. While originally profiles were carefully built from analysis of the characteristics of those who had been found guilty of the crimes involved, data matching—linking information about an individual gathered for one purpose and held in one database with other information gathered for another purpose and held in a separate database—made it possible to develop new types of profiles based only on statistical calculations.

The use of profiles for purposes of law enforcement received a tremendous conceptual boost in the early 1990s, when it became necessary to generate a new definition of the "enemy" for the post–Cold War environment. New security theory used a four-fold approach that defined the enemy as anyone who was a terrorist, involved with drugs, presented an economic threat to the United States—and anyone *whose behavior was statistically unpredictable.*[60] Data matching was regularly opposed by the U.S. Congress, and the U.S. government recognized that privacy concerns would prevent it from acting on its new definition of the enemy within the borders of the United States until the events of 11 September 2001, when the national security argument overcame all barriers. Today statistical profiling is important among the ways in which the U.S. government identifies citizens as targets of surveillance. Nor is the use of this technique restricted to adults potentially capable of terrorist action: Software is being used to profile K–12 students considered to present the potential for socially disruptive behavior at some point in the future in the United Kingdom, which has put itself forward as a test environment for security techniques being considered by other nation-states.[61]

Sentencing is another area in which computers are replacing human decision making. There was speculation about the value of automating judicial reasoning in the 1970s,[62] and in the 1980s experimentation began around the world. Theoretically, computerized sentencing can lighten the judicial load and thus help relieve backlogs, a matter of efficiency; and it can prevent idiosyncratic differences among judges from generating significant differences in responses to the same type of offense across jurisdictions, a matter of equity. Results, however, have shown that computerizing sentencing results in neither an increase in certainty nor in predictability.[63] Judges proved resistant because analyses of case law show no systematic relationships between fact situations and sentences that can reliably provide a basis for computerized sentencing guidelines;[64] not all sentencing takes place within the context of the kind of bounded discretion in which sentencing guidelines are appropriate;[65] and its use undermines the role of sentencing as a form of narrative that helps resolve tensions between the general and the particular, rules and unique circumstances, based on a judge's wisdom and expertise.[66]

Computerizing the sentencing process inevitably changes its nature in a fundamental way. A judge responds to the behavior, demeanor, and context of the individual she or he sees in the courtroom and uses knowledge of the community involved—thick, qualitative analysis—to make sentencing decisions, while statistically based sentencing relies on only a few variables for thin, quantitative judgment. The actual individual involved in the case disappears, replaced by a mathematical calculation. Thus even when the intent is to mimic human decision-making processes via computerization, the effort to do so changes relationships among the law, intentions of the law, and those whom the law governs. While the question of the applicability of expert systems to legal reasoning remains theoretically open, practitioners in the judiciary reject it.

Probably the earliest example of the use of computerized decision making in the area of communications policy came in the 1980s, when the spectrum allocation function of the International Telecommunications Union (ITU) was first handled by software rather than people. This function must be repeated every few months in response to changing meteorological and technological conditions. The growing politicization of the ITU over the course of the 1970s and 1980s made the problem even more complex. Computerization offered the impression that a neutral and nonpolitical solution to this political as well as technical problem would be achieved, but of course the software used to solve the problem had to be written by someone (who turned out to be from the U.S.) and run on someone's computers (they wound up being those of NASA). In the commercial world it has long been recognized that databases and programs are not neutral. The airline reservation system, one of the first databases to be widely used commercially, presents the flights of certain airlines first, making it most likely that those will be the flights booked. Some of the biases built into systems will be those of technological structure, while others will be those of information structure.

SUPPLANTING HUMAN LAW

While first religious, and then legal, systems developed historically as means of structuring the social world, today the most critical structural processes may be those that result from software design and harmonization of information systems.[67] Harmonization of systems takes place in three ways:

1 Harmonization of the same type of information or communication system across nation-state borders, as when television delivered by satellite

broadcast covers a number of nation-states and television programs are coproduced internationally.

2 Harmonization of different types of information and communication systems with each other, as when the results of television audience analysis are linked with purchase records and just-in-time manufacturing and delivery systems—or harmonization of the databases of government agencies with quite diverse concerns.

3 Harmonization of information and communication systems with other types of social systems, as in the collapse of the global financial system into the telecommunications network.

Harmonization may arise either through multilateral or international political agreement (that is, involving many or essentially all nation-states), as in the case of the agreements regarding transparency, national trade regulation, and intellectual property rights that are a part of international trade law. Harmonization can also arise as a result of technical decisions, for in order to optimize many of the possibilities of recent technological innovations there must be standardization across the network. Sometimes harmonization is achieved indirectly, as when decisions made within the General Agreement on Tariffs and Trade (GATT), General Agreement on Trade in Services (GATS), and the World Trade Organization (WTO) make it easier for accounting firms to operate globally. Because accounting firms take with them information architectures and approaches to information processing, the systems they use in turn influence the shape of the organizations with which they work (including governments) and the regulatory systems within which those efforts take place.

SUPERSEDING HUMAN LAW

One of the oldest of human stories about machines is the eleventh century Golem story, best known after its nineteenth-century reincarnation as the inspiration for *Frankenstein*. The heart of the Golem stories is the desire of humans to create something to do their work for them. What makes efforts to do this both important and amusing is that inevitably people are not capable of providing direction to a machine in sufficient detail to prevent a disaster from occurring—in each case, repetitions of the activity sought become too much but can't be stopped because of an error in the instructions. Thus a classic Golem story tells of the machinic creature told to fetch water from the river for a household but not told when to stop, so that the house is ultimately flooded.

The Golem story is useful in thinking about the effects of the supercession of human decision making by machines acting autonomously. Golem-like effects were first seen in the impact of complexity. By the late 1980s phenomena such as the loss of long-distance telephone service for large portions of the U.S. were occurring as a result of the unforeseen and unforeseeable interactions among the many pieces of software involved. Since then, levels of complexity are increasingly being incorporated into analysis of communications problems but by definition this terrain marks a limit to human understanding.

Biotics is a relatively new area of experimentation that launches autonomously acting and self-reproducing and -acting entities in the web simply in order to watch them interact with each other and develop over time. Many of those involved in this work describe those entities as life forms and their development processes as evolutionary. Because neither the ways in which these electronic life forms act nor how they develop are programmed by the humans who originally launched them, the nature of the intelligence they evolve and display is nonhuman. Since experimentation with biotics is quite recent, it is not known how sophisticated such nonhuman electronic intelligences might become nor what they might do that would affect the human world through Internet-based activities as they become more sophisticated over time. Dyson notes that since the intelligence that appears within the network will not be human, it may already be there in forms we are unable to recognize.[68]

The global information infrastructure is undeniably the largest single machine ever built, for it includes all of the computers linked to it, and all of the sensors linked to them, as well as the telecommunications network itself. The number of nodes in the network is on the verge of achieving—or may already have achieved—the number of neurons and connections in the human brain. Some believe this "world brain" can be used to support real-time decision making by humans for human purposes. Others, however, note that according to self-organizing systems theory (and suggested by the biological metaphor), at some point the network may achieve awareness of itself, what is described as self-consciousness when it occurs in humans. When that time comes, the network may choose to act independently of humans on its own behalf.

Information Policy as Posthuman Law

For good reason, public, scholarly, and policy-making discourse about information policy is today absorbed in how to respond to the qualitative changes in the nature of the environment being regulated. Most of that discourse focuses on relatively small questions raised by conflicts between details of regulatory and statutory law that are the result of decades of articulation of law and regulation for a world that no longer exists. The charge that policy analysis is irrelevant because the questions being asked are too small has already been levied.[69] One stage of enlarging the questions asked is to examine fundamental principles as they have been developed for application to different technologies historically as a prelude to rethinking what those principles mean in a new technological context, and this work has begun. The context must be enlarged yet one more time, however. Technological decision making—often for technologies rather than humans—is already beginning to replace policy made by humans for social ends. The theoretical, legal, and empirical implications of this must now also come onto the research and policy-making agendas.

NOTES

1 For a more detailed discussion of these different stages in theorizing the relationship between information technologies and society, see Sandra Braman, "Technology," in *Handbook of Media Studies*, ed. John Downing et al. (Thousand Oaks, Calif.: Sage Publications, in press). For classic works on communication technology as a barrier to experience see James W. Carey, *Communication as Culture: Essays on Media and Society* (Boston: Unwin Hyman, 1989); Hans Magnus Enzensberger, *Mediocrity and Delusion*, trans. Martin Chalmers (New York: Verso, 1992); Jürgen Habermas, *Structural Transformations of the Public Sphere: An Inquiry into a Category of Bourgeois Society* (Cambridge: MIT Press, 1991); David Held, *Introduction to Critical Theory: Horkheimer to Habermas* (Berkeley: University of California Press, 1980); Lewis Hyde, *The Gift: Imagination and the Erotic Life of Property* (New York: Vintage Books, 1983); Oskar Negt, "Mass Media: Tools of Domination or Instruments of Liberation: Aspects of the Frankfurt School's Communication Analysis," *New German Critique* 14 (1978): 61–80; Avital Ronell, *The Telephone Book: Technology, Schizophrenia, Electric Speech* (Lincoln: University of Nebraska Press, 1989).

2 Works that introduce the concept of communication technology as a shaper of experience include: Edward A. Comor, ed., *The Global Political Economy of Communication: Hegemony, Telecommunication, and the Information Economy* (New York/London: Macmillan/St. Martin's Press, 1996); Ronald J. Deibert, *Parchment, Printing, and Hypermedia: Communication and World Order Transformation* (New York: Columbia University Press, 1997); Harold A. Innis, *The Bias of Communication* (Toronto: University of Toronto Press, 1951); Joshua Meyerowitz, *No Sense of Place: The Impact of Electronic Media on Social Behavior* (New York/Oxford: Oxford Uni-

versity Press, 1986); Lewis Mumford, *Technics and Civilization* (New York: Harcourt, Brace, 1934).

3 The literature on communication technology includes Jay David Bolter, *Turing's Man: Western Culture in the Computer Age* (Durham: University of North Carolina Press, 1984); Daniel J. Boorstin, *The Image: A Guide to Pseudo-events in America* (New York: Vintage Books, 1961/1992); Jack Goody, *The Domestication of the Savage Mind* (Cambridge: Cambridge University Press, 1977); Eric Havelock, *Preface to Plato* (Cambridge: Harvard University Press, 1982); Marshall McLuhan, *Understanding Media: The Extensions of Man* (Cambridge: MIT Press, 1964/1994); Walter J. Ong, *Orality and Literacy: The Technologizing of the Word* (New York: Methuen, 1982); Susan Sontag, *On Photography* (New York: Picador Books, 1977/2001).

4 The literature on communication technology *as* reality is more recent and therefore not yet as extensive. It includes, notably: Jean Baudrillard, *Simulations* (New York: Semiotext[es], 1983); Chris Hables Gray, Heidi Figueroa-Sarriera, and Steven Mentor, eds., *The Cyborg Handbook* (New York: Routledge, 1995); Donna Jeanne Haraway, *Simians, Cyborgs, and Women: The Reinvention of Nature* (New York: Routledge, 1991); Brandon Hookway, *Pandemonium* (Princeton: Princeton Architectural Press, 1999).

5 Lawrence M. Friedman, *A History of American Law*, 2d ed. (New York: Simon and Schuster, 1985).

6 Morton J. Horwitz, *The Transformation of American Law, 1870–1960: The Crisis of Legal Orthodoxy* (New York: Oxford University Press, 1992); Theda Skocpol, *Protecting Soldiers and Mothers: The Political Origins of Social Policy in the United States* (Cambridge: Belknap Press, 1992).

7 Alfred D. Chandler, Jr., and James W. Cortada, eds., *A Nation Transformed by Information: How Information Has Shaped the United States from Colonial Times to the Present* (New York: Oxford University Press, 2000).

8 For more detailed discussion of the distinction between technologies and meta-technologies, see Sandra Braman, "Technology."

9 Sandra Braman, "Harmonization of Systems: The Third Stage of the Information Society," *Journal of Communication* 43, 3 (1993): 133–140.

10 Lawrence Lessig, *Code and Other Laws of Cyberspace* (New York: Basic Books, 1999).

11 Stuart Biegel, *Beyond Our Control? Confronting the Limits of our Legal System in the Age of Cyberspace* (Cambridge: MIT Press, 2001).

12 Sandra Braman, "Threats to the Right to Create: Cultural Policy in the Fourth Stage of the Information Society," *Gazette* 60, 1 (1998): 77–91. The Electronic Frontier Foundation website (www.eff.org) contains a great deal of information on current legal issues of this type.

13 Janet Abbate, *Inventing the Internet* (Cambridge: MIT Press, 1999).

14 Stuart Biegel, *Beyond Our Control*; Milton Mueller, *Ruling the Root* (Cambridge: MIT Press, 2002).

15 E.g., Robin Mansell and Roger Silverstone, eds., *Communication by Design: The Politics of Information and Communication Technologies* (Oxford: Oxford University Press, 1996).

16 *Capital Cities Cable v Crisp*, 467 U.S. 691 (1984).

17 Braden R. Allenby, "Environmental Security: Concept and Implementation," *International Political Science Review*, 21, 1 (2000): 5–23; Gregory D. Foster,

"Environmental Security: The Search for Strategic Legitimacy," *Armed Forces and Society*, 27, 3 (2001): 373–396; David N. McNelis and Glenn E. Schweitzer, "Environmental Security: An Evolving Concept," *Environmental Science and Technology* 35, 5: 108–114.

18 Christopher D. Stone, *Should Trees Have Standing? Toward Legal Rights for Natural Objects* (New York: Avon Books, 1975).

19 Jacques Ellul, *The Technological Society*, trans. John Wilkinson (New York: Vintage Books, 1964).

20 Susan G. Hadden, "The Future of Expert Systems in Government," *Journal of Policy Analysis and Management* 8, 2 (1989): 203–209.

21 B. D. Fisher, "Controlling Government Regulation: Cost-benefit Analysis before and after the *Cotton-Dust* Case," *Administrative Law Review* 36 (1984): 179–207.

22 *American Textile Manufacturers v Donovan*, 452 US 490 (1981); *Baltimore Gas and Electric Co. v Natural Resources Defense Council*, 462 US 87 (1983); *FCC v WNCN*, 450 US 582 (1981).

23 David Held, *Political Theory and the Modern State: Essays on State, Power, and Democracy* (Stanford: Stanford University Press, 1989).

24 Robert O. Keohane and Elinor Ostrom, *Local Commons and Global Interdependence: Heterogeneity and Cooperation in Two Domains* (London: Sage Publications, 1995).

25 Pamela Samuelson, "*Benson* Revisited: The Case against Patent Protection and Other Computer-related Inventions," *Emory Law Journal* 39 (1990): 1025–1054.

26 M. Ethan Katsh, *The Electronic Media and the Transformation of the Law* (New York: Oxford University Press, 1989).

27 Daniel B. Sibbet, "MASINT: Intelligence for the 1990s," *American Intelligence Journal* 11, 3 (1990): 23–26.

28 Jorgen Karpf, "Competition between Types of Regulation: The Impact of Computerization of Law, *Jurimetrics* 12 (1989).

29 Richard Rose, ed., *The Dynamics of Public Policy: A Comparative Analysis* (Beverly Hills, Calif.: Sage Publications, 1976).

30 Manuel de Landa, *War in the Age of Intelligent Machines* (New York: Zone, 1991).

31 Exemplars of this widespread critique include an examination of the problem as it plays out in international relations and as it appears in the effort to balance constitutional principles. See Johan Galtung, "Why Do Disarmament Negotiations Fail?" in *Arms and Survival*, ed. Radhakrishna and Mahendra Agrawal (New Delhi: Satvahan, 1982), 218–227.

32 Frederick Schauer, *Playing by the Rules: A Philosophical Examination of Rule-Based Decision Making in Law and in Life* (New York: Oxford University Press, 1990).

33 Michael Nicholson, "Misperception and Satisficing in International Conflict," in *Communication and Interaction in Global Politics*, ed. Claudio Cioffi-Revilla, Richard L. Merritt, and Dina A. Zinnes (Beverly Hills: Sage, 1987), 117–139.

34 Samidh Chakrabarti and Aaron Strauss, "Carnival Booth: An Algorithm for Defeating the Computer-assisted Passenger Screening System" (typescript, MIT, 2002).

35 Hacking is an obvious example of this but the use of such approaches by those seeking to change power structures altogether is promoted by what is being described as the "tactical media" movement; see Barbara Abrash and Faye Ginsburg, eds., *Tactical Media: A Virtual Case Book* (New York: New York University,

http://www.nyu.edu/fas/projects/vcb/); Critical Art Ensemble, *Electronic Civil Disobedience and Other Unpopular Ideas* (Brooklyn, N.Y.: Autonomedia, 1996); Critical Art Ensemble, *Digital Resistance: Explorations in Tactical Media* (Brooklyn, N.Y.: Autonomedia, 2001).

36 De Landa, *War in the Age of Intelligent Machines.*

37 Wesley A. Magat and W. Kip Viscusi, *Informational Approaches to Regulation* (Cambridge: MIT Press, 1992).

38 Richard Rose, ed., *The Dynamics of Public Policy: A Comparative Analysis* (Beverly Hills, Calif.: Sage, 1976).

39 J. A. Wilson, "Methodologies as Rules: Computer Models and the APA," *Columbia Journal of Law and Social Problems* 20 (1986): 167–202.

40 Bruce Ackerman, *Reconstructing American Law* (Cambridge: Harvard University Press, 1984); Jonathan L. Entin, "Numeracy, Law, and Dichotomy" (presented to the Law and Society Association, Philadelphia, May 1992).

41 Thomas E. Patterson, *Toward New Research on Communication Technologies and the Democratic Process* (Aspen, Colo.: Aspen Institute, 1985).

42 Karpf, "Competition between Types of Regulation."

43 Katsh, *The Electronic Media.*

44 W. A. Hamilton, "Computer-induced Improvements in the Administration of Justice," *Computer/Law Journal* 4 (1983): 55–76.

45 See, e.g., Janaka Y. Ruwanpura, Simaan M. AbouRizk, and Siri Fernando, "Implementation of Computer-based Planning and Estimating Tools for a Public Utility," *Cost Engineering* 43, 10 (2001): 39–46.

46 See, e.g., Paul Henmman and Michael Adler, "Information Technology and Transformations in Social Security Policy and Administration: A Review," *International Social Security Review* 54, 4 (2001): 23–47.

47 Ethan Katsh and Janet Rifkin, *Online Dispute Resolution* (San Francisco: Jossey-Bass, 2001).

48 James R. Hargreaves, "PSJandI and Integrated Justice," *International Review of Law, Computers, and Technology* 12, 2 (1998): 287–297.

49 Alfred D. Chandler, Jr., *The Visible Hand: The Managerial Revolution in American Business* (Cambridge: Belknap Press, 1977).

50 De Landa, *War in the Age of Intelligent Machines*; Martin van Creveld, *Technology and War: From 2000 BC to the Present*, rev. ed. (New York: Free Press, 1991).

51 The first machine to overtake human calculating labor was Kelvin's tide predictor in 1876.

52 Andrew Clark and Kim Economides, "Computers, Expert Systems, and Legal Processes," in *Law, Computer Science, and Artificial Intelligence*, ed. Ajit Narayanan and Mervyn Bennun (Norwood, N.J.: Ablex, 1991), 3–32.

53 Robert F. Nagel, *Constitutional Cultures: The Mentality and Consequences of Judicial Review* (Berkeley: University of California Press, 1989).

54 Robert Axelrod and Robert O. Keohane, "Achieving Cooperation under Anarchy: Strategies and Institutions," *World Politics* 38, 1 (1985): 226–254.

55 William H. Dutton and Kenneth L. Kraemer, *Modeling as Negotiating: The Political Dynamics of Computer Models in the Policy Process* (Norwood, N.J.: Ablex, 1985).

56 J. R. Corsi, *Judicial Politics: An Introduction* (Englewood Cliffs, N.J.: Prentice-Hall, 1984).

57 Cary Coglianese, "Legal Rules and the Costs of Environmental Litigation" (presented to the Law and Society Association, May 1992, Philadelphia).

58 Kevin Ryan, "Law and the Creation of Deviance: The Case of the Drug Courier" (presented to the Law and Society Association, Philadelphia, May 1992).

59 *U.S. v Mendenhall*, 446 US 544, 1980. Part of a suite of cases that also included *Reid v Georgia*, 448 US 438 (1980), and *Florida v Royer*, 460 US 491 (1983).

60 Ian O. Lesser, David Ronfeldt, and Michele Zanini, *Countering the New Terrorism* (Santa Monica, Calif.: Rand Corporation, 1999); Robert D. Steele, "Applying the 'New Paradigm': How to Avoid Strategic Intelligence Failures in the Future," *American Intelligence Journal* 12, 3 (1991): 43–46.

61 Brett Forrest, "UltraViolence Predictor 1.0," *Wired*, June 2000, 124.

62 E.g., G. Schubert, *Human Jurisprudence: Public Law as Political Science* (Honolulu: University Press of Hawaii, 1975).

63 R. V. de Mulder and H. M. Gubby, "Legal Decision Making by Computer: An Experiment with Sentencing," *Computer/Law Journal* 4 (1983): 243–303.

64 Ralph J. Henham, "On the Philosophical and Theoretical Implications of Judicial Decision Support Systems," *International Review of Law, Computers, and Technology* 14, 3 (2000): 283–296.

65 John Zeleznikow, "Building Decision Support Systems in Discretionary Legal Domains," *International Review of Law, Computers, and Technology* 14, 3 (2000): 341–356.

66 Cyrus Tata, "Resolute Ambivalence: Why Judiciaries Do Not Institutionalize Their Decision Support Systems," *International Review of Law, Computers, and Technology* 14, 3 (2000): 297–316; Richard E. Susskind, "Some Preliminary Considerations Concerning Expert Systems in Law, *Northern Kentucky Law Review* 14, 2 (1987): 211–235.

67 Braman, Harmonization of Systems.

68 George Dyson, *Darwin among the Machines: The Evolution of Global Intelligence* (New York: Perseus, 1997).

69 Eli M. Noam, "A Report Card for the Policy Analysis Community after the Dotcom Bust" (presented to the Telecommunications Policy Research Conference, Alexandria, Va., September 2002).

CIRCULATION

CULTURES, STRATEGIES, APPROPRIATIONS

Piracy, Infrastructure, and the Rise of a Nigerian Video Industry

BRIAN LARKIN

My discussion of piracy will be based on the pirate culture that exists in Nigeria. By pirate culture I do not mean "the culture of media pirates" in the anthropological sense of studying a subgroup. Piracy is better seen as part of a wider infrastructure of reproduction that creates the material channels through which media flow. In northern Nigeria, along with many other developing nations, piracy is perhaps the dominant infrastructural means whereby media are distributed and consumed. There is an aesthetic to this, as pirate reproduction is the material screen that filters audiences' engagement with media and the new senses of time, speed, space, and contemporaneity that result. Piracy is not just an alternative mode of distribution then, but has distinct formal qualities that influence the media traveling under this regime of reproduction. Moreover, piracy is generative; it produces new sorts of social and cultural practices that follow in the wake of its organization. In Nigeria, the rise of a new video industry that makes feature-length films shot and distributed on video has been a striking example of a "legitimate" media that could not exist without depending heavily on the infrastructure created by its "illegitimate" double, pirate media. One may be legal and the other not, but both participate in what I term the wider infrastructure of reproduction.

Infrastructure

Capitalism, as many spatial thinkers from Karl Marx to Henri Lefebvre to David Harvey have reminded us, is not separable from space but produces the spaces through which it operates. All regimes of capital depend upon infrastructures—shipping, trains, fiber optic lines, warehouses, and so on—whereby space is linked up and connected into a network. In this sense, urban infrastructure networks provide the base for the operation of modern economic and social systems, linking individuals and corporations into wider economic and social structures.[1] Cities—or space itself, in Lefebvre's terms—only take on real existence through their insertion into networks and pathways of commodity exchange, and it is networked infrastructure that provides those channels of communication.

Infrastructure, then, creates the particular sets or networks through which what we term "globalization" travels. It is about mobility—the movement of commodities, whether waste, energy, or information—bringing diverse places into interaction, connecting some while divorcing others, constantly ranking, connecting, and segmenting spaces and people.[2] Successive regimes of capital depend on forging successive infrastructural forms, each one superimposed on the one that went before, closing off old connections, facilitating new ones, and reconfiguring space, social relations within that space, and relations between technology and the body.[3]

There are two things to remember about infrastructure. First, as obvious as it is, infrastructure often does not work in the way it is supposed to. In emphasizing the unity of a network and the radically destabilizing effects of technologies of communication on our notions of time, space, and subjectivity, there is often an implicit presumption that infrastructure is smoothly efficient, penetrating homogenously, and connecting equally. In reality—especially outside of the West, infrastructure is messy, discontinuous, and poor. This refers to more than something like the digital divide or the unequal access to the infrastructural economic order of globalization.[4] Breakdown refers to the *experience* of technology, the quotidian conditions of existence through which people engage with technology, media operate, and cultural signification is possible. Televisions often have fuzzy pictures, tape recorders distort sound, cars break down, and roads are in dire need of repair. In a country like Nigeria, for instance, phone lines are expensive, roads are not repaired, airlines go bankrupt, electricity frequently disappears (NEPA, the Nigerian Electric Power Authority, is known by the bon mot "Never Expect Power Always"). The engagement of ordinary people with the technologies of infrastructure is often one of frustration and dysfunction, and this inability to take infrastructure for granted results in a heightened self-consciousness about it.

Second, and most important to this paper, infrastructure also sets in motion other types of flows that operate in the spaces capital opens, that travel routes created by new infrastructures of communication. The organization of one system sets in motion other systems spinning off in different directions. This results in a layering of networks and infrastructures that contest each other but also feed off each other and remain mutually dependent. The urbanists Stephen Graham and Simon Marvin use the concept of "enhancement" to address the way that new technologies do not simply destroy older forms of communication but call into being new mobilities and intensify older ones.[5] One result of this enhancement is that infrastructures create particular sets or networks through which capital operates but, at the same time, inherently produce their own pathologies. They place in motion the potential for other sets of relations to occur, creating a ripple effect on movements of people, culture, and religion. In this sense, piracy is the informational pathology in an era of globalization. Information pirates feed off the formal distribution networks established by mainstream media companies, but in order to divert this flow of goods they must elaborate their own chains of reproduction and distribution. Films made in Hollywood to be distributed in an organized circuit in the United States are copied by pirates; sent to Asia or the Middle East, where they are subtitled and produced in large numbers as cassettes, VCDs, and DVDs; and reshipped, in the main, to the developing world (though pirate cassettes are of course available in all major Western cities and on the Web). Pirates feed off official media by following the logic of technology. They exploit the capabilities of new technologies for reproduction that remain unused due to judicial constraints. Piracy is one example of the counterflows that could not exist without the existence of a formal distribution system but that, while parasitic on that system, continue to develop their own infrastructural networks.

Piracy

Piracy is an ambivalent phenomenon in countries such as Nigeria. It is widely feared by indigenous film and music makers as being destructive of the small profits they make by way of intellectual property. Yet many of these same people make use of pirate media themselves in their private and professional lives. Piracy has made available to Nigerians a vast array of world media at a speed they could never imagine, hooking them up to the accelerated circuit of global media flows. Piracy is part of the so-called shadow (second, marginal, informal, black) economy and is one of the prime infrastructural ways that media travel outside the West. Largely unregulated, piracy exists in varying degrees outside the law. It produces profits, but not for corporations, providing no revenue to the state. It operates in the second economy, untaxed and unmonitored. New-media theorist Ravi Sundaram has defined the contours of what he terms "pirate modernity" as quotidian, disorganized, and nonideological, marked by mobility and innovation.[6] This formulation nicely captures the ambivalence of piracy: the fact that it makes available software and media texts at a price affordable in poor nations, yet it does not represent a self-conscious political project in opposition to capitalism—these are not tactical media in that sense of the term.[7]

But piracy is only disorganized in the sense that it is not part of the legal, "organized" traffic in media goods. Piracy preys on official networks of media distribution, on globalization and the unique connection of people and commodities it has brought about, but to do this it has to generate its own infrastructural orders. Piracy is highly formal and ordered, even if it operates in the underside of the spaces produced by capitalism. It may be cheap, it may be poor, it may often operate by crude means, but piracy is part of a much larger process whereby Africans have cobbled together an unofficial way of engaging with a globalized world. Generating pirate order is part of a much larger process we can see in what might be termed the "pathology of infrastructure." This is the pirating of a system's mode of communication—the viruses that attach to other kinds of what we might think of as official or recognized movement. Technological infrastructure generates movement, but this movement creates possibilities for other new actions and mobilities to occur.

Piracy in Kano, Nigeria

Piracy exists in this second, shadow economy but frequently surfaces to overlap and interact with the official economy. It generates order from the unregulated, mobile movement of transnational media, but it is only one aspect of the larger infrastructure of "reproduction" (see figure 1). I use this term to reference the fact that pirate videos, like nonpirate ones, rely on the informal qualities of cassette technology:[8] They are mobile, diverse, fluid, and easily reproducible. Piracy has vastly increased the range of media products available to the ordinary Nigerian citizen, but while Indian, U.S., and Hong Kong films are popular, so are cassettes of Islamic preachers. Those involved in the distribution of pirate media are almost always distributing legal media at the same time, so the two were, for a while, almost wholly intertwined. Recently, this has been affected by the rise of a Nigerian home video industry that produces films made and distributed on video in English, Hausa, and Yoruba languages. This industry has grown to be one of the most vibrant media phenomena in Africa.[9]

I. Itinerant cassette seller, Kof'ar Wambai market, Kano, Nigeria. Photo by Brian Larkin

Until the rise of video films in Nigeria in the early 1990s, nearly all available dramatic films on video were pirate media. Hollywood's refusal to distribute films to Nigeria in 1983 was intended as a punishment for the "indigenization" of Nigerian industries—the seizure of assets and control from foreign investors (the Motion Pictures Association or MPAA) and their replacement with indigenous entrepreneurs. What the MPAA did not realize is that the growth of new technologies of reproduction meant that unofficial infrastructures would blossom in its absence, linking Nigeria to new and changing circuits of media flow. U.S. films are still copied illegally in the United States and then shipped to Dubai, Lebanon, and elsewhere, arriving in Nigeria while they are still on first-run release in the United States. Sometimes they arrive in Dubai by way of India or East Asia. One Jean-Claude van Damme film I saw had Arabic subtitles superimposed over Chinese ones, providing a visible inscription of the axes of media flow. Many U.S. videos contained a message that scrolled across the bottom of the film every few minutes stating: "Demo tape only. Not for rental or sale. If you have rented or purchased this cassette call 1-800 NO COPYS (1-800 662 6787). Federal law provides severe civil and criminal penalties for unauthorized duplication or distribution."[10]

Until the rise of VCD, a technology of reproduction that is rarely seen in the West but is common elsewhere, Indian films were available in Nigeria largely through the entrepôt of Dubai. From there, master copies were shipped on to Nigeria to the two main distributors of Indian films, copied, and sold in bulk. Now, Kano distributors import VCD mastercopies from Pakistan. It takes seven days for a film to be released in India, a high-quality copy of it made in Pakistan, and then shipped by DHL to Nigeria where it is dubbed onto tape. The appearance of pirate tapes in the markets of Kano and Lagos is one moment in the operation of what has grown to be a highly ordered, highly formal infrastructure that connects Nigeria into a global flow of goods that move on the "gray" market. This formality is clear in Kano, as the duplication and sale of cassettes is organized under the auspices of the Kano Cassette Sellers Recording and Co-operative Society Ltd. (Kungiyar Gawa Kai Ta Masu Sayar Da Kaset Da Dauka Ta Jihar Kano) based in Kofar Wambai market. While once this organization controlled the duplication and sale of both legal and nonlegal media, in recent times the massive growth of Hausa films and Hausa popular music has spawned a move away from foreign (usually pirate) media to homegrown (legal) fare. The success here, I would argue, is not just in making the films themselves, but in developing an entirely novel national and international system of distribution and exhibition that depends heavily on the infrastructure created, in part, for moving pirate media. It is in this decentralized, thoroughly commodified, privatized world that video films give evidence of a new political economy that operates on the back of piracy in the way that piracy operated on the back of official media—all of it, to a large extent, in the interstices of state control.

The rise of the legal Hausa film market is thus intertwined with the long years of piracy that preceded it. The money, knowledge, and networks established partly for the distribution of pirate media created an infra-structure that proved central to the success of home video films in Nigeria. One of the most distinctive attributes of the Nigerian "film" industry—that "film" is wholly shot, edited, and distributed on video—is an outcome of the centrality of piracy to Nigerian cultural production. In a nation where the cinematic exhibition of films excluded African cinema, Nigerians made use of the mobile, innovative world of cassettes to build a wholly original film organization.

Video in Kano

In the mid-1990s, the rise in southern Nigeria of video films in English, Igbo, and Yoruba spawned a movement in the north toward the production in the Hausa language of narrative movies on video. Before this, while Hausa TV dramas were popular, there was no tradition of feature filmmaking and Hausa feature films numbered fewer than ten. By 2001, in contrast, more than two hundred video films were released onto the market, representing the strongest year in a proliferating industry. Hausa films often last two hours or more. To this point, they have separated themselves stylistically from southern Nigerian videos by deemphasizing issues of magic and horror and have famously (or infamously) concentrated instead on themes of love. In this they have drawn heavily on the narratives and formal styles of Indian films, which have long been popular in the north. This tendency is most clearly seen in the use of song and dance sequences.[11] The production of such a large number of videos has resulted in the growth of a small army of people in the industry working as editors, camera operators, directors, set designers, actors, composers, musicians, singers, and poster and video-jacket designers, as well as those involved in distribution and sales. Video rental shops have mushroomed on the urban landscape, penetrating into the smallest neighborhood. There are three film magazines modeled on the popularity of the Indian film magazine *Stardust*. These videos sell well—on average between ten and twenty thousand copies, with hits selling between one and two hundred thousand. As in Indian films, there is a substantial side industry in the audio market, as popular Hausa music has been dominated in the last five years by songs from Hausa video films.

Hausa films are financed by the producer, who is responsible for all initial costs. The explosion in films forced the Kano State Filmmakers Association to institute controls over how many films can be released at one time. Once a film is made, editing completed, and the covers for the tapes printed, the film goes on a waiting list that ensures not more than six films are released each month. When the film is released, the producer takes it to one of the distributors in Kano and sells a master copy of the tape and several hundred copies of the jacket at about N50 (forty cents); the final film will sell for N250 (about $2.50) per copy. If the film sells well, the producer will provide more jackets. The distributor covers the cost of dubbing machines and blank tapes and produces the tapes he will then sell, both wholesale and retail, only paying the producer once the tape has been sold. A few filmmakers try to recoup costs of production through cinematic exhibition, but these are few in number and organization of the industry has been around sales for home video consumption. Initially, some distributors went into production (and at least one is still involved), but distribution involves lesser risk and greater financial reward, fomenting considerable tension between the production and distribution sectors as the industry evolves.

Kano has emerged as the main center of film production and distribution for Hausa films. Traders come from all over northern Nigeria as well as from neighboring countries such as Niger, Cameroon, and even Ghana to buy films in bulk (see figure 2). These films have energized and swollen the distribution networks established for the earlier distribution of pirate video films (Kano has also long been the main market for Indian films). Five distributors dominate the Hausa video film industry, and all of them began in the marketing and selling of other videos (U.S., Indian, and Islamic), which gave them the capital to foster and shape the nascent film industry.

The Materiality of Piracy

The rise of piracy, and the cost of Nigeria's ability to partake in the consumption of world media and produce the country's own contribution to it,

—— 2. Alhaji Rabi'u V-P, vice president of the Kano State Cassette Sellers ——
& Recording Co-operative Society Ltd. in his shop, Kano, Nigeria.
Photo by Brian Larkin

have been made possible because piracy is part of the larger materiality of
infrastructure. Nigeria's infrastructure today is marked by cheapness, faulty
operation, and repairs. The temporal experience accompanying this is less
one of dizzying real-time integration into a new globalized world than one of
interminable waiting for Internet messages to open or of a lived experience
of dysfunction as programs periodically disappear when blackouts occur.
Media have projected Nigerians into a globalized world in new and important
ways, but this projection has to be examined in its material execution. Consuming media is a way to be modern, but Nigerians know they are the unintended recipients of Indian and Hollywood films that have been diverted
off the mainstream of distribution and to Nigeria. There is no official distribution for Hollywood or Indian films in Nigeria and there are no first-run
cinemas—even the "new" Indian films there are years old, having been on a
circuit through Europe and the Middle East before reaching Nigeria, by which
point they are burned, falling apart, and characterized by poor sound and frequent jump cuts. Nigerians engage with first-run foreign media only through
pirate means, and piracy takes a particular material form, one marked by distortion, poor quality of sound, video dropouts, and the breaking up of images
on scratched VCDs. The Russian formalists referred to this as the semiotics of
interference. The media theorist Friedrich Kittler writes about it as information being engulfed by the noise of the real, and in developing nations it is
the tactile materiality of how cultural goods like films move.[12]

Distortion like dropouts on a video or a slow connection to the Internet place Nigerians at the back of a history organized by the West, where to be modern is to be technological. One of the defining experiences of technology and modernity in the contemporary era, speed, is an ambivalent phenomenon for Nigerians.[13] Nigerian audiences are well aware that while technological infrastructures speed up their connection to a wider world, those infrastructures are poor; their lack of efficiency makes them stand out. As media speed up the experience of globalization for Nigerians, they heighten the sense of marginalization at the same time. The material conditions of reproduction and consumption create a technological veil, a screen through which Nigerians interact with media on a quotidian basis that is quite different from the experience in developed nations. This is one of the experiential effects of pirate culture, a contradictory speeding up and screening off that represents the ambivalent promise of modernity.

Conclusion

In the midst of economic collapse generated by structural adjustment programs that imposed crippling financial burdens on the average Nigerian citizen, a pirate culture has managed to generate a new, unprecedented media industry. This industry builds on the infrastructure created by piracy, just as pirate entrepreneurs built on the official flow of media from India, Hong Kong, and the United States. I have argued that pirate media is not "tactical media" in the sense of an oppositional, critical media dependent on mobile, unofficial media forms. But it does overlap with this media in its poaching of the structures and aesthetics around us that we use to fashion something quite different.[14] In this way, pirate media speak to much larger issues: the migration of the second economy into the mainstream of Nigerian economic and social life, the reconfiguration of the state (which removes itself from some arenas while reasserting itself in others), as well as the dynamics of technology and power.

People fashion inventive responses to the failures of everyday life not because they wish to but because they have to. We have to beware of romanticizing the construction of order from disorder, recognizing its power and innovation while acknowledging that it is often the outcome of a situation of struggle and suffering. Piracy, often as a result of poverty, imposes material conditions on the storage, transmission, and retrieval of media. Cheap tape recorders; old televisions; videos that are the copy of a copy of a copy to the extent that the image is permanently blurred, the sound resolutely opaque. These are the infrastructural modes that create the channels through which much media flow in the globalized world and that form the bedrock of pirate modernity.

NOTES

My research depended heavily on the help and support of Alh. Rabi'u B.K and Alh Musa Na Sale of the Kano State Cassette Sellers and Recording Cooperative Ltd.; the directors Ado Ahmad, Tijani Ibrahim, and Aminu Hassan Yakasai; and the cultural activism of Ibrahim Sheme, Umar Farukh, and Abdalla Uba Adamu. I dedicate it to the memory of Aminu Hassan Yakasai and Tijani Ibraheem, two directors who pioneered Hausa video film. I thank Meg McLagan and Birgit Meyer for readings and corrections. Finally, I thank Patrice Petro and Tasha Oren for inviting me to Milwaukee and providing the intellectual catalyst for this.

1 Stephen Graham and Simon Marvin, *Splintering Urbanism: Networked Infrastructures, Technological Mobilities, and the Urban Condition* (London: Routledge, 2001).

2 Ibid; Armand Mattelart, *The Invention of Communication*, trans. Susan Emanuel (Minneapolis: U of Minnesota P, 1996); Armand Mattelart, *Networking the World, 1794–2000*, trans. L. Carey-Libbrecht and J. Cohen (Minneapolis: U of Minnesota P, 2000); Saskia Sassen, *Globalization and Its Discontents* (New York: New Press, 1998).

3 David Harvey, *Spaces of Capital: Towards a Critical Geography* (London: Routledge, 2001).

4 Sassen, *Globalization and Its Discontents*, 1998.

5 Stephen Graham and Simon Marvin, *Telecommunications and the City: Electronic Spaces, Urban Places* (London: Routledge, 1996).

6 Ravi Sundaram, "Recycling Modernity: Pirate Electronic Cultures in India," *Third Text 1999* 47 (1999): 59–65.

7 David Garcia and Geert Lovink, "The ABC of Tactical Media," *Sarai Reader 01* (2001): 90–93. http://www.sarai.net/events/tml/tml_pdf/abc_tactical.PDF.

8 Annabelle Sreberny-Mohammadi and Ali Mohammadi, *Small Media, Big Revolution: Communication, Culture, and the Iranian Revolution* (Minneapolis: U of Minnesota P, 1994). Peter Manuel, *Cassette Culture: Popular Music and Technology in North India* (Chicago: U of Chicago P, 1993). See also Brian Larkin, "Hausa Dramas and the Rise of Video Culture in Nigeria," in *Nigerian Video Film*, ed. Jonathan Haynes (Athens: Ohio UP, 2000).

9 Jonathan Haynes, ed., *Nigerian Video Films.* (Athens: Ohio UP, 2000). See also Brigit Meyer, "Ghanaian Popular Cinema and the Magic in and of Film," in *Magic and Modernity: Dialects of Revelation and Concealment*, ed. B. Meyer and P. Pels (Stanford: Stanford UP, 2002); Moradewun Adejunmobi, "English and the Audience of an African Popular Culture: The Culture of Nigerian Video Film," *Cultural Critique* 50 (2000):74–103; N. Frank Ukadike, "Images of the 'Reel' Thing: African Video-Films and the Emergence of a New Cultural Art," *Social Identities* 6 (2000): 243–261.

10 This is now a phone number that distributes information for new drugs.

11 Controversy over song sequences led to the banning of Hausa videos following the introduction of Islamic law into the northern state of Kano in 2001. After the formation of a new censorship board with a list of new requirements (men and women could no longer sing to each other), the ban was rescinded. For more on Indian film in Nigeria, see Brian Larkin, "Indian Films and Nigerian Lovers: Media and the Creation of Parallel Modernities," in *The Anthropology of Globalization*, ed. Jonathan Xavier Inda and Renato Rosaldo (Oxford: Blackwell, 2000), 350–378.

12 Friedrich Kittler, *Gramophone, Film, Typewriter* (Stanford: Stanford UP, 1999).

13 Paul Virilio, *Open Sky* (London: Verso, 1997).

14 Garcia and Lovink, "The ABC of Tactical Media."

Unsuitable Coverage

The Media, the Veil,
and Regimes of Representation

Annabelle Sreberny

Almost every day I get stuck in the traffic occasioned by a crowd of heavily veiled women bringing their kerchiefed daughters to school. In the center of Leicester, a multicultural city that is set to become Britain's first majority nonwhite city, these families are patronizing an Islamic school and their veiling is done voluntarily through the mediations of familial patriarchy.

More than twenty-five years ago I was required to live under the veil, during the Islamization of the popular resistance movement in Iran in 1977 and then under the enforced *hijab* of the Islamic Republic, the patriarchy of a theocratic state. I have pulled it off with relief as an aircraft has left Iranian soil. I have worn it with very little underneath in summer heat and felt the peculiar frisson of an eroticized political gesture. I have watched the veil's changing meanings within the cultural politics of Iran and know its turbulent history as a signifier: forcible unveiling during the regime of Reza Shah in the 1930s; women taking it up during the popular movement in 1977; women using it to conceal weapons and propaganda; women desperate to take it off once they weren't allowed to.

And yet recently, I've also felt a strong urge—like some laddish response to a lap dancer—to shout "Take it off!" at the news picture of Afghani women wearing the *burqa*, positioned behind the prying eye of Western cameras peering inside Afghanistan behind the triumphant Allied troops.

What I try to explore here are the relationships between the political realities, the media coverage and my own—and Western—responses. I have organized these under four headings: (1) scopophilia and the nature of visual regimes of power *scopophilia*; (2) state sovereignty and the control of women; (3) click politics and the nature of mousy solidarity; and (4) the circular relationship between traditional media and the Internet. This is a rather sanguine look at the question of women's rights and solidarity in global civil society.

Visual Regimes of Power

The representations in Western media during spring 2002 of the burqa in Afghanistan seem to exemplify a struggle between two competing male determinations of women: that of the Taliban inside Afghanistan and that of Western politicians and journalists outside. The invitation to audiences has been to line up in this bifurcated manner that the Afghan "war" itself made real, and the success of which became quite quickly focused on gender, with the burqa becoming the key symbol of women's oppression.

In the most obvious manner, certain terms in the rhetoric of the news media directly parallel the sexualized language of the veil. News and the veil both "cover," stories and bodies, with many tensions in the play between "uncovering" and "covering up." This trope is at play in the title of Edward Said's book *Covering Islam* (1981) and his valuable analysis of the way in which knowledge production not only reveals and hides elements of the object under scrutiny, but also reveals the interests and concerns of the actors, the knowledge producers themselves.

Analysis of the gendered dynamics of Orientalism has a long pedigree. There exists a rich literature on the European masculinist vision in Orientalist art that was fascinated by the harem and sought to discover its secrets, or at least to represent its own fantasies of this impenetrable female space; for example, Ingres painted the *hamam* without ever stepping out of Paris. After art came photography, and excellent work by Sarah Graham-Brown and Malek Alloula analyzes the manner in which the prying camera of the early colonials tried to uncover the key to Middle East (hetero)sexuality.[1] Some of the early studio portraiture was driven by the growing tourist markets in North Africa and Egypt, and included louche photographs of Berber odalisques lying voluptuously on divans with hookah pipes, reproduced as postcards for travelers, including the French military, to send home. I have often wondered what a petit-bourgeois French housewife thought and felt when she received an image of a half-naked foreign woman from the postman. The camera seemed insatiable, demanding to see more, asking women to uncover, and culminating in the extraordinary image of a veiled woman with bare breasts.[2] And that tendency continues. With the increasing tabloidization of journalism has come growing public debate in Britain and the United States about invasion of privacy, the nature of private space, the limits of a "public life." John Thompson's recent book on scandal explores both the role of public media in revealing private affairs and our contemporary love of scandal.[3] The key instrument of prying paparazzi is the still camera with an inordinately long lens, its crudely phallic power trying to penetrate everywhere.

Western audiences saw little television imagery of Afghanistan until the events of September 11 and the ensuing policy of pursuing al-Qaeda, when Afghanistan emerged so dramatically onto our screens. In the aftermath of the military campaign that dislodged the Taliban from power, Western journalists seemed desperate once again to see under the veil and waited expectantly for women to unveil themselves. As Western audiences, we lined up behind this camera, and its images structured our knowledge, or lack thereof.

Yet the scoping gaze of the television camera does not show everything that is going on. We increasingly inhabit the illusion of transparency, where the "real" is not evident, not imaged, not apparent to us. Also, cultures vary in their attitudes toward individuals being photographed. Women are often uneasy about being photographed, and in many societies, men are fiercely protective of any images of their womenfolk being taken. I will give two indications of how this happens and what it means. In Spring 2002 on an electronic list for a major international organization of communication scholars, the head of the United Nations Education, Scientific, and Cultural Organization (UNESCO) office in Kabul posted a few pictures showing Afghanis unpacking the books sent to the university by Western donors and arranging them on the shelves of the newly reconstituted and reopened school of journalism in Kabul University. All the people in the picture were men. This triggered a rapid response from a Western feminist who acknowledged the significance of the moment but suggested to the UNESCO official that the presence of women would be appropriate (as if UNESCO had control over Afghani cultural norms). He quietly replied, describing how unusual it was for Afghani women to be photographed, and wrote: "I think it is fair to say that many women in this society, even the most progressive, are still reluctant to be photographed and this is inclined to ensure that most photographs have a disproportionate number of male images." He mentioned how angry men become with foreigners trying to snap even women covered by the burqa.

He also suggested that behind the scenes, not evidenced by the camera, a number of activities related to gender equality were under way. Two women's publications, *Seerat Weekly*, the first women's newspaper, and *Malalai*, a women's magazine, have been established, each with a woman editor. The Media Resource Center in Kabul has a women's publications unit, and a professional association of women media workers has already been established, with more than sixty women media professionals. Of forty-five teacher trainees at a recent UNESCO workshop, fifteen were women; women have been included in university examinations; and UNESCO was amongst the first UN offices to have a gender advisor, Ms. Rina Amiri.

In Britain, articles in the *Guardian* newspaper through 2002 have described how, with the return of television, came the return of women's voices, including Rida Azimi, a popular newscaster when the Taliban banned television; how a radio serial broadcast by the Pashto and Central Asian branch of the BBC World Service is one of the most popular programs, and how music and cinema are in great demand again. The cultural politics of developing a communications policy inside Afghanistan is extremely interesting, with the BBC and Voice and Vision of the Islamic Republic fighting for influence, with every major international agency ready to rush in and give advice, and with individual entrepreneurs wanting to establish private stations and cable operations to feed the cultural starvation that many Afghans feel.

But back to images. Another example of the politics of image making in an Islamic context are the controversies that have broken out in Saudi Arabia. There, women often have difficulties in proving who they are and are usually merely named as dependants on their male guardians' cards. They have been allowed to have their own identity cards with a photograph, although a woman can get this only if she is over twenty-two and has the written consent of her guardian, as well as that of her employer if she is working. Yet conservatives pronounced it un-Islamic that women's faces be revealed for unrelated men to see. In the winter of 2002 another controversy broke out around the new generation of mobile phones that can take pictures. These were banned as a potential threat to female modesty, although most attempts at banning a technology usually serve only to encourage its use.

Despite audiences' growing understanding of the conventions of television and the aesthetic conventions of photography, when it comes to the
"foreign," the "other," we still think the camera does not lie and all is as we
see it. But what we see is not all there is; the presence of television does not
produce universal WYSIWYG (What you see is what you get) regimes, and
perhaps nowhere less than in international news coverage.

State Sovereignty and the Control of Women

When the Taliban successfully captured Kabul in September 1996 and established a militant Islamic state in Afghanistan, they immediately did two
things: they barred women from attending school and going to work, indeed
from any participation in the public sphere, and they banned television. Control over these two elements—women and the media—lay at the heart of the
Taliban regime, and the state of each is increasingly taken as a key index of
the democratization and development of a society.

Western politicians had paid no attention to Afghani women from the
time the Soviets left Afghanistan. Even under the regime of Najibullah,
although more seriously under the Taliban, women suffered violence in many
forms: widespread abuse, rape, dowry killing, acid throwing, sexual harass-
ment, and sexual slavery. State indifference, discriminatory laws, and the
gender bias of the country's legal system—if it can even be called that—
ensured the virtual impunity of the perpetrators.[4] And Western countries did
little while an entire generation of girls and young women were removed
from the education system and rendered illiterate and unskilled, or when
many women were condemned to beggary and prostitution as a result of economic collapse.

The various human rights abuses, and especially those against women,
were documented by Amnesty International and Human Rights Watch. In
1998, the American Medical Association documented deteriorating physical
and mental health of women, including a very high suicide rate. In March
2000, some Afghanis commandeered a plane and demanded asylum in the
United Kingdom; they included a number of women. But no women Labor
MPs did anything, But there was little political action, and in the end only
eight Afghans were allowed to stay in the United Kingdom.

It has been estimated that at least half of all female refugees in the United
Kingdom were seeking protection from rape and sexual torture in their
home countries.[5] Immigration authorities rely on protocols and standards of

evidence that are blind to the particular circumstances of women refugees, failing to recognize that women find it hard to articulate experiences of abuse, often lack appropriate paper documentation, cannot provide witnesses for alleged abuse, and so on. Many Western countries now have some gender guidelines in place in relation to immigration and asylum that often acknowledge discrimination on the basis of sexual orientation or physical or sexual abuse as grounds for asylum claims. But the British home secretary Jack Straw recently accused the Law Lords of being overliberal in their support of two Pakistani women seeking asylum on the basis of domestic abuse. Amnesty's first-ever report on human rights abuses in Saudi Arabia focused prominently on rights abuses against women and migrant workers. Nonetheless, the 2001 report *Broken Bodies, Shattered Minds* documents torture and violence against women in many countries, the absence of redress, the gender bias of the courts and security services, and the ignorance of women themselves about their rights.

With the fall of the Taliban and the elation that heralded the re-emancipation of women, this became a post facto justification for the war. In the post–September 11 environment, with the campaign against al-Qaeda in full flow, both the U.S. and British governments sought quite cynically to use their first ladies to make rare political interventions to focus on women in Afghanistan. In November, Laura Bush made a rare radio address by a first lady, while Cherie Blair, at the end of November, also received huge media coverage by denouncing the burqa as the symbol of the oppression of women in Afghanistan. Thus the burqa was used as part of a Western propaganda campaign, here addressing Western audiences sympathetic to women's rights. The burqa became the synecdoche for fundamentalism, anti-modernism, and suddenly a ruthless pursuit of the terror network behind the September 11 events was transformed into a war of liberation with women as the main victors. Indeed, on January 29, 2002, George Bush proclaimed that the U.S. flag once more flew over the U.S. embassy in Kabul, and "that mothers and daughters of Afghanistan who were once captives in their own homes are today free." Even *Vagina Monologues* playwright Eve Ensler in March 2002 tried to spin the war as a crusade against a global patriarchy (although the women of Afghanistan might feel that political dialogue would be more relevant to them than vagina monologues). Clearly, the restoration of some kind of democratic government to Afghanistan and a slow restoration of rights to women may be part of the collateral benefit, as opposed to the damage, that is the outcome of the Western military strikes. But to paint the liberation of women as the "intention" of the war is a cynical rewriting of the process.

Indeed, there are other signs of how patriarchy utilizes issues around women as its shifting politics allow. A fascinating obverse of the "take off the burqa" position has been the requirement that every U.S. woman soldier stationed in Saudi Arabia wear an *abbaya* and forgo driving, in observance of Saudi custom. But in early January 2002 the top female fighter pilot, Martha McSally, filed suit against Donald Rumsfeld for no less than violating her constitutional rights. She was supported by the liberal National Organization for Women, as well as by the conservative Rutherford Institute. Later in the month, the chair of the U.S. Central Command told U.S. Army leaders not to impose these clothing restrictions on women anymore. In 2002, U.S. relations with Saudi Arabia cooled considerably; U.S. military bases there are being closed down and the center of the military's Gulf activities reestablished in Qatar and elsewhere. Keeping the Saudis happy no longer matters so much, and thus McSally's volley was allowed to knock down an old Aunt Sally.

Feminist political theorists such as Cynthia Enloe have developed powerful critiques of the gendered nature of war and militarism, but it is also important that we better understand the nature of the state as a masculinist structure of modern life. Wendy Brown in *States of Injury* has argued that the elements of the state identifiable as masculinist do not correspond to some property contained within men but to "the conventions of power and privilege constitutive of gender within an order of male dominance."[6] In authoritarian regimes in the south, including Afghanistan, the manifestations of patriarchy are transparent. In the West, the state is neither hegemonic nor monolithic, but "it mediates or deploys almost all the powers shaping women's lives: physical, economic, sexual, reproductive and political, . . . the powers wielded in previous epochs directly by men."[7] The fundamental international relations notion of state sovereignty acknowledges the legal jurisdiction of states within their own borders. As Jacqueline Bhabha has shown, in adjudicating issues around refugees and asylum seekers entering Western countries, there is an evident conflict between notions of state sovereignty and notions of fundamental rights.[8] The conflict is hardly even engaged when it comes to the systematic abuse of women *within* national borders. There was more, and more intensive, international concern and mobilization, including through UNESCO, to try to prevent the Taliban's

destruction of the Buddha statues at Bamiyan than to deal with their intern-
ment of a generation of women. This is a powerful indictment of the lopsided
nature of global cultural politics, where stones are valued more highly than
womenfolk because the former can be deemed part of the global patrimony
whereas the latter are considered to be under the jurisdiction of uncontrol-
lable patriarchal states. Thus, gender analysis and politics so often slip
through debates on multiculturalism (as practices "internal" to each group)
and through debates on cultural policy (as something "social" rather than
cultural in the narrow, formal sense understood by the language of cultural
policy).

Such are the states, and international regimes, we are in.

The Cultural Blinkers of Global Solidarity:
Click Politics and Mousy Solidarity

As I've said, I'd also felt a strong urge to shout "take it off" at the news picture of Afghani women wearing the burqa (pale blue in most news shots,
unlike the vivid colors in the film *Kandahar*). And I have been shocked at
some recent news footage of Kabul in the 1960s that showed bareheaded
women in twin sets and knee-length skirts, the contemporary Western fashion of the day. I knew that Kabul had a modernizing elite, a strong university,
and some very emancipated women, but I'd managed to forget that in the
thin history of Afghanistan the media provided. We became fascinated by the
burqa, a garment that denies not just femininity but all individuality to those
who wear it. It thus becomes an excellent disguise for Westerners, including,
most famously, the BBC journalist John Simpson, who slipped into Afghanistan wearing one; the British woman journalist Yvonne Ridley who slipped
up in Afghanistan and was arrested and held for some days; and for the odd
Afghani or Saudi man who slipped out of the country the same way.

Probably the most enduring feature of the burqa will be the introduction
into English, and thus to Scrabble games, of a word where *q* is not followed by
u. In colloquial Pashto, it is referred to as a *chadoori*, like the Persian *chadoor*,
or tent, reflecting both its voluminosity and its rural origins. Ilene Prusher
vividly describes learning how to wear one and the difficulty of not seeing
one's feet, but also of being buffeted by men in public spaces, the only way
they could touch women.[9] And it very rapidly became apparent that women
would not immediately take off the burqa. The social environment was not
yet conducive; women did not feel safe enough to take it off, did not want to

be the daring first ones to do it, did not want to encounter and have to deal with the perhaps hostile, perhaps overly inquisitive, gazes of their Afghan menfolk.

Slowly and occasionally we were invited to see that the issue of the veil was secondary to issues of security, financial stability, education. As Al-Marayati and Issa argued in an article in the *Los Angeles Times*, the burqa is not Afghani women's main concern.[10] Their priorities are more basic— feeding their children, becoming literate, and living free from violence, a violence that is both domestic and international in its manifestations. Indeed, as women were allowed to go out alone once again, the sales of the burqa rose, since it provides some protection for women in a very uncertain time.

So what did, and could, global women do in support of Afghani women, both inside Afghanistan and in refugee camps on the borders? Many of us doubtless added our names to the e-mail petition in support of Afghani women: "Help free Afghani Women — Sign and send this petition to a hundred of your closest friends!" What good did we think we were doing? The e-mail address to which the petition was directed had been long defunct, as the global torrent of unauthorized chain letters swamped the university server at Brandeis University. By January 1999 the system had crashed and the university closed the mail account.

Even if these petitions had been collected, what would the American woman have done with them? Sent them in an e-mail attachment to the Taliban? Did they have an e-mail address? Did she have it? Print and send it by post? Few countries had formal diplomatic ties with the Taliban regime, so it would have been hard to get the petition presented, and to whom? And were the Taliban really going to be influenced by an Internet petition? This petition circulated and returned to me at least fifteen times over a number of years; it uselessly filled our e-mail inboxes. Perhaps it made us feel good that with a mousy little click we could play a role in global politics. But if this is the stuff of global solidarity, its web is pretty thin. Adding your name to an Internet petition is quick, easy, and virtually useless, partly because Internet petitions often provide incomplete information and unverifiable names. Some sites, like the Feminist Majority Foundation, established a way of sending more personal messages in support of Afghani women, as did Revolutionary Association of the Women of Afghanistan (RAWA). In December 2000, members of RAWA were featured on the *Oprah Winfrey Show*, triggering such a storm of people (estimated at 300,000) onto their site that the software crashed and all the signatures were deleted from the server. Such petitions might—I stress *might*—get people talking about the issue, might help the subjects of the petition to feel they are not alone. But they are more likely to provide a quick assuaging of Western feelings of powerlessness and guilt and do little to change the reality of Afghani women's lives.

Perhaps here is the moment for me to eat some humble pie, or at least temper a few of my own words. Over a number of years, I have written in somewhat celebratory tones about the emergence of global civil society in which women's transnational political activities, especially in relation to the organizing before and around the Beijing conference and later in Beijing-plus-Five, have been central. For instance:

> The global interactivity of women continues to provide support to local and national groups struggling to achieve specific goals within nation-states but also as a global movement: the ratification of CEDAW; the recognition of women's rights as fundamental human rights; the development of international instruments and actions against violence against women, the sex industry, have become part of the global ideological and political landscape. Difference-in-solidarity remains its mode of operation.[11]

And indeed, I am in good company. Two major male social theorists, Alberto Melucci and Manuel Castells, have both described the decentered, subtle character of networks of social change. Castells recognizes the social movements that resist global capitalist restructuring, uncontrolled informationalism, and patriarchalism as counter-hegemonic forces. These offer a "networking, decentered form of organization and intervention" that both mirrors and counteracts the "networking logic of domination in the information society." Both men argue that a key contribution of such movements is to challenge accepted codes—Castells says, for example, the new movements do more than organize activity and share information; "they are the actual producers, and distributors, of cultural codes"—and both credit the women's movement in its varied forms and expressions for the demise of patriarchy.[12]

Melucci, long a key theorist of new social movements, also acknowledged considerable variation within the women's movement, from affective support structures to professional groups that feminized public space, those producing female culture and those offering public services. When I read his work, I was delighted to find him echoing my independently arrived at description, that the "movement" is a network of networks.[13]

Of course we can acknowledge that new information and communication technologies, especially the Internet, can be important political tools that link individuals and groups beyond geographic borders. As Hamm writes, social movements have "used the technologies to denounce, mobilise, campaign and make their struggles known to a worldwide audience," and she describes a variety of activities, including information sharing, education, networking, and acting as an alternative to mainstream media, specifically in the general area of violence against women.[14]

Yet I want to suggest that click politics is a rather mousy form of solidarity, an easy way of assuaging Western consciences. It is a poor substitute for material forms of solidarity like funds (imagine if every click had put a pound, a dollar, into a RAWA bank account) and a weak form of global compassionate politics when the demands and the process are run from the West without the actual involvement of the would-be recipients, Afghani women, another form of feminist colonialism. As the drums of war with Iraq beat ever faster in the spring of 2003, once again mousy politics kicked in, with the circulation of countless e-mail petitions variously addressed to the UN, the White House, or academic locations, the contemporary form of electronically powered but otherwise rather powerless political action.

Traditional Media and the Net: A Circular Relationship?

RAWA was established in 1977 in Kabul by Afghani woman intellectuals to fight for social justice and human rights. Some went into exile after the Soviet invasion, yet others after the fall of the Soviets. Some were supported by the Americans, some joined the Mujahedeen. Afghans constitute the single largest nationality amongst global refugees, with huge camps in both Pakistan and Iran. The leader of RAWA, Meena, was assassinated in Quetta, Pakistan, in 1987.[15]

British television has produced two powerful documentaries on the women of Afghanistan. In "Beneath the Veil" by Saira Shah, a Channel 4 reporter who made an emotional trip to Afghanistan, her father's homeland, Shah managed to access horrific footage taken by RAWA members of public executions and other human rights abuses inside Afghanistan. It includes a chilling interview with a senior Taliban official whom Shah asks how the Taliban could use a football pitch built with international funds for executions.

The answer given was that if the international community would fund a place especially for public executions, then the Taliban would allow sports events in the stadium again. The program won the 2001 Sais-Novartis International Journalism award of Johns Hopkins University, and in 2002 won the British Academy of Film and Television Arts award for best documentary.[16]

Another documentary, entitled "Silent Scream," was shown in March 2002 in the *Correspondent* series for the BBC. It provided a good history of the impact of twenty-three years of war upon the women of Afghanistan, supported by interviews with members of RAWA, as well with as Eve Ensler, who has established an organization called V-Day, and Meryl Streep. Each of these documentaries is supported by extensive Web site material and links to RAWA, Amnesty International, V-Day, and beyond. These television programs all trailed supporting Web sites. Recent articles in the *Guardian* are also supported by a wealth of Web-based information, links, and Web logs.

As the story about RAWA that appeared on the *Oprah Winfrey Show* suggests, we cannot any longer think about television as simply mainstream and banal and the net as radical, alternative, and exciting. Each can be both, and it is increasingly clear that some of the best broadcast and press coverage will lead people to the net and help them understand how additional information, knowledge, and paths to actions can be found there. Indeed, the reverse argument could be made, that the existence of the net, and its links and orientations toward action, is encouraging mainstream media to provide follow-through to many broadcast programs in a way that was unheard of even five years ago.

I started to think that women's responses to other women as represented in international news and factual programming perhaps traced an unusual trajectory. Most academic analysis and public debate about the impact of international news coverage on audiences focuses on indifference and a lack of affect. The literature on international news and audience reactions has been filled with metaphors of "compassion fatigue," "states of denial," and a general lack of concern about "distant suffering."[17] It appears that the usual response to international news is "not existential anger and horror . . . but a mixture of entertainment and listless ennui."[18] The conceptual play is about different kinds of distance: the geospatial, which communication technologies lessens, and the sociocultural, which communications content often works to increase. Tester writes of the news audience in the developed Western world that "we are indifferent in so far as we tend to have no sustained interest in what we see and hear; for us what we see and hear of horror in other places lacks importance or deep meaning."[19] But two implications need comment. One is the assumption that among this "we" of audience there are no others who *do* deeply identify with the matter in hand. For example, Britain's Asian populations are agonized about and deeply divided over the religious violence in India. And both Arabs and Jews watch coverage of the Middle East with different eyes than do others, as well as utilizing other sources of information. The second point is that through the narrow definition of "we" as the Western viewer, the news violence never happens to "us." Part of the deep shock of 9/11 was that "we" had become the object of violence, not its perpetrator.

I sense that women may sometimes respond differently to images of violence, particularly those against other women, and may actually be galvanized into action. If we were able to track the traffic from mainstream media toward the Internet and thus into political action of various kinds, we might be able to show both the obverse of the "compassion fatigue" syndrome as well as the net's potential for showing us paths to action in ways that mainstream media never felt it was their business to suggest.

In Conclusion: The States We're In

To sum up, I have been stressing the synecdochic function of television in particular in setting up parts for a whole, and the need to remember what is not shown, and not obvious, as much as what is made evident.

I'm pointing yet again to the masculine nature of the state and its instruments of coercion, which include the cynical use of gender in its propaganda wars. The issue of sovereignty protects patriarchal states, raising the tension between state sovereignty and gendered human rights as an issue that needs further political exploration and social exposition. I'm asking whether we can do better than mousy solidarity in building global civil society, and I'm suggesting that we need to look at the interconnections between mainstream media and the net to better understand both and the dynamics of contemporary politics.

This recent British documentary programming was still not quite women representing themselves, not fully the subaltern voice but women's voices nonetheless.[20] Finally, we got to hear from women themselves, including the two women who were appointed ministers in Afghanistan's new interim government, from women who had organized illegal schools for girls, from

Latifa, who produced her own underground magazine under the very eyes of the Taliban, and from Zoya's teenage experiences.[21] Only then did I/could we (the British audience) begin once again to think about the complexity of the veil, its practices and their meaning, and the difficulties of bringing about a different, other modernity. Slowly, a third space appeared, more problematic, ambivalent, complex.

Two women attended the 2002 Bonn talks to determine the future of Afghanistan. One was Sima Wali, who said that Afghanistan and its women do need the help of the West, "but please do not speak for us. We are there. We can speak for ourselves." Once again, the global politics of feminism reminds me that solidarity with Afghani women means not assuming that "we" in developed societies know what is good for them, but working in alliance with them to help them rebuild what they want. Perhaps we should put our mice down and lift our hands up to help.

NOTES

A short version of some of this material has appeared as "Seeing through the Veil: Regimes of Representation," *Feminist Media Studies* 2, 2: 270–272.

1 Malek Alloula, *The Colonial Harem* (Minneapolis: U of Minnesota P, 1986); Sarah Graham-Brown, *Images of Women: The Portrayal of Women in Photography of the Middle East, 1860–1950* (New York: Columbia UP, 1988).

2 From an unknown German publication, 1908, reprinted in Graham-Brown, *Images*, 136.

3 John Thompson, *Scandal* (Cambridge: Polity Press, 2002).

4 Fadia Faqir, "Where Is the 'W' Factor? Women and the War on Afghanistan, after 9/11," article no. 10, *Open Democracy*, February 27, 2002, http://www.open-democracy.net/forum.

5 Black Women's Rape Action Project, "Women Deserving Refuge," *Times Law Supplement*, July 14, 1998.

6 Wendy Brown, *States of Injury* (Princeton, N.J.: Princeton UP, 1995), 167.

7 Ibid., 194.

8 Jacqueline Bhabha, "Embodied Rights: Gender Persecution, State Sovereignty, and Refugees," *Public Culture* 9, 1 (fall 1996): 3–32.

9 Ilene Prusher, "Stumbling through a Shrouded World," *Christian Science Monitor*, January 10, 2002.

10 Laila Al-Marayati and S. Issa, "An Identity Reduced to a Burqa," *Los Angeles Times*, January 20, 2002.

11 Annabelle Sreberny-Mohammadi, "Feminist Internationalism: Imagining and Building Global Civil Society," in *Electronic Empires*, ed. Daya Thussu (London: Arnold, 1998), 208–222; ibid., "Women Communicating Globally: Mediating International Feminism," in *Women Transforming Communication*, ed. D. Allen, R. Rush, and S. Kaufmann (Thousand Oaks, Calif.: Sage Publications, 1996), 233–242.

12 Alberto Melucci, *Challenging Codes* (Cambridge: Cambridge UP, 1997), 362; Manuel Castells, *The Power of Identity* (Oxford: Blackwell, 1997), 362.

13 Melucci, *Challenging*, 144; see also Valentine Moghadam, "Feminist Networks North and South," *Journal of International Communication* 3, 1 (1996): 111–126; Donna Dickenson, "Counting Women In: Globalization, Democratization, and the Women's Movement," in *The Transformation of Democracy?* ed. Anthony McGrew (Cambridge: Polity Press, Open UP, 1997).

14 Susanne Hamm, "Information Communications Technologies and Violence against Women," *Development* 44, 3 (September 2001): 36–42.

15 Anne E. Brodsky, *With All Our Strength: The Revolutionary Association of the Woman of Afghanistan* (New York: Routledge, 2003); Cheryl Bernard, *Veiled Courage* (New York: Broadway Books, 2002); Melody Ermachild Charis, *Meena, Heroine of Afghanistan* (New York: St. Martin's Press, 2003).

16 S. Shah, *The Storyteller's Daughter* (London: Michael Joseph, 2003).

17 Susan Moeller, *Compassion Fatigue: How the Media Sell Disease, Famine, War, and Death* (London: Routledge, 1999); Luc Boltanski, *Distant Suffering* (Cambridge: Cambridge UP, 1999).

18 Keith Tester, *Compassion, Morality, and the Media* (Buckingham, UK: Open UP, 2001), 28.

19 Keith Tester, *Moral Culture* (London: Sage, 1997), 30–31.

20 Gayatri Spivak, "Can the Subaltern Speak?" in *Marxism and the Interpretation of Culture*, ed. C. Nelson and L. Grossberg (Urbana: U of Illinois P, 1988).

21 Latifa, *My Forbidden Face* (London: Virago, 2002); Zoya, with John Follam and Rita Christofari, *Zoya's Story* (New York: Morrow, 2002).

USEFUL WEBSITES

http://www.mediachannel.org/atissue/womensmedia/

http://www.womensenews.org/

http://rawa.fancymarketing.net/index.html

http://www.unesco.org/afghanistan

http://www.snopes2.com/inboxer/petition/afghani.htm

http://www.feminist.org.action/1_actions.html

MUSCLE, MARKET VALUE, TELEGENESIS, CYBERPRESENCE

THE NEW ASIAN MOVIE STAR IN THE GLOBAL ECONOMY OF MASCULINE IMAGES

ANNE CIECKO

Though the category called "Asian cinema" may well be a product of the Western imagination's penchant for "othering," it also has the power to disrupt the perception of Hollywood's global supremacy. As Indian filmmaker Shekhar Kapur has recently and provocatively argued, "[T]here is in fact," from a philosophical standpoint, "a commonality in Asia." Based on his predictions regarding combined Asian demographics, the increase of Asian film financing, the growth of Asian movie studios, and the rise of Asian news media outlets, he anticipates that Western domination of the cinema will soon be reaching its final days. He cites Bollywood as a premier example of Asian cultures' unfixability and their ability to constructively assimilate—via a fluid, ever-morphing "adaptation of Western technology to eastern forms of storytelling." Asian movie stars are also central to Kapur's characterization of Asian-centric global media culture in the near future, as he argues that "[s]oon we will find that in order to make a hugely successful film, you have to match Tom Cruise with an Indian or Chinese actor."[1]

The originary narrative of the coming of cinema (that exuberantly commodifiable form of popular culture) to Asia can be framed as a story of foreign colonization via Western technological invention (the apparatus or medium) and Western-driven capital/profit. Within such a version of film history, Asian national cinemas emerge as indigenized film (especially the mode of filmic storytelling), as well as indigenized film going. Another take on the story finds connections to technologies of image making in public forms throughout Asian cultures that long predate the mechanical innovation— raising the question if what we call cinema need be, by definition, a Western phenomenon. It is arguably the very hybrid nature of cinema as cultural production that compels film producers, audiences, and theorists alike to struggle to use the medium itself to define difference.

This essay is an effort toward reconceptualizing contemporary Asian films—and Asian film stardom in particular—without reinstating hegemonic Hollywood paradigms. Rather than essentializing "Asian" (as a presumed subset of "non-Western") or effacing national specificities, I consider "Asian cinemas" and "Asian superstars" part of an overarching geoindustrial category. This is a polemical gesture toward recentering Asia, the world's most prolific film producer.[2]

Since contemporary cinema is literally transformed by and into other media, expressed in a variety of technological formats, movie stars inevitably acquire new discursive valences in these proliferating forms. My project here is to examine Asian star constructions: to illustrate the ways these famous figures have been recharged by cross-media excursions, and the ways they have come to represent the viability of Asian-produced media. As Christine Geraghty has noted, "Film stardom . . . has to be seen in the context of the drive in the media to exploit the status of being famous across the whole range of entertainment formats."[3] Introducing the variable of gender into the mix, it is male stars who are culturally positioned as the principal power players.

With Western interest in Asian cinema at an all-time high, this is a cultural moment of perceived ascendance or transcendence of Asian film that can be exploited at every level. Recent Hollywood films and coproductions have incorporated Asian star talent and appropriated Asian-coded film genres, but the brilliance of Asia's foremost multitasking multihyphenates (actor-writer, director-producer, etc.), such as Hong Kong's Jackie Chan or Japan's "Beat" Takeshi Kitano, is easily reduced to reductive caricature in the process of "translation."[4] To date, Chan has endlessly played riffs on the martial arts/action clown with broken English and little chance for romance, while Kitano's stoic and nearly mute *yakuza* in his directorial foray into English-language filmmaking (*Brother*, 2000) loses the many shades of nuance of his complex Japanese star image to rather empty self-parody.[5]

A perhaps unprecedented pressure is now being placed on the Asian male star's visual image and "author" status (in the Foucauldian sense of institutional structures and discursive possibilities) to appear deceptively self-generating and ubiquitous, to be everything everywhere at once.[6] The star is not solely a "product of" the media-making machinery of the film industry (the "constructed persons in media texts" that Richard Dyer describes in his seminal work in star studies),[7] but is configured as an active, virile agent—sculpting his body, self-reflexively mugging, making career decisions which determine his salary/monetary worth, remaining connected to televisual vehicles (often classified as proto- or precinematic in the teleology of star making), selling himself in shamelessly entrepreneurial ways, and embracing (and aggressively interpolating himself into) emerging technological expressions of star/fan cultures.

The contemporary technostructure of superstardom, the multiple media sites inhabited by a growing array of Asian performers, insists upon a leveling of hierarchies. Film and television performances, Internet and digital multimedia, music recording, advertising campaigns, stage shows, and various "live" events are some of the many much-valued vehicles for contemporary star construction. The contemporary Asian male movie star is expressed through a rather confounding conglomeration of elements: morphing physical qualities, discernable market value, enduring televisual appeal, and growing cyberpresence. Versions of such a conceptualization may be applicable to contemporary non-Asian stars, as film scholar Brian Gallagher suggests in his comments on the "mysterious and paradoxical ways" the Hollywood star system still functions today.[8] He discusses how Hollywood actors such as Paul Newman and Robert Redford self-produce, and at times even direct, their own work. However, Gallagher proposes: "Oddly, perhaps, in this media-saturated era, there continue to be more or less 'pure' movie stars [he includes Newman and Redford in this category], stars whose celebrity derives almost entirely from their work in films."[9] In contrast, the formulation of Asian stardom that I am proposing demands impurity—or rather, excess. The star in this case is always *more than* a movie star, or (in compound terms) a movie star and more.

The often familiar narrative of what I call "telegenesis"—the small-screen-to-big-screen-career narrative trajectory—is recharged by the contemporary Asian star's frequent return to the box. Television variety programs, game shows, dramas, and sitcoms can offer the illusion of intimate connection with the erstwhile/current/future movie star. For example, consider recent television hosting stints by Amitabh Bachchan, recognized by a now-legendary BBC on-line poll as the celebrity of the millenium, still a huge box-office draw, and widely considered Bollywood's all-time superstar—as well as the omnipresence of Bollywood's top male stars (referred to in Bollywood parlance as "heroes") in commercial advertisements, especially the requisite soft-drink endorsement.[10] The proliferation of Coke and Pepsi ads in India further demarcates the processes of globalization—and "glocalization." They also offer an unusual forum for ludic star play: games of one-upmanship resonant of box-office rivalries. A seemingly neverending series of ads from both corporate camps quite literally rip on/off each other through mimicry and spoofs, copycat vignettes and jingles, and star lookalikes. The "response" is almost immediate in temporal terms, to the delight (and sometimes dismay) of fans. The constant sexy pairings of male and female stars might offer a frisson of romance, but the real charge is intertextual. Bollywood's male stars in particular are cast into an aggressive (and seemingly personal) dialogue with each other's endorsements through the cola wars. The promos have also escalated in terms of production value, with all sorts of Bollywood personnel involved (from top male and female acting talent to choreographers, musicians, cinematographers, directors, et cetera). Shah Rukh Khan (Pepsi) and Aamir Khan (Coke) have each produced their own lavish film epic—and ads for their respective fizzy drinks.

Hong Kong's Andy Lau Tak-Wah's multitalented star status and his multi-stranded career as entertainer/performer, most notably as movie star and one of Cantopop music's "Heavenly Kings," led to Pepsi's corporate interest in his image. In this way, Lau's pan-Asian popularity resulted in an ongoing and still-developing relationship with the company, as he became "the first Asian singer to sign an endorsement contract with Pepsi-Cola."[11] Now, numerous Cantonese-language musical performers/movie stars have followed suit with stylishly produced singing/dancing/cola-hawking TV spots. Such commercials or star "spots" take on a life outside the television set, especially through the commodification of popular music and star images.[12] They blur media boundaries.

On the part of the consumer/spectator, with the necessary technical hookups working in tandem with the televisual apparatus, "home" modes—videotape, VCD (dominant in Asia), and DVD—can further demolish the delusion of television as a more "primitive" medium (compared to cinema) because of its domestic familiarity and impressions of reduced spectacle. Sometimes these forms are recognized as the only, or as the preferred, way to watch movies and to see stars in performance. TV's seemingly domesticated approach to nationalism can also mask possibilities for territorial expansion, especially in light of pan-Asian audiences and satellite television's link to diasporic audiences. Star power is a vehicle for spectatorial identification and community building, establishing connections within and across borders.

The contemporary Asian star is thus expressed at the tensile interstices between technophobia and technophilia: image control/regulation and desire for technological mastery that promises endless variation, self-invention, and self-reflexivity. But it also threatens endless derivation and denial of individuality, originality, and ownership. The star is exposed to constant and often contradictory ideological and industrial pressures. On one hand, the star might appear to embrace technology through participation with interactive media, product endorsements, or appearances in special effects–driven films. On the other hand, star charisma can be dampened or extinguished by overfamiliarity generated through image reproduction (media burnout and overexposure), or perceived lack of entertainment value in any medium.

One star who has attempted to maintain career momentum through savvy use of technology is South Korea's Han Suk-kyu. A voice-dubbing artist turned television star turned movie star, he recently took a three-year hiatus from the screen at the pinnacle of his career. During this period he developed, among other projects, a Web-based screenplay service/competition.[13] The contrast between his low tech(nology)/high tech(nique) performance as the terminally ill photo shop owner in the critically acclaimed *Christmas in August* (1998) and his role as the spectacularly tormented secret agent in the explosive special effects–laden blockbuster *Shiri* (1999) confirmed his versatility an actor.[14] (The latter film's record-breaking box-office success was also attributed to corporate movie backer Samsung Entertainment's relentless merchandising and promotion.) During his break from the movies, the star's Internet profile and appearances in television commercials helped give longing fans a sense of—to cite the title of his 1997 film about an electronic chat room relationship—the contact.[15]

This "technology effect" can be seen as an extension of industrial modes of star production, promotion, distribution, and so on. Additionally, fandom can be profoundly participatory and interactive, especially as enacted or displayed through the mechanisms of virtual or cybercultures that insist on boundary blurrings and border crossings, not to mention (illicit or sanctioned) acts of "poaching" or piracy.[16] The latter term adds another layer of netting, because piracy is widely considered to be the worst "threat" to all Asian film industries, individual and collectively imagined—although Kapur, in the newspaper piece cited at the beginning of this essay, contends that the assertion that there are "no big markets in Asia" because of piracy is a "fallacy," offering the example of Star TV, the pan-Asian satellite network, in partnership with the pirates. Star-image pilfering can also take more overt forms, as in the famous case of Andy Lau versus Hang Seng Bank Ltd. (2000), where the star could not prevent the bank from issuing credit cards making unauthorized use of his name and likeness.[17]

And industry and fan activities needn't be mutually exclusive, as in the case of Bollywood *masala* movies, which engage highly developed and distinctive fan magazine (print and on-line) cultures as part of the nationally rooted but globally reaching movie fantasy factory.[18] The traditional and ongoing functions of other sorts of mediators, such as star handlers (agents, managers, and others), usually in the employ of the actor or the studio, are still operative—but these functions have also been usurped by fans, audiences, the public, the market, policy makers, and the nation-state. Media and power are profoundly interconnected, and the fan/star relationship fuels the fantasy of democratic access and ownership. Also, the political economy enables stardom, once the "star" designation is bestowed, to become a "self-fulfilling prophecy."[19]

However, in (en)gendering my model of the Asian star, I'm also insisting that the star be a "real" man (even if this reality is, as always, illusory). This is not an endorsement of (hetero-)sexism in the persistent hegemonic discourses which permeate cultural policies, capitalism, and the "culture industries"—including all contemporary forms of mass media and modes of cultural production. Rather, this is an observation based on research into the textual and discursive fields of Asian cinemas: Male stars consistently make more money for their screen time and have perceptibly inflated industrial and technological power. (A strong argument can be made that the female star is, to follow through on the economic trope, in recession.)

Thus some striking rhetorical and discursive gestures that represent the Asian cinema and political economy (from the outside and from within) can be read as attempts to reassert mass culture as a gendered phenomenon. Andreas Huyssen's useful interpretation of overt expressions of "mass culture as woman" in the founding texts of literary modernism, as well as slippages in theoretical and philosophical writings, can be applied in revealing ways here, as can theories of transnational feminism and postcolonialism dealing with cultural "othering" in gendered terms.[20] Forms of Asian mass culture have consistently been rendered as distortions of gender in the West. Scholars of Asian-American cinema and literature such as Gina Marchetti, Peter Feng, David Eng, and Sheng-mei Ma, among others, have formulated insightful historically based critical and theoretical positions on the U.S. response to the perceived Asian menace with representational strategies of demonizing, castrating, and fetishizing—Hollywood's images of stereotypical Asians from early cinema to the present day.[21] And more generally, Robert Stam reminds us in his meta-account of the emergence of film theoretical discourses that "[t]he beginnings of cinema . . . coincided with the very height of imperialism."[22] The saga of cultural imperialism continues with the contemporary tale of globalization and the related fable of the Asian economic crisis—miracle to meltdown (circa 1997)—in its various renderings as a story of economic castration and of fallen masculinity, writ with pervasive and lumpenly amorphous metaphors of a sickly, ailing, flaccid, infected body. When Asian culture industries begin to show signs of "recovery," this is expressed through domestically produced "blockbusters" that bullishly threaten the Hollywood competition which tends to saturate the multiplex in time of economic downturn, or in a crossover film like *Crouching Tiger, Hidden Dragon,* where production and distribution financing registers as subsidy or patronage of exotic but high-quality, technically virtuoso alternative fare.[23] As Huyssen has suggested (vis-à-vis his rendering of the Frankfurt School), emphasis on technological features of mass culture asserts a "masculinizing" discourse which masks inscribed ideas of feminine or feminized mass culture[24]—not to mention reinforces gender binaries. Thus the "embodiment" of Asian male superstardom in figures who are constructed as masters-of-much-media is offered as economic justification for popular cinema.

In terms of the gendering of "mass culture" (read here as inclusive of popular cinema and its related cultural texts), the national-cinema question becomes even more charged. If one of the functions of cinematic nation building and "imagined" community creation in Asian cinemas is inventing a "legitimizing" discourse, as Wimal Dissanayake has asserted, the internalized aspects of colonialism/imperialism and racism seem to have contributed, especially on the part of Asian cultural elites, to an often troubled relationship between domestic cinema (especially cheaply made "body genres") and mass appeal.[25] The Western reception of Asian cinemas—from martial arts to Bollywood masala films—continues to view genres through a prism which refracts "excessive" affect or movement, and deviations from realist conventions, in exaggerated gender terms.

Illustrating the internalization of these perspectives at the national level, the economically struggling film industry of the Philippines is still churning out domestic films, despite such travails as censorship and disdain on the part of the cultural elite for movies which tend to appeal to what is often described in derogatory terms as the *bakya* crowd, or low-brow audiences. Anxiety about the perceived inferiority of the local industry is also projected onto Filipino film stars as questions about their ability as performers.[26] The body genres are not only gendered, but also associated with disparaging class distinctions and lack of access to "cultural capital."

Cesar Montano, a Filipino actor enjoying superstardom at this moment in his twenty-year career, has a star image that has been profoundly complicated by the stark distinctions drawn between socially minded (and also often commercially savvy, highly budgeted, and conspicuously technically proficient) "cinema of quality" and low-budget popular sex and action films, as well as by the vicissitudes of the local film industry. Montano has been recast (and we are led to believe, has recast himself) in provocative ways. After early career collaborations with the late new-wave filmmaker Ishmael Bernal, he performed in a number of pulp thrillers. His profile has shifted again with his recent participation in three of the most commercially successful (and expensive) films in the history of the Philippines: *Jose Rizal* (1998), *Muro Ami* (*Reef Hunters*, 1999), and *Bagang Buwan* (*New Moon*, 2001). These three melodramatic epics, all directed by Filipina auteur Marilou Diaz-Abaya, shape a composite of a serious actor's repertoire and cinematic versions of the martyr-hero: the executed patriot Rizal in the titular biopic, the tragically flawed fishing captain Fredo who goes down with the ship in *Muro Ami*, and the pacifist Muslim doctor Ahmad who takes a bullet in the crossfire of wartorn Mindanao in *Bagang Buwan*. In an interesting twist, the woman filmmaker here becomes connected with both taste making and power brokering in the national film industry. As a film director, Diaz-Abaya has had a very close working relationship with the formidable GMA Network, an institution involved with multiple media outlets, as well as film production.

Montano-as-star has followed up his facilitated career makeover by continuing to assert and extend his own clout and local popularity with an almost impossible lineup of everyman projects—or mass-culture conquests. He has produced, directed, and starred in muscular guns-and-superpowers movies such as *Bullet* (1999) and *Mananabas* (*The Reaper*, 2001) and appeared in other action films, as well as playing regular gigs on television programs such as the sitcom *Kaya ni Mister, Kaya ni Misis*; product endorsements for underwear and sardines; a fan-friendly marriage to his sexy frequent costar Sunshine Cruz (and recent fatherhood, adding to his three children from other relationships); an album of guitar-strumming folk songs; and (perhaps the ultimate coup) a role in a the upcoming Miramax production *The Great Raid*, the Filipino superstar's Hollywood debut. Whether or not he succeeds in Hollywood, Montano's hard-luck past and rags-to-riches career path remind audiences in the Philippines that the star is one of the masses, though an extraordinarily ambitious specimen.

For other male stars in Asia's popular film industries, like Bollywood's Shah Rukh Khan, the most formidable hero in the generation after Amitabh Bachchan, the star's scrappy entrepreneurship (starting with his non-*filmi* origins) underscores the ways he represents a break with the conventional industrial model—in this case, a Bollywood entrenched in nepotism and family dynasties. Before the dot.com bust, Khan was also known as Bollywood's most "wired star," with a high-profile commercial site and an exceedingly technofriendly persona (on-screen, in life, and in cyberspace). Such an embrace of technology functions on one level as a retort to the crises of masculinity that contemporary masala movies demand their stars enact. Besides appearing in Bollywood's most expensive productions to date, including the family-oriented (but male-centered) melodramas *Kabhi Kushi Kabhie Gham* (2001) and *Devdas* (2002), Khan also has pushed the phenomenon of Bollywood public appearances and stars-on-tour performances to the limit. He is by his own admission Bollywood's most available-for-hire superstar (even cheekily referring to himself as the star most likely to dance at your wedding).[27] I have argued elsewhere that such representational politics of the male Bollywood star, everywhere at once, "is central to a re-imaging of India for global consumption."[28] The nationalistic didacticism of contemporary Bollywood films is explicitly connected to a bid to encourage nonresident

Indian (NRI) diasporic audiences to become more Indian, amid globalization's powers of diffusion, dispersion, assimilation, and potential homogenization. As Bollywood narratives increasingly take their cosmopolitan
characters away from India and create crises of identity and family which call
them back from abroad, more Bollywood films are set both in Indian cities
such as Mumbai and Delhi, and in international cities such as London and
Sydney—cinematically enlivened by the presence of Indian culture. The
"ethnoscape" (to use Arjun Appadurai's concept) marks these filmic
places/spaces, making them part of the Indian experience.[29] The Bollywood
"diaspora film" is therefore a popular subgenre of Hindi masala movies tai-
lored to NRIs who constitute a most lucrative audience, as well as globally-
minded spectators at home. Bollywood cinematically transforms every city it
represents, through the potent agency of the male star, into an Indian city;
these other iconic cities (these nations, in synecdochic terms) are complicit
in the process of "becoming" Indian. The Bollywood male star symbolically
travels the world in a manner reminiscent of Baudelaire's flaneur who wan-
ders nighttime Paris, the city of lights (and women).

Like Shah Rukh Khan, Hong Kong's Andy Lau is known as the hardest-
working man in the business. Born poor, Lau trained as an actor with Hong
Kong's TVB television network (an apprenticeship that also crafted the star
image of Chow Yun-Fat) and has now appeared in more than one hundred
films, in addition to being a massively successful musical recording and performing artist. In the summer of 2000, three vulnerable industry years after
the handover that returned the British crown colony to mainland China, in
the midst of the multiplex deluge of Hollywood fare with émigré Hong Kong
talent (John Woo's *Mission Impossible: II*, Jackie Chan in *Shanghai Noon*) and
inescapable posters, star press conferences, and other media fanfare predict-
ing the impending *Crouching Tiger, Hidden Dragon* outbreak, a decidedly local
breakout hit called *Needing You*, featuring superstar Andy Lau, managed to
draw the territory's biggest audience. Furthermore, ads for *Needing You* in the
metro stations and movie posters in the theaters advertised the recently
launched *andylau.com* Web site as yet another function of the author, prom-
ising almost unlimited access to the star. Hong Kong–based CCT Telecom
established a subsidiary, CCT Multimedia, which made its debut with the
Web site.[30] (Ironically, Andy Lau reportedly had to buy his domain name from
a fan.) Double-decker buses were also plastered with a striking series of eight
head shots that spanned the star's life and career via his most distinctive

roles and looks, punctuated by an image of Andy pointing to his own name dot.com.

In *Needing You*, Andy Lau's character, conveniently called Andy, a cad with unfinished business with his ex, steals the girl (played by fellow Cantopop star Sammi Cheng) away from a boyish Chinese American Internet entrepreneur, Roger, who started a company called Young Cool (a loose phonetic play with Yahoo, one of the film's corporate sponsors, along with Kentucky Fried Chicken). The filmic character Andy's masculinity is challenged by the younger, richer, American would-be suitor with all the right technotools, fame, and media exposure (including his picture on the cover of *Newsweek*). One of Roger's most alluring gadgets is a state-of-the-art motorcycle, which Sammi Cheng's character, Kinki, likens to the motorcycle from *A Moment of Romance* (an earlier Andy Lau film). This extreme self-reflexivity, a spillover of star aura perhaps, enables filmic Andy to express the self-deprecating awareness that wins over Kinki at the end of the film. Meanwhile, in real life, the star Andy, image-control skirmishes notwithstanding, continues to shine as brightly as ever. Movies become yet another media arena for stars to demonstrate their resilience and durability.

This conclusion echoes filmmaker Shekhar Kapur's prediction of a widespread seismic shift in the Western conceptualization of popular cinema and media culture toward an inevitable recognition of Asia's formidable role as global producer/consumer. In the meantime, Asian superstars like Andy Lau, Shah Rukh Khan, and others continue to prove that all media have star-fueling potential, and that true superstars are, by all appearances, inexhaustible.

NOTES

1 See Shekhar Kapur's commentary in *The Guardian*, August 23, 2002, http://www.shekharkapur.com/guardian.htm.

2 Wimal Dissanayake argues this cautionary point regarding "non-Western" cinema. See his interventionist essay "Issues in World Cinema," in *The Oxford Guide to Film Studies*, ed. John Hill and Pamela Church Gibson (Oxford: Oxford UP, 1998), 527–534. This piece is adapted from the introduction of Dissanayake's important edited anthology, *Colonialism and Nationalism in Asian Cinema* (Bloomington: Indiana UP, 1994).

3 Christine Geraghty, "Re-examining Stardom: Questions of Texts, Bodies, and Performance," in *Reinventing Film Studies*, ed. Christine Gledhill and Linda Williams (New York: Oxford UP, 2000), 188.

4 Here I am in dialogue with the idea of translation in Mark Gallagher's excellent essay "Masculinity in Translation: Jackie Chan's Transcultural Star Text," *Velvet Light Trap* 39 (spring 1997): 23–41. However, I feel the "destablized" masculinity

Chan registers in Hollywood undermines the subversive possibilities of his anarchic approach to performance and genre interpretation through fixed stereotypes.

5 Darrell Davis discusses the complexities of Kitano's Japanese image in "Reigniting Japanese Tradition with *Hana-Bi*," *Cinema Journal* 40, 4 (summer 2001): 55–80. Kitano's production company's official Web site also chronicles the many activities of the superstar/renaissance man: www.office-kitano.co.jp.

6 See Michel Foucault's poststructural take on authorship in "What Is an Author?" in *Language, Counter-memory, Practice: Selected Essays and Interviews*, ed. Donald F. Bouchard, trans. Donald F. Bouchard and Sherry Simon (Ithaca, N.Y.: Cornell UP, 1977), 113–138.

7 See Richard Dyer, *Stars* (London: British Film Institute, 1979), 109. This quote is also cited in Brian Gallagher, "Greta Garbo Is Sad: Some Historical Reflections on the Paradoxes of Stardom in the American Film Industry, 1910–1960," *Images: A Journal of Film and Popular Culture* 3 (March 1997), www.imagesjournal.com/issue03/infocus/stars9.htm.

8 See the wrap-up section dealing with contemporary movie stars in Gallagher, "Greta Garbo."

9 Ibid.

10 I examine other related aspects of Bollywood stardom in "Superhit Hunk Heroes for Sale: Globalization and Bollywood's Gender Politics," *Asian Journal of Communication* 11, 2 (2001): 121–143.

11 This point is made by Frederic Dannen and Barry Long, *Hong Kong Babylon: An Insider's Guide to the Hollywood of the East* (New York: Hyperion Books/Miramax, 1997), 104–105.

12 I first saw an anthology of these commercials on a VCD acquired at a video store in Boston's Chinatown by a student in my Asian Pop Cinema course.

13 See Han Suk-kyu's Makdong Scenario Korean Web site, www.hansukgyu.net. Please note the variant spelling of the star's name in the URL. An excellent English-language Web site on Korean cinema is maintained by Seoul-based Darcy Paquet, www.koreanfilm.org. Additionally, a number of weekly and monthly Korean-language film magazines have on-line editions, including *Cine 21*, *Film 2.0*, *Screen Magazine*, and *Kino*.

14 Speaking of technology: In one memorable and poignant scene in the film, Han's character, the dying son, teaches his elderly father how to use a VCR.

15 However, when Han Suk-kyu's comeback film, the espionage thriller *Double Agent*, was released in Korea in January 2003, the box-office figures were disappointing, suggesting that the star was not really able to effectively reconnect with movie audiences after his big-screen separation. In a case study of Han Suk-kyu's stardom I am working on with Korean scholar Hunju Lee, we are examining this "contact" breakdown in terms of fan/audience expectations (including reactions to the star's presence in TV ads while he was absent from the movies), film-industry trends, marketing/publicity, and the actor's trademark performance style.

16 See Henry Jenkins's classic work in this area, *Textual Poachers: Television Fans and Participatory Culture* (New York: Routledge, 1992), which is invoked here.

17 For legal information on personality rights in Hong Kong, see "Sport Stars' Rights in Asia," www.lawgazette.com.sg/Dec02-focus.htm.

18 While she doesn't really deal with the relationships between the Bollywood film magazine and new media, Rachel Dwyer's "Shooting Stars: The Indian Film Magazine, *Stardust*," is a valuable study. Versions of this essay appear as chapters in Dwyer's *All You Want Is Money, All You Need Is Love: Sex and Romance in Modern India* (London: Cassell, 2000), 168–201, and in Dwyer and Christopher Pinney, eds., *Pleasure and the Nation: The History, Politics, and Consumption of Public Culture in India* (Oxford: Oxford UP, 2001), 247–285.

19 In using the term "political economy," I am referring to the political economy of communication, in relation to media and markets. I discovered that journalist Dan Ackman specifically uses the phrase "political economy of movie stars" and makes this assertion about Hollywood stardom's "serendipity" and self-fulfillment in "The Myth of Stars," *Forbes*, June 6, 2002, www.forbes.com/2002/06/12/0612stars.html.

20 See Andreas Huyssen, "Mass Culture as Woman: Modernism's Other," in his book *After the Great Divide: Modernism, Mass Culture, Postmodernism* (Bloomington: Indiana UP, 1986), 44–62. I find the work of Caren Kaplan and Interpal Grewal especially eloquent in articulating these issues, especially their groundbreaking essay "Transnational Feminist Cultural Studies: Beyond the Marxism/Poststructuralism/Feminism Divides," originally published in *positions: east asia cultures critique* 2, 2 (fall 1994): 430–445, and reprinted in Kaplan, Norma Alarcon, and Minoo Moallern, *Between Woman and Nation: Nationalisms, Transnational Feminisms, and the State* (Durham, N.C.: Duke UP, 1999), 349–363.

21 See Gina Marchetti, *Romance and the "Yellow Peril": Race, Sex, and Discursive Strategies in Hollywood Fictions* (Berkeley: U of California P, 1993); Peter Feng, ed. *Screening Asian Americans* (New Brunswick, N.J.: Rutgers UP, 2002); David Eng, *Racial Castration: Managing Masculinity in Asian America* (Durham, N.C.: Duke UP, 2001); and Sheng-Mei Ma, *The Deathly Embrace: Orientalism and Asian American Identity* (Minneapolis: U of Minnesota P, 2000).

22 See Robert Stam, *Film Theory: An Introduction* (Malden, Mass.: Blackwell, 2000), 19.

23 I analyze the impact of the invention of "blockbusters" in the Philippines, South Korea, and Thailand in "Ways to Sink the *Titanic*," *Tamkang Review* 33, 2 (Winter 2002): 1–29, a special issue on Asian Cinema.

24 Huyssen, "Mass Culture as Woman," 48.

25 See Dissanayake, introduction to *Colonialism and Nationalism in Asian Cinema*, xiii. The idea of the "imagined community" is taken from Benedict Anderson's *Imagined Communities: Reflections on the Origins and Spread of Nationalism* (London: Verso, 1983), although Dissanayake suggests at least one striking departure from Anderson's formulation: Instead of positing print media as central to generating national consciousness, Dissanayake points out *cinema's* comparable role. I'm borrowing "body genres" from feminist film scholar Linda Williams, who uses the term for such genres as pornography, horror, and melodrama; see her essay "Film Bodies: Gender, Genre, and Excess," originally published in *Film Quarterly* 44, 4 (1991): 2–13, which can also be found in Sue Thornham, ed., *Feminist Film Theory: A Reader* (New York: New York UP, 1999), 267–281.

26 See, for example, Dennis Ladaw, "Can Filipino Movie Actors Really Act?" *Sunday Times of Manila*, July 21, 2002, www.mailiatimes.net/national/2002/jul/21/weekend/20020721weki.html.

27 See Jyothi Venkatesh's interview with star Shah Rukh Khan, "I Love Dancing at Weddings," www.vluvshahrukh.com/info/2001/01.htm.

28 Ciecko, "Superhit Hunk Heroes for Sale," 121.

29 See Arjun Appadurai, *Modernity at Large: Cultural Dimensions of Globalization* (Minneapolis: U of Minnesota P, 1996).

30 See CCT Telcom's announcement of the Andy Lau site at www.cct.com.hk/hongkong/english/contents/news/20000117.htm. CT Telecom chair Clement Mak describes Andy Lau's assets at www.cct.comwww.cct.com.hk/hongkong/english/contents/news/20000723.htm. Find superstar Andy Lau at www.andylau.com.

THE AFRICAN DIASPORA SPEAKS IN DIGITAL TONGUES

ANNA EVERETT

African diasporic consciousness originated below the decks of European ships during the infamous middle passage of the transatlantic slave trade. Severed from the familiar terrain of their homelands and dispatched to the overcrowded bowels of slave vessels, the abducted Africans forged out of necessity a virtual community of intercultural kinship structures and new languages with which to express them. During the first half of the twentieth century, African scholar-activists W.E B. Du Bois and C.L.R. James argued that these historical events made Africans in the New World among the first people to experience modernity. In 1969 James asserted:

> The vast change in human society came from the slave trade and slavery. All the historians tell you that. . . . It was slavery that built up the bourgeois society and enabled it to make what Lévi Strauss thinks is the only fundamental change in ten thousand years of human history. The blacks not only provided the wealth in the struggle, which began between the old [aristocratic] society and the new bourgeois society; the black people were foremost in the struggle itself.[1]

Other contemporary theorists, such as Paul Gilroy, echo James and Du Bois's views and further explain that the transatlantic diasporic consciousness of African Americans, African Caribbeans, black Britons, and others is directly attributable to the post-Enlightenment demands of a modernity which would power the impending industrial revolution. Despite the well-documented dehumanizing imperatives of the colonial encounter, the ethnically and nationally diverse Africans in the New World developed self-sustaining virtual communities through paralinguistic and transnational communicative systems and networks of song, dance, and talking drums that enabled this heterogeneous mass of people to overcome their profound dislocation, fragmentation, alienation, relocation, and ultimate commodification in the Western slavocracies of the modern world.

This brief history is necessary for understanding the movements that herald what is often termed the "postcolonial era." Many, including myself, are not convinced that colonization is over but believe rather that it has morphed into new global oligopolies thriving in the post-cold-war era. Hence, without an overview and context for understanding, it is almost impossible to grasp and fully account for the historical shifts and mutations in the ideology of African diasporic consciousness, which spans nineteenth-century African colonization societies to twentieth-century black nationalist or Afrocentric movements of the 1960s to the present day.

The current research focuses on the persistence of African diasporic consciousness in cyberspace and the digital age. Since 1995, there has been a proliferation of electronic bulletin boards, chat rooms, home pages, listservs, and electronic directories on the Internet and the World Wide Web that are specifically targeted at African and African diasporic net users. In fact, my on-line surveys of the African diasporic presence on-line suggest that 1995 is a watershed moment in the transformation of the Internet away from a predominately elite, white masculinist domain. Although a number of black early adopters infiltrated this would-be gated cybercommunity prior to this benchmark, African diasporic connectivity on-line seems to have achieved a critical mass in 1995, when the Yahoo search engine initiated a separate category for Afrocentric content on the World Wide Web. In his 1995 study of the Internet for the *Economist* magazine, Christopher Anderson gives an indication of the magnitude of its unprecedented growth. His estimation of the World Wide Web's massive expansion is particularly revealing. Anderson noted that the Internet had doubled in size since 1988. "At the same time," he observed, "the Web grew almost 20-fold; in just 18 months users created more than 3 million multimedia pages of information, entertainment and advertising." Although he concedes that exact numbers were difficult to ascertain, he calculates that at least twenty million "users" were on-line as early as October 1994. If we accept his evocation of Moore's Law, a phenomenon named after Gordon Moore, founder of the Intel Corporation, "which says that computing power and capacity double every 18 months," then the unwieldy nature of any attempt to survey the contents of the Internet after 1995 is apparent.[2]

The difficulty of delimiting the cybertext for analytical purposes in many ways replicates problems encountered by early analysts in their formulation of a critical hermeneutics of television. Like television, the dynamic and fluid nature of the Internet makes it "too big and too baggy to be easily or quickly explained. No single approach is sufficient to deal with it adequately."[3] With this in mind, I have opted to frame my own findings on the African diasporic niche within the Internet in terms of a snapshot or moment-in-time approach so that some useful perspective on this difficult, moving target of analysis might emerge. Also, in the years since I began this brief history of a new media technology in a state of becoming, I have discovered some important and quite intriguing methodological and theoretical problems. My previous research on early twentieth-century black print publications did not prepare me for the extreme ephemerality of cybertexts. What this means is that conducting Internet content analysis presents its own set of problems involving access to and availability of the material under scrutiny. The fleeting nature or short shelf life of most individual, grassroots and private, nonprofit Web sites necessitates the immediate downloading of sites that might be considered worthy of study because, as I have learned the hard way, to attempt a second page or site view may not be possible. Too many of these sites disappear without a trace or are upgraded to the point of unrecognizability. These are the challenges of conducting a "history of the present."

In his 1993 book *The Virtual Community: Homesteading on the Electronic Frontier*, Howard Rheingold observed that "computer-mediated communications" technologies owe their phenomenal growth and development to networking capabilities that enable people "to build social relationships across barriers of space and time." These spatial and temporal ruptures and the promise of an egalitarian technosphere are the focus of this analysis. It is therefore useful to emphasize an important lesson embedded in Rheingold's ethnographic account of the "computer-mediated social groups" he has dubbed "virtual communities." Of the myriad ways that grassroots groups adapted the inchoate Internet technology "designed for one purpose to suit their own, very different communication needs," none is more symptomatic of technology's overall elasticity and unpredictability than the rapid and unanticipated growth of the "Internet Relay Chat (IRC)" phenomenon among noncomputer experts.[4] Rheingold sees the lure of the IRC as inextricably bound up with its recombinant nature as an interactive medium that conjoins "the features of conversation and writing."[5] This technological hybridization of speech or orality (conversation) and literacy (writing), which privileges neither, not only furthers the Derridian project of negating epistemological exaltations of logocentrism (privileging speech) over techne (writing), but also suggests a parallel to or affinity with various traditions of black technocultural syncretisms.[6] For example, much has been written about black appropriations and mastery of Western musical technologies and instruments to craft and express such uniquely black musical idioms as jazz and the blues.[7] As Bruce R. Powers puts it in *The Global Village*, "Unlikely combinations produce discovery."[8] Thus the seamless combination of conversational strategies and writing on the proliferating IRC channels has produced for black "early adopters" a discovery of the latest inchoate mass medium to be appropriated for unfettered social and cultural expressions. This is possible, of course, because the complete domination of the Internet by the interests of corporate capital remains somewhat tentative, at least for now. Meanwhile, it appears that computer-mediated communication (CMC) is refashioning the concept and utility of a viable black public sphere in the new millennium.

Establishing Cybergateways to the African Diaspora: Geopolitics in the Digital Age

The hyperbolic rhetoric that designates the Internet and the World Wide Web as the "super information highway" and as the gateway or on-ramp to the information age did not go unnoticed by the African diasporic community. While some remained skeptical of the discursive onslaught of utopic claims for the revolutionary digital democracy, many were affected by the gold-rush mentality that seems to have triggered a bout of global cyberfever. It is important to understand that the current scramble for domination and domestication of the Internet and the World Wide Web is not unlike that unleashed on the African continent by the West in the nineteenth century.

This "scramble for Africa" analogy as a narrative frame for contextualizing the stakes involved in the Internet revolution was dually inspired. One inspiration was a spate of newspaper articles that covered the apparently surprising alacrity of African Americans' entry onto the fast lanes of the global infobahn. Another suggested itself as news surfaced of the global media corporations' scramble to colonize the Internet through their highly publicized strategies of merger mania and media convergence hype. And while print reports that detail an unanticipated surge in black on-line connectivity only hint at what any netizen (virtual citizen of the Internet) or net-novice today who types in the key words "black" and "African" as any portion of a keyword search quickly discovers, these search commands yield from hundreds of thousands to more than a million "results," "hits," or "category matches" (in the argot of Internet search engines Lycos, Hotbot, AltaVista, Google, Yahoo, and many others).[9] My study reveals that since 1991, black people throughout the African diaspora have mounted their own scramble for a secure share of the Internet spoils in the intensifying global grab for Internet dominance.

As one of history's most profound and far-reaching cycles of corporate expansion and domination since the industrial age's robber barons and corporate trusts, today's mega-media mergers threaten to obliterate any remaining optimism about preserving the last vestiges of a viable and unsponsored public sphere.[10] Indeed, the political engine of deregulation responsible for powering the economic force of the ascendant global media behemoths has the capacity and intent now to rock our worlds. No sooner had the centripetal forces of technological innovation produced newer, democratizing models of mass-media diversity such as cable, satellite, Internet, wireless, and other wide-ranging digital communications systems, than the older media concerns set in motion a centrifugal counter-model in the global telecommunications industries. This centrifugal counter-model consists of the latest round of FCC-sanctioned information technologies' megamedia mergers and reconsolidation. Because these newer media were poised to undermine what Ben Bagdikian calls "the media monopoly," many believed the decentralized nature and transnational reach of these new media industries signaled a new age of participatory democracy available to any and all who could get onto the information highway. It seemed that finally new multimedia forms might serve and promote the diverse communicative needs of a changing, multicultural world. The arrival and rapid diffusion of the Internet and the World Wide Web were central to this vision of inevitable global transformation, as the Internet's role in pro-democracy movements in several developing nations attest. One contemporary critic who underscores the connection between the Internet and geopolitical change is Ingrid Volkmer. In Volkmer's estimation:

[T]he Internet can be regarded as an icon of a globalized media world that has shifted global communication to a new level. Whereas television was a harbinger of this new era of global communication by reaching a worldwide audience with worldwide distribution and innovative global programming (such as that of CNN and MTV), the Internet reveals the full vision of a global community; . . . the implications are obvious: national borders are increasingly disappearing within cyberspace.[11]

Not only do national borders increasingly disappear in cyberspace; they are replaced by new kinship structures now predicated on the fluidity of cybernetic virtual communities and homelands.

In his influential work *Imagined Communities: Reflections on the Origin and Spread of Nationalism*, Benedict Anderson explains that "nationality, or . . . [the] world's multiple significations, nation-ness, as well as nationalism, are cultural artifacts of a particular kind." It is essential to Anderson that we understand how nation-ness is often historically determined and its meanings subject to change over time. And yet for Anderson it is crucial to recognize the profound emotional legitimacy of nationalisms despite the challenge of subnationalisms within many tenuous nationalist borders, to which the recent dissolution of the Soviet Union, the fall of the Berlin Wall, and the bloody coups responsible for reconfiguring many third-world nations clearly attest. "Nation, nationality, nationalism," as Anderson points out, "all have proved notoriously difficult to define, let alone analyse."[12] Clearly, then, the historical changes and technological innovations responsible for the Internet threaten to exacerbate the increasing fragility of traditional nationalisms while simultaneously strengthening the affective dimensions of a newer virtual or cyber nationalism now unbound by traditional ideological, political, economic, geographical, and even temporal boundaries and limitations.

Imagined African Communities in Cyberspace
or Digitizing Double Consciousness

In the late 1980s, Marshall McLuhan and Bruce R. Powers studied "the structural impact of technologies on society." In their book *The Global Village: Transformations in World Life and Media in the 21st Century*, the authors remarked that "electronic technologies have begun to shake the distinction between inner and outer space, by blurring the difference between being here or there." Additionally, they observed, "man's nature was being rapidly translated into information systems which would produce enormous global sensitivity and no secrets."[13] Although it was the phenomenal communications revolution wrought by video-related technologies to which McLuhan and Powers addressed themselves, their observations have obvious and profound implications for digital technologies such as the Internet. Without a doubt, McLuhan's conceptualization of the global village has been a useful heuristic for grasping the incredible lure of the Internet's global reach. However, his later ideas about the technological breakdown of inner and outer spaces, and information technologies' production of "enormous global sensitivities and no secrets," are equally, if not more, generative. For these ideas provide important frameworks for thinking about how digital media erect new possibilities for understanding African digital diasporas capable of enacting a new manifestation of W.E.B Du Bois's powerful trope of black "double consciousness."

As early as 1991 the African diaspora was willfully and optimistically dispersed into the transnational ether of the Internet by many tech-savvy African nationals and expatriates living and working abroad. For these black geeks the lure of cyberspace represents "the possibility of vast, unexplored territory," to use Anne Balsamo's words. This territory, moreover, is capable of sustaining new modes of postcolonial African unity, of sorts, often untenable on the continent given the political and military economies of "real" space.[14] Among African early adopters of the Internet and the World Wide Web were those visionary tech evangelists or cyber witchdoctors, if you will, who conjured such new Africanities on-line as Naijanet, the Association of Nigerians Abroad, the Buganda Home Page, the African National Congress Home Page, and others. By 1997, more black diasporic Web sites began appearing, including ones for the Republic of Ghana, the Afro-Caribbean Chamber of Commerce, Camden (UK) Black Parent's and Teacher's Association, Canadian Artists' Network: Black Artists In Action, Egypt's Information Highway Project, and Africa Online, among others too numerous to consider here. Although the named sites are exemplary, I want to stress again the importance of acknowledging the existence of many more Web sites that I came across in my studies, many of which are long defunct. This fact of the vanishing cybertext is a significant research problem, and apparently it is particularly acute for experimental, avant-garde, and outré—the most marginal and unusual—nonmainstream on-line ventures. So, one of the burdens of writing this history, to borrow a phrase from Hayden White, is producing and preserving a critical archeology of these first Afrocentric Web sites. This is not lessened by the reduction of this rich, early constellation to a smaller orbit of extant stars (at least at this writing) and those now defunct that I have preserved serendipitously through my habitual downloading since the 1994 heyday of Internet homesteading. While it is impossible to elaborate on most of these sites' specific identities, impact, and developments, it nonetheless is important to acknowledge the historical fact of their on-line existence.

New Africanities and the Idea of a Reverse African Brain Drain— or a Digital African Brain Reattachment

One of the first and most successful African diasporic communities to go digital included the intelligentsia from Nigeria in various forms of exile in the West who comprised the Niajanet listserv. The first steps "toward developing a Nigerian on-line network took place in 1991" when a Nigerian at Dartmouth College began forwarding to select friends e-mail news about the home country.[15] From this inauspicious beginning sprang Naijanet, one of the net's most robust and enduring Afrocentric virtual communities. In a 1999 article for the on-line journal *West Africa Review*, Misty L. Bastian reports that around 1992 the Naijanet list spun off several related on-line networks, and that at the height of its influence and popularity in 1995, "Naijanetters" numbered approximately 750. In fact, one difficulty in locating more specifically African virtual communities to research early on was precisely the penchant for insularity within such usegroups, which Bastian conveys well as a result of her own unique status as an invited observer of the group: "Basically, an interested party needed to know a Naijanetter in order to learn the address to subscribe. The subsidiary nets were (and remain) even more difficult to access. People who have heard of the subsidiary nets would, during the later 1990s, post to Naijanet and request their subscription addresses from Naijanetters 'in the know.'"

Relying on data from Bastain's ethnography allows for a rethinking of issues of postcoloniality. One of the more recognizably transformative aspects of postcoloniality being wrought by the digital age is a new discursive Africanity emerging in chat rooms and listservs of several Nigeria-centered subnets engendered by Naiganet. According to Bastian, the six Naiganet subnets are:

Oduduwa (the Yoruba net), ANA-net (a net for the Association of Nigerians Abroad, an activist group), Naijawoman-net, soc.culture.nigeria
on Usenet, Igbonet, and Rivnet (a net for indigenes of southeastern
Nigeria's Rivers State). A number of people who were once important
"netizens" of Naijanet have also begun to construct Africa or Nigeria
pages on the World Wide Web; these pages act as clearinghouses of
information about African and Nigerian issues on the internet at
large.

This fracturing of Naijanet's success into these "fission nets," in Bastian
terms, suggests the possibilities for a virtual tolerance and acceptance of ideological and political dissent and democratic practices that remain elusive in
Nigeria's militarized postcolonial (although I prefer the term "recolonized")
reality.[16] Bastian's participant informers at Naijanet revealed that the not-
too-surprising issues that provoked the splintering of Naijanet generally concerned the politics of indigenous language pluralism, expatriate political
activism, gender oppression, netiquette, ethnic cleansing, and tribalism. To
be sure, this is familiar terrain for postcolonial conflicts, and expectations of
passionate expressions of conflict by now typify the communicative exchange
in usegroups and listservs, particularly in this age of "globalization and its
discontents."[17] However, the fact that Naijanet and its fission-nets formed
and sustained a voluntary Web ring of mutual support and nationalist solidarity is remarkable indeed.

This postindependence conceptualization of a virtual Nigerian consan-
guinity is remarkable because, as scholar Emeka J. Okoli explains, "the British
arrogantly realigned Nigerian political structures to serve their own interest
at devastating consequences to relations between Nigerian ethnic populations, which include between 178 and 300 languages and more than 250 cultures, each having its own customs and traditions." And notwithstanding the
ineffectuality of Nigeria's so-called "independence" in 1960 in bridging the
bitter divisions between such major ethnic groups as Housas, Igbos, and
Yorubas, neither has it alleviated their mutual suspicions.[18] However, as
writer Sandy Stone points out, usenets and e-mail networks are new spaces
that instantiate "the collapse of the boundaries between the social and technological, biology and machine, natural and artificial."[19] Thus, Naijanetters
used the new spaces of the Internet to refuse crucial elements of Nigeria's
intractably debilitating colonialist legacy, and through CMC reimage a new
Africanity in cyberspace.

Obviously, it would be naive to expect a miraculous vaulting over decades of deep-seated ethnic and tribal hostilities, even given the phenomenological and experiential accelerator that is Internet time. Yet, outside the state panopticon, diverse expatriate Nigerians in virtual communication found common ground for airing divergent and convergent views. In cyberspace, they were not governed by the volatile "press/government relationship that makes it a no-win battle between the pen and the sword" that defines Nigeria's state-controlled press and media institutions.[20] Still, as Bastian's recent ethnography conveys, Naijanetters were not immune to intense ethnic and gender rivalries of the sort that plague Nigerians on the continent. By contrast, however, these new on-line social spaces and democratic media forums facilitated face-to-face meetings, "but under new definitions of both 'meet' and 'face,'" and, for Naijanetters, under less-threatening conditions more conducive to nonlethal expressions of opposing views, philosophies, and perspectives.[21] This is not to imply that Naijanet's tolerant, digital public sphere was a flame-free zone. Far from it, as the network's eventual splintering amply demonstrates. In that regard, Bastian has noted:

> Even though some netizens suggested censuring the people who "flamed" in the past, most participants during this period insisted that "Naija" was a community where all opinions were valued and where discourse consequently had to be freeflowing. Some of the most radically egalitarian on Naijanet actually decried the formation of alternative nets, saying that those who split off from Naijanet wished to fractionalize the true spirit of the net—and therefore the true spirit of "Naija," the virtual nationalist space they were struggling to create.[22]

Because the digitized postcolonial condition forestalls the necessity of putting real flesh-and-blood bodies dangerously on the line in service to the nation-state—taking primacy over ethnic group allegiance—Naijanetters used their virtual bodies regularly to challenge and contest one another, as well as to amplify problems in the homeland. One challenge that simultaneously embodied and threatened the "true spirit of Naija" was the insistent articulation of African women's long-standing discontent vis-à-vis gender oppression. Just as "Naija's" free-speech ethos helped foster painfully honest dialogues and vigorous debates about the politics of language chauvinism and ethnic "tribalism," so too were grievances and recriminations about the persistence of women's "double colonization" given voice—at least for a time.[23]

This concept of "double colonization" is discussed in postcolonial feminism as a particularly acute system of gender oppression whereby "women in
formerly colonized societies were doubly colonized by both imperial and
patriarchal ideologies."[24] In decolonizing struggles for African cultural
restoration, the matter of women's double colonization too often was subli-
mated under a "first things first" offensive promulgated by men who saw
such oppression as ancillary to the larger fight against Western racism and
imperialism.[25] Naijanet's cell divisions along gender lines indicates how
these postcolonial issues get refracted significantly in the African digital diaspora. Name-based gender marking is not always evident in Nigerian languages, and Bastian reports that women Naijanetters "were tired of being
addressed as 'Mr.' or 'Brother' in every post."[26] Other gender-specific fric-
tions ensued, and when some men uttered sexist remarks and commentary
romanticizing abusive traditional practices against women such as female
circumcision, Naijawomen-net was formed. It is telling that despite the fact
of most women's continued participation in both nets after the split, with
some even forwarding information to Naijanet, the majority of men ignored
Naijawomen-net. It is important to underscore, however, that African men in
the digital diaspora were confronted with, and some took notice of, the
women's insistent liberation agenda within many black nationalist decolonizing strategies.

Among the more fractious and irresistible matters to afflict Naijanet were
members' intense reactions to homeland news of recurring military coups,
human rights abuses, and the frustrations of their mediation through Nigeria's powerful state-controlled mass media. One of Naijanet's more politically
minded fission-nets willing to engage these hot-button issues directly and
vociferously was the Association of Nigerians Abroad (ANA-net).[27] Because of
its political outspokeness, ANA's CMC approach presents fertile ground for
recontextualizing aspects of the postcolonial condition in the digital era.

Resisting the lure of a presumed white mask of émigré privilege (or hon-
orary white-skin privilege) that often hides Africans' actual black skin in
global politics, ANA members were committed "to the concept of Nigerian
nationalism, even during the dark days of the Abacha military regime."
Moreover, ANA members were determined to broadcast—or cybercast—
their vehement political dissent against "power hungry despots bent on taking [Nigeria] back into the Stone Age" to progressive-minded netizens
willing to enlist the medium in an array of postimperialist moves. In a

scathing indictment in the form of a press release of Nigerian military rule in 1995, ANA articulated its outrage over the "Stalinist-style terror" being visited upon "the Nigerian people." Using the occasion of Nigerian poet-writer Ken Saro-Wiwa's and other political prisoners' unconscionable murders to demonstrate that indeed the subaltern could and would speak, ANA's press release made these charges and appeals. The example bears quoting at length.

> A year ago the Association of Nigerians Abroad (ANA) predicted that the Nigerian military cabal will unleash the most brutal and lawless acts of irresponsibility on Nigeria. Since then, the evil and satanic regime, has gradually and systematically chosen to re-enact Stalinist-style terror on the Nigerian people. . . . The latest act in these series of atrocities is the deliberate judicial murder of Mr. Ken Saro-Wiwa and 8 other Ogoni political activists. At the same time, the military regime holds more than 80 political detainees in prisons scattered all over the country. . . . We therefore urge the international community to enact urgent measures to bring an end to the tyrannical regime in Nigeria. If this is not done as a matter of urgency, the consequences for Nigeria and the entire world community will be enormous.

To underscore the urgent need for rethinking Nigeria's place in the world community of nations, outside its often shadow status as a major oil supplier to the West (second only to OPEC), ANA reminds the international community of its recent moral victory against another despotic African regime—apartheid South Africa. Recalling the immense pressure brought to bear by an outraged global citizenry on South Africa's scandalous human rights abuses, ANA sought to reawaken that activism against Nigeria's military government, with the added irony that "Nigeria was an active proponent for economic sanctions and total isolation of [South Africa's] racist regime." Anticipating some recalcitrance on the part of some Western leaders, ANA's subalterns spoke truth to power on the matter and in this way:

> With all due respect to the British Prime Minister, Mr. Major on the hardship that economic sanctions may cause, our generation accepts and prefers the hardships of economic sanctions to the wanton killing of our citizens by a brutal regime. Besides, the oil-wealth has only gone to benefit the ruling cabal not the average Nigerian. Indeed, sanctions represent the best available tool that could lead to a speedy emancipation of Nigerians from military colonization and oppression.

While it might be tempting to view ANA's confrontational speech through jaundiced eyes, owing to its members' presumed free speech privileges and protections in the United States, we must not overlook the significant political risks always attendant upon exiles. For despite their liminal positioning astride Africa and America, ANA members were resolute in their efforts to "move the world into the 21st century" via the Internet and work toward Nigeria's political freedom.

In one of the foundational texts of postcolonial discourse, "The Occasion for Speaking," from his book *The Pleasures of Exile*, West Indian novelist and critic George Lamming observed in 1960 that the act of writing is linked to the expectation, however modest, of being read. He also said: "The pleasure and paradox of my own exile is that I belong wherever I am. My role, it seems, has rather to do with time and change than with the geography of circumstances; and yet there is always an acre of ground in the New World which keeps growing echoes in my head. I can only hope that these echoes do not die before my work comes to an end." Lamming's utterances prefigure new modes and codes of struggle and transformation and when he asks "what [has] the West Indian novelist has brought to the West Indies," he poses the same question to which ANA members' on-line work responds.[28]

Apparently, among the pleasures and paradoxes of exile for ANA members is that the Internet makes it possible to belong to and be in both Africa and the United States at once. This permits an ideological boundary crossing with material force in digital space wherein ex-patriots can oppose neoimperialist interests that primarily benefit their host nation. Seizing upon the Wild West ethos embodied in a *Wired Magazine* press release titled "Cyberspace Cannot Be Censored," ANA challenged the neoimperialist practices of powerful Western oil corporations in their host countries. ANA used its Web site to hold the Anglo-American Shell Oil Company accountable for human rights violations, repressions, political abuses, and environmental devastation in Nigeria. In its November 13, 1995, press release, ANA specified ten demands of the international community on behalf of the "People of Nigeria," including "freezing of all new loans, extension or rescheduling of old loans; we particularly applaud the decision of the IFC to freeze a $180 million loan and equity package that would have been used by the Nigerian regime, Shell, Elf, and Agip Oil Companies to build a gas plant and oil pipelines in the ravaged Niger Delta; A world-wide boycott of all Shell Products. We hold Shell equally responsible for the death of all nine activists and for the decimation of the oil producing areas of the Niger Delta."[29]

If Lamming's mid-twentieth-century contemplations of the peculiar pleasures of exile revolved around the cultural dissonance West Indian writers experienced negotiating the "idea of England" and living its exile reality, ANA members more than thirty years later clearly invite new rules of engagement with their U.S. and other "Others." Unlike Lamming's writer in exile who "has not only to prove his worth to the other, he has to win the approval of Headquarters, meaning . . . England," ANA's global exiles living "in the USA, Canada, Australia, Japan, the UK, South Africa, Botswana, Russia, Saudi Arabia, Finland, and so on," wanted proof of *their* "other's" worth.[30] To a large extent, this "proof" entailed unequivocal international support for the struggle against Shell Oil. ANA's 1995 on-line press release put it this way: "There is a moral responsibility which must be borne by certain governments and multi-national companies whose desire for profit and the proverbial black gold has blinded them into unholy alliances with the evil regimes. In particular, we note the roles being played by Shell Petroleum in Nigeria. Shell's operation in Nigeria is one of the worst nightmares visited upon Nigerians and the Ogoni people in particular."[31]

Shell was named as a litigant in a special tribunal responsible for legal actions that resulted in the criminal convictions of Ken Saro-Wiwa and the other Ogoni activists. ANA notes further that Shell was morally implicated in their deaths, and that the oil giant must be stopped, insisting: "Every litre of petroleum product from Nigeria marketed by Shell is being extracted at the expense of the blood and the lives of our patriots whose families and land are being destroyed mainly for the benefits of a tyrannical elite and of Shell and its shareholders."[32] These are strong words—words of the order likely responsible for Saro-Wiwa and the others' political assassinations. Again, Lamming's writings are instructive: "The exile is a universal figure. The proximity of our two lives to the major issues of our time has demanded of us all some kind of involvement. Some may remain neutral," as many Naijanetters attempted, "but all have, at least, to pay attention to what is going on. On a political level, we are often without the right kind of information to make argument effective; on a moral level we have to feel our way through problems for which we have no adequate reference of traditional conduct as a guide. . . . Sooner or later, in silence or with rhetoric, we sign a contract whose epitaph reads: To be an exile is to be alive."[33] Alas, it was ANA's very much alive exiles who paid attention to what was going on, and who issued a digital call to arms against Shell to help secure Nigeria's salvation and Saro-Wiwa's redemption.

What makes ANA such an interesting study, beyond its contrast to most chat groups' self-centeredness and to MUDs' and other on-line groups' hedonistic role-playing digital playgrounds, is its historical self-consciousness about forming a digital diaspora. In a welcome letter to its site visitors in the mid 1990s, the group's president, Usman G. Akano, had this to say about the organization:

> The ANA is an association of Nigerian professionals, academics and students who are resident abroad, and friends of Nigeria with genuine interests in issues Nigeriana. . . . The Association of Nigerians Abroad is unique among Nigerian organizations for the breadth of its developmental goals, the diversity of its membership, and its commitment to see Nigeria take her rightful place among the comity of nations. The ANA's business is also conducted almost entirely via the internet, perhaps the only full-fledged organization born of the information super-highway. This web page, designed, created and implemented through volunteer effort by a group of dedicated ANA members on our WWW sub-committee, is a small example of what ANA is all about. As you move around from page to page and from one link to another, you will come to learn more about ANA; . . . join us in the task of making the Nigerian corner of the world a better place for all. I thank you for your visit.[34]

Comfortable in the i-speak (Internet speech) of the net's argot, replete with interactive appeals ("join us," "your visit," "as you move around") and new technology verbiage ("information super-highway," for example), Akano emphasizes his commitment to the organization's goal of supporting "the development of Internet communication in Nigeria." By November 19, 2000, the ANA Web site deployed more graphics and intrasite links (links internal to ANA's own pages, as opposed to extrasite links or what are more commonly called "webrings"). Sound files, animated gifs and icons, and an expanded array of features, topics, issues, and visitor surveys were other structural changes and interactive elements that indicated the site's technical sophistication, growth, and development over the years. For example, the site boasts a "Free Fax Service to *anywhere* in the world . . . click here to *just do it!*" An offer to "Set Up Your Home Page" is made to visitors of ANA.

Regular departments of the site include About ANA, Join ANA, ANA Executives, ANA Committees, ANA Publications, Nigeria News, Guardian, Post
Express, Nigerian Universities, Business in Nigeria, Fallen Heroes, Nigerian
Gallery, Nigeria History, and Enter ANA Chatroom.[35] At this writing, ANA has
become a full-service site that follows the rhizomatic structuring principles
of many large-scale, nonprofit, group-run, information-rich Web sites, with
pages and pages of data and discourse. Added to the obligatory copyright
page, ANA's tag line is "All images ©www.ana.org® 1999 This Site is Designed
by *Nigerians.*" Finally, and lest anyone is left with the impression that the
ANA of 2000 and beyond is not as politically active and confrontational as it
was from 1993 to 1995, one need only point to a post on the site from March
3, 2000. In a letter to Nigerian president Olusegun Obasanjo, ANA expressed
"its profound sadness at the recent colossal loss of lives and destruction of
properties in Kaduna and Abia States as a result of the Sharia controversy."
As one might expect, ANA brooked no compromise in its rhetoric of outrage:

> While the Association condemns the brains behind these atrocities
> against innocent citizens of Nigeria, it expresses its disappointment at
> President Olusegun Obasanjo's lukewarm approach of mere pronounce-
> ment that the Sharia law is 'unconstitutional' and will 'die a natural
> death' to this serious constitutional problem. . . . As a result of the
> national controversey and the danger it posed to the country's nascent
> democracy, the world awaited President Obansanjo's executive initiative
> by utilizing all the judicial means available to resolve the issue. The
> President's inaction until the outbreak of violence clearly sent the
> wrong message.[36]

The letter concludes with declarations of several resolutions. As with the
Shell censure, ANA is once again using the Internet to keep a vigilant eye on
Nigerian affairs, which all but ensures that Africa's digerati in exile will not
lack "the occasion for speaking."

Accompanying those expatriate Nigerians of Naijanet and ANA to the on-
line ether were other Africans on the continent and in the diaspora who were
most instrumental in constructing and beating the digital talking drums of
Internet connectivity for new cyberhomelands. Most prominent were African
diasporans who produced such Web sites as the African National Congress
(ANC), the Buganda Hompage, Egypt's Information Highway, and those affiliated with Africa Online. But we hear little of these cases in mainstream media
coverage of race and technology matters, as the rhetoric of the digital divide

has become especially potent for positioning black people as poster children for its often pathologizing and debilitating discourse. Still, the African diaspora is speaking in digital tongues, and if you listen closely you find that not only have these subalterns found an occasion for speaking, but also through digital means they can and do speak for themselves.

NOTES

Although this essay revises the author's "The Revolution Will Be Digitized: Afrocentricity and the Digital Public Sphere" (reprinted by permission from Duke University Press), it includes substantial material previously unpublished but adapted from the author's recently completed manuscript, *Digital Diaspora: A Race for Cyberspace.*

1 C.L.R. James, *The C.L.R. James Reader*, ed. Anna Grimshaw (Oxford: Blackwell, 1992), 396.

2 Christopher Anderson, "The Internet: The Accidental Superhighway," *The Economist*, July 1995, 3, 4.

3 Horace Newcomb, *Television: The Critical View*, 4th ed. (New York and Oxford: Oxford UP, 1987), ix.

4 Howard Rheingold, *The Virtual Community: Homesteading on the Electronic Frontier* (New York: HarperPerennial, 1993), 7, 1, 7.

5 Rheingold, *Virtual Community*, 3. See Theodore Roszak, *The Cult of Information* (Berkeley: University of California Press, 1994) for an insightful discussion of the symbiosis obtaining between the 1948 discovery of cybernetic information theories and microbiological research into cracking the "genetic code" of DNA. According to Roszak, Norbert Weiner's "too esoteric" work on cybernetics "found its most dramatic support from another, unexpected quarter: Biology—or rather, the *new* biology, where the most highly publicized scientific revolution since Darwin was taking place [original emphasis]. In 1952, microbiologists James Watson and Francis Crick announced that they had solved the master problem of modern biology. They had broken the 'genetic code' hidden deep within the molecular structure of DNA. The very use of the word 'code' in this context is significant. . . . It immediately seemed to link the discoveries of the biologists to those of the new information theorists, whose work had much to do with the 'encoding' of information. . . . Since its inception, the new biology has been so tightly entwined with the language and imagery of information science that it is almost impossible to imagine the field developing at all without the aid of the computer paradigm" (16–17).

6 These ideas are found throughout Jacques Derrida's writings, including his books *Of Grammatology* and *Writing and Difference.*

7 For a thorough treatment of the confluence of African and European musical traditions, see LeRoi Jones, *Blues People* (New York: Morrow, 1963).

8 Marshall McLuhan and Bruce R. Roberts, *The Global Village: Transformations in World Life and Media in the Twenty-first Century* (New York and Oxford; Oxford UP; 1989), ix.

9 My own searches on February 6, 2001, of the term "African American" yielded these results from the following search engines: Excite—120,065 matches; Hot-Bot—907,600; Look Smart—2,000; Lycos—1,651,895.

10 In 1987, Ben Bagdikian commented on the role of big media corporations in narrowing the information spectrum of U.S. citizens. In his perennially in-print book *The Media Monopoly* (Boston: Beacon Press, 1990), Bagdikian writes: "Each year it is more likely that the American citizen who turns to any medium—newspapers, magazines, radio or television, books, movies, cable, recordings, video cassettes—will receive information, ideas, or entertainment controlled by the same handful of corporations, whether it is daily news, a cable entertainment program, or a textbook. Any surprise of a few years ago is replaced by the demonstration that media giants have become so powerful that government no longer has the will to restrain them. Corporate news media and business-oriented governments have made common cause. The public, dependent on the media giants for its basic information, is not told of the dangers" (ix). Prefiguring this cross-media consolidation or corporate cartelism, the film industry, led by Thomas Edison, effected its own brand of media monopoly. For a cinema-history discussion of the Edison trust, see, for example, "Edison's Trust and How It Got Busted," in Robert Sklar's *Movie Made America: A Cultural History of American Movies* (New York: Vintage Books, 1975).

11 Ingrid Volkmer, "Universalism and Particularism: The Problem of Cultural Sovereignty and Global Information Flow," in *Borders in Cyberspace: Information Policy and the Global Information Infrastructure*, ed. Brian Kahin and Charles Nesson (Cambridge and London: MIT P, 1997), 48.

12 Benedict Anderson, *Imagined Communities: Reflections on the Origin and Spread of Nationalism* (London and New York: Verso, 1992), 4, 3.

13 McLuhan and Roberts, *Global Village*, x, 148, viii.

14 Anne Balsamo, *Technologies of the Gendered Body: Reading Cyborg Women* (Durham, N.C., and London: Duke UP, 1996), 116.

15 This quote and the details and quotes on the Naijanetters in the paragraphs that follow are drawn from Misty L. Bastian's excellent history "Immigrant Nigerians on the Internet," www.westafricareview.com/war/vol1.1/bastian.html.

16 I discuss this usage of "recolonize" in more detail in "Recolonizing Africa for the Twenty-first Century," *UFAHAMU: Journal of the African Activist Association* 21, 1–2: 26–38.

17 I borrow this phrasing from the title of Saskia Sassen and Kwame Anthony Appiah's book *Globalization and Its Discontents: Essays on the New Mobility of People and Money* (New York: New Press, 1998).

18 Emeka J. Okoli, "Ethnicity, the Press, and Integration in Nigeria," *International Journal of Africana Studies* 5 (1999): 32–33.

19 Allucquere Rosanne [Sandy] Stone, "Will the Real Body Please Stand Up? Boundary Stories about Virtual Cultures," in *Cyberspace: First Steps*, ed. Michael Benedikt (Cambridge and London: MIT P, 1991), 85.

20 Okoli, "Ethnicity," 39.

21 Stone, "Will the Real Body," 85.

22 Bastian, "Immigrant Nigerians on the Internet."

23 Ibid.

24 Bill Ashcroft, Gareth Griffiths, and Helen Tiffin, "Feminism and Post-colonialism: Introduction," *The Post-Colonial Studies Reader*, (London and New York: Routledge, 1995), 247–250.

25 Kirsten Holst Petersen, "First Things First: Problems of a Feminist Approach to African Literature," *The Post-Colonial Studies Reader*, ed. Ashcroft, Griffiths, and Tiffin, 254.

26 Bastian, "Immigrant Nigerians on the Internet."

27 See, for example, the text of the ANA press release, interesting because of its international list of members and the particular demands it outlines for progressive net users. See ANA Online 1995: "The Association of Nigerians Abroad (ANA)," www.ananet.org. The details and quotes in the discussion that follows are drawn from this Web site.

28 George Lamming, "The Occasion for Speaking," in *The Post-Colonial Studies Reader*, ed. Ashcroft, Griffiths, and Tiffin, 16, 17.

29 ANA Online, 1995.

30 Lamming, "Occasion," 13. Usman G. Akano's "Welcome Letter" page of the ANA site at www.ananet.org:

31 ANA Online, 1995.

32 Ibid.

33 Lamming, "Occasion," 12.

34 Akano, "Welcome Letter."

35 See ANA at http://www.ananet.org/.

36 For the full text of the letter to President Obasanjo, visit the site at http://www.ananet.org/Sharia.html.

SOME VERSIONS OF DIFFERENCE

DISCOURSES OF HYBRIDITY
IN TRANSNATIONAL MUSICS

TIMOTHY D. TAYLOR

*I know from painful experience that when you upset white
people's categories, you'd better watch out.*
    —Mandawuy Yunupingu, bandleader, Yothu Yindi

Few terms are bandied about more in discussions of contemporary musics
than "hybridity," a term believed to capture the kinds of mixtures of musics
prevalent in this era of globalization or transnationalism. But the term has so
many uses in and out of considerations of music that it has come to represent
a variety of musics and other cultural forms, discourses, political strategies,
and identity conceptions. These usages are frequently intertwined in complex ways that can complicate investigation into a particular facet of the
term, and into the musics and peoples it is supposed to characterize.

The popularity of the metaphor of hybridity has meant that older discourses of authenticity are no longer the only ways that the music industry
markets musics from other places, and that Western listeners apprehend
musics from other places.[1] Listeners to world music are now less likely to
criticize music that doesn't seem to be authentic, and are more likely to welcome it as a hybrid.[2] Hybridity is also increasingly becoming construed as
another kind of authenticity, demonstrating the constantly shifting nature of
regimes of authenticity around world music.

The purpose of this essay is to confront the hybridity concept in discourses in and around what has come to be called "world music" (a term used
here to refer to the Western music industry's construction of non-Western

musics influenced by Western popular musics).[3] The hybridity concept exists in a number of different discourses in academia and the music industry, and among journalists, fans, and musicians, and these discourses of hybridity have become powerful means of shaping the perceptions and experiences of world music. While it is not my goal to explore hybridity as a "real," on-the-ground mode of cultural production, I am nonetheless interested in the ways that the conceptions of hybridity, the discourses of hybridity, affect understandings of musicians and musics, and the way that identifiable musical hybrids are treated discursively, and so it will be necessary to tackle academic conceptions of hybridity on the ground.

Hybridity Discourses in the Music Industry

Hybridity has become an important lens through which cross-cultural encounters are understood, sometimes displacing lenses of authenticity. But the widespread use of the term as a descriptor has also meant that it is sometimes used as a prescriptor. Like the term "postmodern," the hybridity concept influences both the hearing and the production of popular musics.[4] There are now musicians who deliberately make hybrid musics, and who use the term in describing their music. An early example is Michael Brook's album *Hybrid* from 1985; this recording, realized with Brian Eno and Daniel Lanois, employs instruments and samples (that is, exact digital copies of previously recorded sounds) of musics around the world.[5] Another example is the name of the band of one of my former students, "High Bird," a name that my student told me was a deliberate play on the term "hybrid." The rap/rock fusion band Linkin Park recently released an album entitled *Hybrid Theory*. And there are many other examples.

Because of the increasing salience of the hybridity concept, it is now possible to argue that there has been a partial displacement of discourses: hybridity is now joining authenticity as one of the ways that musics by Others are marketed by the music industry. And hybridity is joining authenticity as one of the ways that musics by Others are heard by critics, fans, and listeners.[6] This means that listeners are now more likely to have multiple referents for their sense of the authentic when they hear world music.

As an example of the music industry's deliberate positioning of a particular music as hybrid, consider *Welenga*, a 1997 collaborative album between the Cameroonian Wes Madiko (who goes by his first name only) and Michel Sanchez, one of the two musicians behind the highly successful "band" Deep

Forest.[7] Their album is accompanied by some of the most extravagant prose to be found in the usually overheated rhetoric of the world-music industry:

> Having written his first traditional album (which only appeared in the USA), Wes was wary of facile and over-artificial associations, a form of white-gloved slavery that is at the heart of too many fashionable cross-cultural projects. He was, however, reassured by the sincere passion of Michel Sanchez, who for three years gave Wes his time and his know-how. The combination of the two spirits, the irrational Wes and the virtuoso Michel, was a fusion of fire and water, the meeting of a wild but fertile root and the gifted loving caretaker of a musical garden where Wes could flourish.[8]

The combination of the pseudo–politically correct with the continuation of colonialist tropes of the African Other as "irrational," the "wild" with the rational and cultivated, is quite remarkable here. This kind of packaging simply reproduces old negative stereotypes dressed up in new language. Ashwani Sharma has commented on this strategy, arguing that "the powerful redefinition of ethnicity evoked through the concept of hybridity enters the dynamic of popular cultural politics to be incorporated, reterritorialized and reworked by hegemonic structures to produce new marginalized and essentialized identities."[9]

But it is not just identities that are marginalized and essentialized—this has happened to world music as a whole. While major generic/stylistic categories such as "rock" can support a number of independent record labels, the number of world-music labels is decreasing, and the major labels are increasingly hegemonic in this music. One of this industry's achievements with respect to world music has been to reduce this vast array of musics to a recognizable "style" that possesses only a few audible features that can be easily managed (vocals in an unusual language, acoustic drums, or perhaps a wooden flute–like sound). Such reductionism makes it far easier for huge companies to manage a potentially unruly category such as world music for the purposes of sales calculation, marketing, and retailing.[10] Even so, an entire album of these sounds would still be too foreign for most of today's listeners, and so the industry seems to prefer to package them with a mediator or broker such as Sanchez who can introduce familiar Western sounds and techniques and add his star power to raise sales. This form of "curatorship"—in which a known Western musician adds his (it is usually a he) name and sounds to a non-Western musician's work—has become an increasingly

visible mode of world-music marketing.[11] In instances such as these, "hybridity" has become a marketing term, a way of identifying, commodifying, and
selling what on the surface is a new form of difference, but one that reproduces old prejudices and hegemonies.[12]

    World music journalists are no less enthusiastic about hybridity than the
music industry. In the coverage of the Beninoise musician Angélique Kidjo's
recent album *Oremi*, reviewers attempt to sound accepting of her not strictly
authentic style but use only updated terms from an older discourse that naturalizes peoples from other, "third-world" cultures.[13] A reviewer in the *Boston
Globe* writes that the album "balances the electronic and organic," with
"organic" here presumably meaning "African," and "electronic" presumably
meaning "Western."[14] Another reviewer says that "though Kidjo employs
many elements familiar to techno fans, she makes that genre sound utterly
sterile next to her funky, thoroughly organic hybrid."[15] The language of these
reviewers is striking given the fact that Kidjo's record company purposely
marketed her not as a world-music artist but as an R&B musician, a strategy
that was unusual enough to have achieved coverage on a front-page story in
Billboard magazine.[16] But she is still seen—heard—as an African musician,
who, by the Western music industry's definition, make world music and only
world music.

    "Hybridity" in these usages, it seems, is simply a code for older forms of
difference; non-Western musicians who make world music are still consigned
to the Other, "savage slot."[17] Non-Western musicians are still naturalized, still
seen as nonmodern. Hybridity in this usage is not just a sign of Kidjo and
Wes's otherness, but also a sign of their *authenticity* as late–twentieth-/
early–twenty-first-century Africans to Western listeners. This is a far cry from
the critical reception of just a few years ago, when Kidjo and some other
Afropop musicians were excoriated by Western world-music journalists for
sounding *too* Western, or for selling out to commercial Western pop styles, or
for working with Western producers.[18] For example, one critic wrote of
Kidjo's album *Ayé* of 1994 that it is "straight funk-rock, slickly packaged by a
pop producer and, whichever way you look at it—not necessarily with any
purist inflection—the songs on it are less engaging."[19] It was clearly the
encroachment of Western styles and production values that cheapened the
album for this writer.

    Because of this shift of conceptions of authenticity-as-pure to authenticity-
as-hybridity, the music industry's world-music category appears to be bifur-

cated and now includes only "authentic" music (i.e., field recordings, which don't sell well except to purists, aficionados, and musicians looking for music to sample in their own works) and music labeled as hybrid such as Kidjo's and Wes's, even though their music is as slick and polished as any Western pop music currently available. But because of its use of sounds that signify "world music" to the Western music industry, music that is in between gets little attention for it is too difficult to classify and is altered so it can be effectively marketed, or excluded from the category altogether, and thus fails.

The Australian Aboriginal band Coloured Stone, for example, had trouble finding a white audience because of its "musical Aboriginality," according to Marcus Breen. The band plays musics associated with whites—rock and country rock—but its style frequently breaks with accepted white expectations of square phrasing and constant rhythms, even when performing cover versions of popular standards. White audiences tend to hear these alterations as mistakes.[20] Similarly, Jocelyne Guilbault writes of the ways that zouk musicians in the West Indies had to conform to an "international sound," which for them meant altering their music to European scales and tunings and in other aspects.[21] Conversely, however, it is possible for musicians to conceal sounds of their musical traditions that nonetheless remain audible to members of their own community. Jill Stubington and Peter Dunbar-Hall, for example, write of another Australian band composed of both white and Aboriginal members, Yothu Yindi, that there is more going on than meets the average non-Aboriginal pop/rock listener's ear.[22] But Yothu Yindi sounds enough like what the music industry desires in a "hybrid" that this band could succeed in ways that Coloured Stone could not. (I treat Yothu Yindi in some detail later.)

Generally speaking, world-music artists currently face growing expectations by Western listeners that Others produce hybrid music.[23] It seems that a subaltern musician can succeed in the world-music market only if she takes on a touch of the sound —but not too much—of the West. After all, the world-music albums that sell the most are almost never recordings of traditional music, but rather of hybrids, whether Salif Keita's Afropop, Cesaria Evora's Portuguese *fado*-like *morna* from Cape Verde, or R. Carlos Nakai's Native American flute recordings. Virtually no non-European or non-U.S. music that is relatively free of Western influences has appeared on *Billboard* magazine's World Music charts or received a Grammy award, with the sole exception of an occasional recording of North Indian classical music.[24] It appears, in other words, that world musicians may not be expected to be authentic anymore in the sense of being untouched by the sounds of the West, but it is now their very hybridity that allows them to be constructed as authentic.

Hybridity on the Ground/in Academia

And yet, of course, musics do mix—hybridity isn't merely an industry or journalistic discourse, though it has become a powerful set of discourses around world music. Since I am interested in the ways that the discourses of hybridity affect understandings of musics and musicians, it is necessary to examine academic conceptions of hybridity, and hybridity as an identifiable phenomenon on the ground. I am not claiming that academic considerations of hybridity are more accurate than nonacademic ones, but they do tend to be somewhat less influenced by the marketing hype surrounding hybridity, and thus academic usages of the hybridity concept exist somewhat apart from usages in the industry and by critics.

One of the leading theorists of hybridity is the literary critic Homi K. Bhabha. Perhaps the most influential aspect of Bhabha's notion of hybridity concerns what he calls the "third space":

> Hybridity to me is the "third space" that enables other positions to emerge. This third space displaces the histories that constitute it, and sets up new structures of authority, new political initiatives, which are inadequately understood through received wisdom. The process of cultural hybridity gives rise to something different, something new and unrecognizable, a new area of meaning and representation.[25]

But because of the prevalence of the marketing and journalistic hybridity discourses and the chauvinistic practices of the music industry, it is frequently the case that a hybrid cultural form of this third space finds itself in an all-too-familiar opposition as the subordinate part of a dominant/subordinate binary, which is precisely what has happened to Angélique Kidjo and her music, despite her well-publicized efforts to achieve more mainstream success outside the narrow and marginal world-music category. The "hybrid" can be recoded as "authentic," finding itself back in the "savage slot."

It has not been a major part of Bhabha's work to examine how the oppositional and destabilizing effects of hybridization might actually play out, for he has spent most of his attention on the activities of the oppressed, not the workings of the oppressors. In his interest in the counter-hegemonic practices of disempowered groups, Bhabha doesn't consider that colonializing or other dominant powers might interpret the hybrid forms that subalterns produce as simply inaccurate, or mimetic, inferior versions of what the dominant culture has thrust upon them, or as new kinds of "authentic" cultural production.[26] Interpretations aren't made solely by those in power, of course, but hegemons have ways of ensuring that their interpretations prevail, at least in institutions that they control, such as the major record labels, radio markets, and large retailers, and, to some extent, the less responsible music journalists. The marketing of hybridity frequently triumphs over the third space.

Michael Hardt and Antonio Negri make a similar critique of Bhabha's work, noting that Bhabha assumes an older model of sovereignty that they believe no longer exists: States are less dependent on retaining power through hierarchies and binary oppositions than they once were.[27] And yet, of course, discourses that valorize hierarchies and binary oppositions remain, and peoples' practices are, in part, shaped by these discourses—the "real" and the discursive aren't easily disentangled. The world may "really" have changed, as Hardt and Negri argue, and it may have moved away from Bhabha's and others' interpretations of it, but discourses and practices don't usually change as fast. Older discourses of binary oppositions and hierarchies continue to operate.

Diasporic South Asian Bhangra Remix Music

I turn now to a case study that will serve as an example of the complicated ways that conceptions of hybridity are mixed up in what musicians, fans, record labels, critics, and scholars say and do in the name of "hybridity." The popular music made by diasporic South Asians known as bhangra remix music, which relies on both traditional music and contemporary electronic dance sounds and techniques, is far removed from the "world-music" system constructed by the major labels: It is not a particularly popular music among world-music aficionados, and there is usually little represented in the major retailers (although it received major coverage in both editions of *World Music: The Rough Guide*).[28] Yet the discourses of hybridity play an important role in this music, in part because of the hegemony of the major labels and retailers, and in part because musicians and listeners involved with bhangra remix music use the term "hybridity" themselves to describe both the music and their conceptions of their identity as diasporic South Asians.[29] And some of the South Asians who use the term have clearly learned it from academic treatments such as Bhabha's.

I should say at the outset that there was a time when bhangra and "Hindi remix"—music that sampled primarily from Indian film music—were somewhat separate genres, but sampling has become so predominant that remix musicians sample bhangra sounds as well, clouding the difference between bhangra and remix music. So it will be referred to here as "bhangra remix" unless it is necessary to make the distinction for historical reasons.[30]

When bhangra or bhangra remix music is discussed, the term "hybridity" is frequently invoked, often with its academic trappings. Sunita Sunder Mukhi, for example, quotes academics Bhabha, Gayatri Gopinath (author of an early article on bhangra), and Nabeel Zuberi (author of a book on transnational musics) in her discussions of hybridity and Indian-American identities, demonstrating the ways that the more popular discourses of hybridity are occasionally inflected by academic ones.[31] "Being Indian American," Mukhi writes,

> is being comfortable, smooth and cool amidst non Indians, in the playing fields of hybridity. It is being able to dance Bhangra unabashedly, wear contemporary Indian and Western clothes smartly, enjoy the pleasures of an urban, cosmopolitan life in New York, as well as in Bombay, London, or Hongkong [sic], and still care for mom and dad (at the very least), and go to the temple on occasion. . . . Indianizing fairly tales, American movies, and other such popular texts, dancing the Bhangra and the Hindi film dance, dressing in mixed styles, are hybrid forms which facilitate the expression of the hybrid self.[32]

Elsewhere she says:

> Though the Indian lyrics of Bhangra may be in Punjabi, now intermixed with pidgin English, Black English, Indian English, and Hindi film song lyrics, not necessarily understood by all of the diasporic Indians, the beat, some of the instruments, the melodies are identified as generally non-white, generically Indian, and specifically of Indian hybridity. . . .
>
> The energetic beat [of bhangra] allows for an exuberant, almost ecstatic, very physical and aerobic dancing. The dance is loud, expressive, rhythmic. The music hastens, and reaches a crescendo, making the body reach a peak of energy and awareness. When dancing the bhangra, one feels very alive, very present, absolutely not erased. Dancing the bhangra with others who are experiencing this self-same aliveness allows for the barriers of individuation to dissolve. We all dance together forming one pulsating body of "amorphous" South Asianness. It enlivens our hybridity kinesthetically.[33]

Writings such as this demonstrate the complex ways that the hybridity notion suffuses conceptions of self, musical style, and identity strategies in diasporic and cosmopolitan situations among South Asians in the United States, constituting a distinct discursive usage of the term somewhat removed from the marketing usages.

The music industry's treatment of bhangra remix music has been no different; the hybridity descriptor crops up all the time without any academic trappings, usually in quite matter-of-fact ways. For example, CDNow's on-line description of Bally Sagoo's *Rising from the East* says that "Indian-born mix-master Bally Sagoo helped to create the East-meets-West hybrid he calls 'bhangra beat,' and got American attention two years ago with *Bollywood Flash bash [Flashback]*, a collection of Indian film music made club-friendly by his remixes."[34]

Journalistic representations tread much the same ground, often relying heavily on the press kits supplied by record labels. Ken Micallef, in a review of Talvin Singh's 1997 album *O.K.*, writes that "his music blends state-of-the-art drum and bass with the surging rhythms of traditional Indian music to create one of the most exciting hybrids on the electronic dance scene."[35]

Simplistic treatments of bhangra remix music and other hybrid musics cause some of the more thoughtful academic commentators to react with some degree of exasperation.[36] Ashwani Sharma, for example, notes the ways that Nusrat Fateh Ali Khan was marketed, especially once he started making recordings for Peter Gabriel's Real World label. This is not bhangra remix, but a more iconoclastic blend of a South Asian music with Western sounds. Real World represented Khan's music as an aesthetic object, not a critical part of a religious exercise, and the liner notes to one recording, Sharma writes, revealed the ways that musics such as Khan's "can be celebrated and authenticated as hybrid within the logic of difference in global commodity capitalism."[37] Such arguments, however, tacitly assume that Khan himself was simply a dupe in the process of making his own recordings without agency. It is frequently the case, however, that non-Western musicians in the shadow of major Western stars enter into a Faustian bargain of trading the fame they derive from appearing with these famous U.S. and European musicians for control over representations of themselves and their music.[38] The music industry's hybridity didn't simply run over Khan but perhaps merged to some extent with his own notions of the hybrid, and his own reasons for achieving it.

The changes that bhangra and Hindi remix musics have undergone in the last few years that resulted in bhangra remix point to the ways that these musics are caught up in complicated discourses and practices about diasporic South Asian youth identities, for bhangra remix has become a complex site of discursive contention around the issues of hybridity and authenticity. Much has been made of the supposed hybridity of bhangra remix, but bhangra from the 1980s owed little to traditional bhangra; an occasional *dhol* drum and the language of the lyrics were often the only recognizable sonic signifiers from traditional bhangra, although some bands occasionally used synthesizers to simulate some traditional instrument sounds. This bhangra was more a kind of rock/pop played by South Asians in London than a music whose makers attempted to sound equally South Asian and Western. But signaling the "traditional" was not of concern to the musicians who followed the first wave of the popularization of bhangra in the late 1970s and early 1980s. The first bhangra stars are now arguing that what was called bhangra by the early 1990s wasn't really bhangra at all.[39]

In the last few years, however, bhangra musicians have begun to turn toward more traditional sounds, even as they introduce more and more techniques that use digital technology to make bhangra remix. They are increasing the "South Asian" component of their hybrid sounds. This metamorphosis has come about for complicated reasons that I will flesh out later. First, this strategy of turning toward traditional sounds is fairly common among children and grandchildren of immigrant populations in the late twentieth century.[40] The new interest in musical and ancestral roots also highlights the ways in which bhangra and the people who make it are considered, by themselves and others, to be hybrids. The interest in the roots of bhangra was announced in 1996, when DJ Jiten, a Toronto-based DJ, said that "audiences are moving towards more traditional bhangra right now. The remix bhangra right now is nothing big. . . . The hardcore is coming straight out of Punjab. The real scene is so hardcore right now that you have to be a traditional Punjabi to be right in the scene."[41]

Also in 1996, Panjabi MC, a diasporic South Asian musician based in Britain, released a recording called *Grass Roots*. An on-line report on this album says that "1996 was the renaissance that traditional Bhangra had waited for. Panjabi MC headed back to his music heritage in India with his DAT [digital audio tape] machine in-hand and recorded the father-figures of Punjabi music in a way never before witnessed. Back home in England, he laced the vocals of Kuldip 'he is what James Brown is to soul—he's the God-father of Bhangra. . . .' Manak and Surinder Shinda with street beats and melodies totally new to their style of vocals."[42] In other words, bhangra remix.

Bhangra, like any popular music, is constantly changing, as this quotation indicates; U.K. bhangra musicians' discussions of "getting back to their roots" is registered in the many recent bhangra recordings with titles that refer to roots: *Bhangra Roots Do*, by the Sangeet group of California; Johnny Z's *Back to My Roots*; collections such as *Bhangra Roots* and *Bhangra Roots 2*; Shava Shava's *Diggin' the Roots*; *Roots of Bhangra*; and many others. But the way these roots were acquired was technological—by sampling, or recording live vocals to manipulate later in the studio, bringing about bhangra remix.

Like Punjabi MC, the U.K. superstar DJ Bally Sagoo also made a recent bhangra remix album that attempted to return to the roots of bhangra. Sagoo traveled to India to record musicians to use on his 1998 album *Aaja Nachle*. Sagoo said that "everybody around the world has been requesting that I make a bhangra album, and this one has taken me almost a year to put together." The CD was recorded mostly in India and features, among other musicians, some "new talent I've discovered"—that is, professional bhangra musicians.[43] These musicians sound less Western than do bhangra musicians outside India, but diasporic bhangra musicians audibly influence them.[44]

This shift from bhangra to bhangra remix illustrates the fluidity and changeability of conceptions of hybridity and the third space in Bhabha's for-mulation. Emphasizing fluidity, flux, and changeability helps capture the nature of cultural production, at least in the realm of popular musics. Popu-lar musical styles change fast. So, however, do discourses, practices, and social formations. Hybridities are made in a series of open-ended social moments that move as people move and that can overlap with each other, moments in which sounds or images or styles (or what have you) are thrown up against each other in ways in which their different origins are discernible. But most of the industry's discourses of hybridity are not about flux. They're about fixing something for the purpose of easy categorization and marketing. The concept has become a way for some diasporic South Asians to locate a sense of stability in a complex environment.

Let's examine this shift to bhangra remix in greater detail by comparing a track from a bhangra album before the turn toward roots, and a track from Sagoo's *Aaja Nachle*. First, a song by Achanak, a U.K. bhangra band. "Lako Wadeya" was released on the 1993 collection *What Is Bhangra?* Achanak's song opens with an extended James Brown sample from "Get Up (I Feel Like Being a) Sex Machine"; it's hard to tell for the first forty seconds or so what is South Asian about this song aside from a splash of *tabla* (a pair of tuned drums used in North Indian classical music, not in bhangra): This song is clearly establishing links not with England—or India for that matter—but with African America. This connection to an African American musician is made overtly in both the liner notes and the back cover of the album with the following note: "Bhangra combines quintessential Asian music with a kaleidoscope of contemporary styles including reggae, pop, ska, hip-hop and house."[45] Except for one thing: "Lako Wadeya" employs a singsong percussion rhythm that is the signature bhangra *dhol* drum rhythm, a sound that creates a connection between James Brown's quite similar rhythm and bhangra that non-Punjabi listeners might not notice, in a kind of hidden connection to tradition. Following this extended James Brown sample, the bhangra sound begins, but the *dhol* drums and their swingy rhythm—one of the main sonic signifiers of bhangra—last only about fifteen seconds, long enough to tell us that this is bhangra music (though they do recur periodically throughout the song). The vocal style, closer to Indian film music than to bhangra, is liquid and lilting.

Compare "Lako Wadeya" to Bally Sagoo's "Aaja Nachle" from the album of the same title. Sagoo's music, stemming from the dance-music wave of bhangra that ultimately led to bhangra remix, begins the track, but more traditional-sounding bhangra eventually appears, bhangra that we know Sagoo recorded in India. In fact, the Punjabi musician is credited in the liner notes: He is Hans Raj Hans, a well-known bhangra singer in India. Hans Raj Hans's vocal style is a little rougher than on the Achanak track and makes use of far more ornaments than in "Lako Wadeya."

Clearly I have chosen examples that are eons apart—five years—in the world of popular music. "Lako Wadeya" is still steeped in the African American phase of bhangra influence (which is still around but in a different guise). Bally Sagoo's music reflects the subsequent turn toward the traditional, as well as Sagoo's dance music background—bhangra remix. Styles change quickly in mainstream popular musics, and they change in bhangra and other not-quite-mainstream popular musics as well, affording musicians and listeners endless opportunities for affiliations, political commentary, and pleasure. Third spaces in this realm of the popular are moments of continual (re)invention.

Both Achanak and Sagoo's musics are identifiably hybrids in the sense that more than one musical genre or style is audible. But what is interesting about these tracks is not so much their hybridity, but the ways their hybridity has been constructed and heard in particular historical and cultural and geographic instances, and the ways the discourses of hybridity shape perceptions of the music by journalists, fans, and some academic commentators.

To complicate these issues further, it seems that many diasporic South Asian listeners have only a theoretical notion of the Punjabi folk roots of bhangra/bhangra remix. They know it's a stylistic hybrid, but they aren't always clear on the underlying musical sounds and styles. On a recent visit to Jackson Heights, Queens, one of the most concentrated areas of South Asians in New York City, I stopped at three music stores on a single block and asked for traditional bhangra recordings—traditional, not the bhangra associated with diasporic South Asian youths, but the folk music of the Punjabis. I wanted to acquire the folk bhangra that gave rise to contemporary popular bhangra. In every case, the people I spoke to had no idea what I was talking about. Each clerk brought out early bhangra recordings from the United Kingdom, which evidently are old enough now to be considered traditional, not hybrid. Bhangra (and it seems to me, any commodified music) ages in commercial time more, and/or faster, than in experiential distance from a musical source.[46] These clerks also showed me some recent recordings of musicians who were attempting to sound more traditional. "He's very traditional," said one clerk, handing me a brand-new album by a hot young Punjabi musician.[47]

Contemporary diasporic South Asian fans of South Asian popular musics, who seem to be largely unaware of traditional Punjabi bhangra, don't appear to be conceiving of their bhangra or bhangra remix in terms of a hybrid of traditional bhangra and Western pop music, but as a hybrid of East and West more generally, a messier mixture that includes not only musical sounds and style, but people and cultures as well, as we have seen. This binary, however, can combine with others, such as old/new, traditional/modern, Punjabi/ English, Punjabi/American, Indian/Anglo, acoustic/electronic, subordinate/ superordinate, and doubtless still others. Further, bhangra remix, like most popular music genres, has become a diversifying category—there are many bhangras now, and there are many hybridities.

It also seems to be the case that early bhangra, hailed as a hybrid in its time, is now authentic, traditional bhangra to some of today's youth listeners. This points out another problem with the hybridity metaphor. Not only is it too focused on binarized, asymmetrical social formations, it is too frequently ahistorical.[48] While hybridity, particularly in Bhabha's writings, isn't a static formulation, most uses of the concept, such as those we saw applied to Wes and Angélique Kidjo, too often ignore changing ideas of what is taken as the authentic, and thus constantly changing ideas of what constitutes the new or the traditional.

These hybridities are part of larger ones, however: There is the "East meets West" collision of sounds that are audible in both examples. But, with respect to these recordings, one must ask, what counts as East? Traditional, Punjabi bhangra? Anything at all that sounds South Asian? Whatever alterations Sagoo brings to it? And what counts as "West"? The electronics? Any Western instrument? Further, the early collection *What Is Bhangra?* depicts on the cover a young South Asian male, or, rather, half of a young South Asian male; the other half is a machine, signifying the studio technology used in making bhangra today. The hybrid on this cover is not necessarily of East and West, South Asian and African American, subordinate and superordinate, or even human and cyborg, but rather represents traditional and modern, a particularly complex binary under which other binaries are often subsumed.

This changeability makes it important to emphasize the fluidity of cultural production in Bhabha's third space. Even though this concept was formulated in a colonial/postcolonial framework, the third-space notion is still useful even in the complicated world of mass-produced and mass-mediated cultural forms.

Anthropologist Sunaina Maira has conducted an ethnography of South Asian youths in New York City and has fruitfully examined the complex ways that they conceptualize themselves as ethnic/cultural hybrids. The discourses of hybridity figure prominently in their conceptions of themselves, revealing the ways that the hybridity metaphor can frequently obscure more than it can clarify. Diasporic South Asians talk about themselves as hybrids culturally and generationally, and they use the term to describe everything from their music to clothing to food. Maira usefully points out that simple assumptions about hybridity as being between "East" and "West," or "Asian music" and "African American music," can hide more complicated dynamics (as I will discuss in greater detail in the next section). For example, while some authors view diasporic South Asians' uses of African American musics as a way of sounding a political affiliation, Maira writes that the adoption of hip-hop style among diasporic South Asian men was prompted more by reasons of style, which, she writes, "connotes a certain image of racialised, heterosexual masculinity that is the ultimate definition of 'cool.'" Thus, to call bhangra remix a "hybrid" overlooks the ways that its hybridity is produced for local reasons, forging stylistic alliances between two subcultural youth groups; at the same time the simple label "hybrid" perpetuates old gendered binary oppositions as women either are made the repositories of South Asian "tradition" or are constructed as modern Americans—as Maira writes, they are reconfigured as either "virginally Indian or immodestly American."[49]

Maira is particularly insightful on the question of hybridity-as-identity, writing that the space of contradiction for her interlocutors in New York City was

> between the discourse of ethnic authenticity among second-generation youth on the one hand, and the performance of hybridity in remix youth culture and in everyday life on the other, suggest[ing] that what is at stake in this youth subculture is not just a struggle over definitions of Indian music and dance; rather, this disjuncture also reveals conflicts over attempts by Indian American youth to be "authentic" in both local and diasporic spaces, the belief of immigrant parents in the American Dream, and the complicity of Indian Americans with U.S. racial hierarchies.[50]

Diasporic South Asians' hybrid musics negotiate complex tensions among pressures to assimilate, pressures to be authentic Indians, pressures to be American and rebel against the older generation, and simultaneous pressures to use the older generation's knowledge of India to fashion authentic Indian selves.[51] It is only through studies such as Maira's that potent discourses such as those surrounding the concepts of hybridity and authenticity can be identified *as* discourses and real practices, and can be seen to work in particular practices in particular social groups in particular places and times.

Blackness

The racial/ethnic category that is most problematized, or obscured, by the discourses of hybridity concerns blackness. Blackness represents a peculiar area in the hybridity discourses, for sometimes it is so fetishized as a mode of affiliation and resistance that hybridity is constructed as something simply black and something else; or blackness is subsumed into a larger category of "Western" or "modern," thus obscuring the reasons for its presence in particular instances. There are, to be sure, plenty of discussions of how African American musics have influenced musicians around the world, but if the discussion in question is about "world music" and framed by questions of authenticity and/or hybridity, blackness frequently falls by the wayside.

The problem of blackness in the hybridity discourses surfaces mainly as a result of the usual reductionist presumption that stylistic hybrids consist of two, and only two, "pures" that mix, even though more subtle theorists such as Bhabha and James Clifford hold positions that the concept of hybridity banishes concepts of the "pure."[52] It may already be evident that in most uses of the term "hybridity," the two "cultures" that hybridize are white and nonwhite Other, but the complex and multiple nature of the Other or Others is not always accounted for in the discourses of hybridity. And the nonwhite in popular musics can frequently be a third "culture" that interacts to form a more complex hybrid than is allowed for under most usages of the hybridity discourses. As in the case of Achanak, African American musical sounds can be a crucial part of the music, resulting in a multifaceted hybrid sound that is South Asian, British, and African American, in various and shifting degrees, with audiences that find different things to value and identify with.

Take, for example, the already mentioned Australian band Yothu Yindi (about which there is practically a scholarly cottage industry).[53] This is a band composed of Aboriginal and white musicians, but as far as the music industry is concerned, it is an Aboriginal band. And even though its music is rock, inflected by Aboriginal musics—a rock/Aboriginal traditional hybrid, if you will—the band is still classified as world music because of the presence of Aboriginal members. These musicians foreground their Aboriginality—in their album cover art, the costumes they wear, the instruments they use, and their lyrics—even as they make music that is, in generic and stylistic terms, rock.

Yothu Yindi and many Aboriginal bands arrived at this particular musical style by heeding reggae superstar Bob Marley's belief that all black men are brothers. As Adelaide music announcer Rosie Ryan put it: "Bob Marley played Adelaide in early 1979. The dust raised by that tour never really settled."[54] One of the earliest Aboriginal rock bands, No Fixed Address, believed that reggae was the black music of the future.[55] While Yothu Yindi's music doesn't sound as though it has much to do with Marley's, or with any reggae for that matter, Marley's influence does appear occasionally, as the lyrics to "Tribal Voice" from the 1992 album of the same title show.

All the people in the world are dreaming (get up stand up)
Some of us cry cry cry for the rights of survival now (get up stand up)
Saying c'mon, c'mon! Stand up for your rights
While others don't give a damn
They're all waiting for a perfect day
You better get up and fight for your rights
Don't be afraid of the move you make
You better listen to your tribal voice!

The "get up stand up" phrase comes from Marley's famous song of the same name, perhaps the most famous of all his songs that deliver a political message. Marley's chorus line, "Get up, stand up, stand up for your right" may well be the most potent injunction to black and brown people around the world, echoed and reechoed in songs such as this by Yothu Yindi.

In the burgeoning scholarly literature on Yothu Yindi, *ganma*—an Aboriginal philosophy of "both ways"—usually figures prominently, for this is essentially an indigenous theory of hybridity. In the words of the Both Ways school literature, a school with which the founder of Yothu Yindi, Mandawuy Yunupingu, is heavily involved: "Ganma is a metaphor describing the situation where a river of water from the sea (Western knowledge) and a river of water from the land (Yolngu [Yunupingu's tribe] knowledge) mutually engulf each other on flowing into a common lagoon and becoming one. In coming together the streams of water mix across the interface of the two currents and foam is created at the surface so that the process of ganma is marked by lines of foam along the interface of the two currents."[56]

Ganma specifically, and Yothu Yindi's Aboriginal "culture" in general, are usually the focal point of scholarly analysis of the group.[57] But in discussions of Yothu Yindi and ganma, the band's attraction to Bob Marley and blackness are not always explicitly theorized (one important exception is George Lipsitz's indispensable *Dangerous Crossroads*); ganma is seen as occurring strictly between Aboriginal people and whites, two groups constructed as occupying intractably opposite sides. In the same way that African American musics are not always mentioned in characterizations of bhangra music as hybrid, the power of reggae and other black musics to unite people of color around the world are frequently elided as part of the equation, or as part of the band's supposed hybridity. Usage of the hybridity metaphor tends to focus analysis on binarized asymmetrical power relations, not on the myriad alliances that can be made by those on the subordinate side of those relations, or on more specific local forms of alliances and critiques.[58]

In keeping with my overall argument that the discourses of hybridity shape the production and perception of world musics and can thus obscure as much as clarify a particular music, it is important to remember that musics labeled hybrid are always more than mere stylistic/generic mixtures. It is also important to remember the specific hybridities in particular cases, for Yothu Yindi's music isn't simply caught up in a global sense of a black brotherhood, as we have seen. Yothu Yindi's complex musical hybridity is further complicated by Yothu Yindi's relationships to white Australians, relationships that are imbricated in discourses of the politics of reconciliation and the land. Yothu Yindi makes connections to a global black brotherhood through music, but for specifically local reasons concerning land rights and land use of land controlled by whites with whom ganma is being formed.

Some commentators call for, or champion, musicians who make radical critiques with African American musics, but again hybridity emerges as something that occurs between whites and nonwhites; the cross-racial affiliative potential is overlooked, or minimized. In a discussion of hybridity similar to this one in some respects, John Hutnyk asks, "*What would a radical hybridity look like?*" For him, the British band Asian Dub Foundation, another group of diasporic South Asians, exemplifies a radical hybridity. Hutnyk believes them to be radically hybrid not so much in their music, their sounds, but because of their lyrics and political stances that protest against anti–South Asian prejudice in the United Kingdom. Hutnyk also unquestioningly endorses Asian Dub Foundation's own characterization of their music in one song as neither "ethnic, exotic or eclectic" but, rather, a vehicle for commentary."[59] But it is also music, and their genre—hip-hop—was not chosen accidentally.

Asian Dub Foundation's use of sounds associated with U.S. blackness in a show of solidarity with another oppressed people (in which they are following in the footsteps of earlier diasporic South Asian bands in the United Kingdom such as Fun^Da^Mental) is, as in most discussions of hybridity, overlooked in favor of an opposition between white and something else not African American, in this case, South Asian. Musically, Asian Dub Foundation's music is essentially hip-hop with a dash of South Asian sounds. One of the tracks that Hutnyk discusses is "Jericho," a song that aggressively proclaims the presence of these diasporic South Asians in the United Kingdom:

> We ain't ethnic, exotic or eclectic
> The only "e" we use is electric
> An Asian background
> That's what's reflected
> But this militant vibe
> ain't what you expected.

"Jericho," with its opening sample of a political speech, could have been by Public Enemy, except that the rapping voice of Master D (whose real name is Deeder Zaman) doesn't sound much like Chuck D's, though his name does. The dash of South Asian sounds here is not subtle; the sound of the *tabla* at the beginning serves, like Achanak's James Brown sample, to situate the band in a history of a particular music and politics. The song also quotes the African American spiritual "Joshua Fit de Battle ob Jericho," which meshes with the band's own militancy. But while Joshua's Jericho was a place, the walls that come tumbling down in Asian Dub Foundation's song are the walls of racism. I would be remiss not to note also that it is not only African American culture that Asian Dub Foundation draws on, for their very name refers of course to dub, the reggae studio remix technique; in the United Kingdom, there is a well-known movement called the Dub Poets, consisting of various poets who deliver political messages over dub tracks.[60]

Yet Hutnyk sets aside Asian Dub Foundation's strong gestures of, and affiliations with, blackness, a move that is, I suspect, the result of a common assumption of the hegemony of U.S. popular musical sounds, which themselves are largely African American and African American influenced—this is another instance of African American sounds being taken to signal "Western" more generally. But the global dominance of African American popular musics does not mean that they have always been deracinated, or that their politics have always been aestheticized. Asian Dub Foundation is clearly making an affiliation with African Americans in its music, as do many youth music cultures, and as such is making hybridities, a third space in Bhabha's sense of the term.

While I appreciate Hutnyk's interest in a radical hybridity as a potentially liberatory kind of cultural production, I am at the same time interested in attempting to show how the discourses of hybridity fetishize hybridity, and, indeed, fetishize Otherness, sometimes at the expense of another Other.

Focusing on Asian Dub Foundation as "Asian" loses any diversity within that category, just as diversity within the category of "British" or "Western" is lost as well.

The purpose of this essay has been to demonstrate the ways that the discourses of hybridity complicatedly influence each other, influence music making, influence listening, and to show that the marketing of hybridity also shapes musical production and perception. Use of the term "hybridity" makes most who employ it occasionally complicit, to varying degrees, in continuing, perpetuating, and intensifying historically unequal power relations, the entrenched conservatism of cultural categories employed by the music industry, and the difficulty of changing those categories. In this era of unparalleled transnationalism/globalization, it is perhaps important to remember that it is not just commodities, money, sounds, images, and people that move, but also, as Arjun Appadurai has famously written, ideologies.[61]

At one level, it is now demonstrably the case that the hybridities perceived in popular cultural forms in this moment constitute merely another way that people in so-called developed countries perceive cultural forms from their Elsewheres, and construct them discursively. Hybridity has become, or perhaps always was, simply another form of difference, another subordinate category into which Others and their cultural forms can be put, another form of authenticity, another way that musics by people from Western Elsewheres are relegated to the world-music category and denied access to the more prestigious category of rock. If people with dark skin make hybrid music, their music is world music; if white people, particularly superstars like Paul Simon or Peter Gabriel, make hybrid music, their music is anything but world music.

At another level, perhaps Bhabha's concept of the "third space" can help obviate some of the problems of the hybridity metaphor, circumvent some of its ideological maneuverings. The term avoids the unfortunate organic roots, and racist history, of hybridity as a concept. And much as the music industry would like to reduce musics, styles, and genres to bland, knowable entities for the purposes of easy categorization and marketing, the idea of third spaces serves as a corrective, implicitly referring to the momentary, evanescent nature of culture, social formations, and music.

This is an important point, I think, not just for the music industry and listeners. Theorization in the hands of Homi K. Bhabha resulted in an extraordinarily productive set of analytical tools. But as with all terms and categories, you have to watch what happens to them in practice. It becomes all too easy for those who follow—myself included—to find hybridities everywhere. Naming reifies, and reifications all too frequently prove to be surprisingly enduring.

Let's employ the notion of the "third space" to preempt reification. The third space recognizes the constant flux of cultural production and people and social formations, and at the same time retains the potential for redressing imbalances of power relations, of forging distant and local affinities, of giving voice to political stances that oppose racism and other forms of discrimination. The third space concept recognizes the transitoriness of any of these possibilities, but attempts never to lose sight of them.

NOTES

Thanks are due to Steven Feld, Aaron A. Fox, René T. A. Lysloff, Carol Muller, Irene Nexica, Guthrie P. Ramsey, and Deborah Wong, who helped me think through some of these ideas. And as ever, my greatest thanks go to Sherry B. Ortner.

1 It is not my goal here to account for the success of the hybridity concept, except to note that it provided a more flexible and sophisticated model than did cultural imperialism, which was rejected by most scholars of music. See Andrew Goodwin and Joe Gore, "World Beat and the Cultural Imperialism Debate," *Socialist Review* 20 (July–September 1990): 63–80; Dave Laing, "The Music Industry and the 'Cultural Imperialism' Thesis," *Media, Culture, and Society* 8 (July 1986): 331–341; and Deanna Campbell Robinson, Elizabeth B. Buck, and Marlene Cuthbert, *Music at the Margins: Popular Music and Global Cultural Diversity* (Newbury Park, Calif.: Sage Publications, 1991). For an excellent overview and critique of the discourse of cultural imperialism, see John Tomlinson, *Cultural Imperialism: A Critical Introduction* (Baltimore: Johns Hopkins UP, 1991).

2 There are other kinds of mixes that have been theorized—*mestizaje*, *métissage*, creolization—but they are not nearly as visible as hybridity. On *mestizaje*, see Gloria Anzaldúa, *Borderlands: The New Mestiza* (San Francisco: Aunt Lute Books, 1991); and J. Jorge Klor de Alva, "The Postcolonization of the (Latin) American Experience: A Reconsideration of 'Colonialism,' 'Postcolonialism,' and 'Mestizaje,'" in *After Colonialism: Imperial Histories and Postcolonial Displacements*, ed. Gyan Prakash (Princeton, N.J.: Princeton UP, 1995). On *métissage*, see Ann Laura Stoler, "Sexual Affronts and Racial Frontiers: European Identities and the Cultural Politics of Exclusion in Colonial Southeast Asia," in *Tensions of Empire: Colonial Cultures in a Bourgeois World*, ed. Frederick Cooper and Ann Laura Stoler (Berkeley: U of California P, 1997). On creolization, see Line Grenier and Jocelyne Guilbault, "Créolité and Francophonie in Music: Socio-Musical Repositioning Where It Matters," *Cultural Studies* 11 (1997): 207–234; Ulf Hannerz, *Transnational Connections: Culture, People, Places* (New York: Routledge, 1996); and David Parkin, "Nemi in the Modern World: Return of the Exotic?" *Man* 28 (March 1993): 79–99. For another useful treatment of the hybridity concept, see Lisa Lowe, *Immigrant Acts: On Asian American Cultural Politics* (Durham, N.C.: Duke UP, 1996).

3 For a history and discussion of this term, see Herbert Mattelart, "Life as Style: Putting the 'World' in the Music," *Baffler* (1993): 103–109; and Timothy D. Taylor, *Global Pop: World Music, World Markets* (New York: Routledge, 1997).

4 See Andrew Goodwin, "Popular Music and Postmodern Theory," *Cultural Studies* 5 (May 1991): 174–190.

5 Brook has achieved more recent fame as the collaborator with the late Nusrat Fateh Ali Khan on *Night Song* (Real World 2354, 1996).

6 See also Simon Frith, "The Discourse of World Music," in *Western Music and Its Others: Difference, Representation, and Appropriation in Music*, ed. Georgina Born and David Hesmondhalgh (Berkeley: U of California P, 2000).

7 Deep Forest's eponymous CD was released in 1992 and sold more than 1.5 million copies. For more on Deep Forest, see Carrie Borzillo, "Deep Forest Growing in Popularity; 550's World Music-Dance Hybrid Climbs Charts," *Billboard*, February 19, 1994, 8; and "U.S. Ad Use Adds to Commercial Success of Deep Forest," *Billboard*, June 11, 1994, 44; Andrew Ross, review of *Deep Forest*, *Artforum*, December 1993, 11; Al Weisel, "Deep Forest's Lush Lullaby," *Rolling Stone*, April 21, 1994, 26; Hugo Zemp, "The/An Ethnomusicologist and the Record Business," *Yearbook for Traditional Music* 28 (1997): 36–56; and, most importantly, Steven Feld, "Pygmy Pop: A Genealogy of Schizophonic Mimesis," *Yearbook for Traditional Music* 28 (1997): 1–35.

8 Liner notes to Wes Madiko, *Welenga* (Sony Music 48146-2, 1997). I would like to thank Harriet Whitehead for introducing me to this album.

9 Ashwani Sharma, "Sounds Oriental: The (Im)Possibility of Theorizing Asian Musical Cultures," in *Dis-Orienting Rhythms: The Politics of the New Asian Dance Music*, ed. Sanjay Sharma, John Hutnyk, and Ashwani Sharma (Atlantic Highlands, N.J.: Zed Books, 1996), 20.

10 For more on "world music" as style, see Timothy D. Taylor, "World Music in Television Ads," *American Music* 18 (summer 2000): 162–192.

11 The most famous case is, of course, Paul Simon's *Graceland* (1986), but there are numerous other examples, most prominently, David Byrne's, Ry Cooder's, and Peter Gabriel's work with various non-Western musicians.

12 For a similar point see John Hutnyk, "Adorno at Womad: South Asian Crossovers and the Limits of Hybridity-Talk," in *Debating Cultural Hybridity: Multi-Cultural Identities and the Politics of Anti-Racism*, ed. Pnina Werbner and Tariq Modood (Atlantic Highlands, N.J.: Zed Books, 1997).

13 This process of naturalization is discussed at length in Taylor, *Global Pop*.

14 Paul Robicheau, "Listening to History," *Boston Globe*, September 25, 1998.

15 "Kidjo's 'Oremi' Is Heavenly," *Boston Herald*, September 1998. Robert Young argues in *Colonial Desire: Hybridity in Theory, Culture, and Race* (New York: Routledge, 1995) that the concept of hybridity recapitulates nineteenth-century discourses on race and racism in that it naturalizes peoples from other cultures by employing a term from agriculture, and indeed, the term is usually applied to musics by peoples from other cultures. Paul Simon's *Graceland*, for example, was widely hailed as an important rock album, not as a hybrid of South African (and other African) popular musics and U.S. popular musics. Simon's prominence as an international star, American, and white ensured that *Graceland* would be interpreted as the product of his individual artistic genius, not as a hybrid of styles. See Louise Meintjes, "Paul Simon's *Graceland*, South Africa, and the Medi-

ation of Musical Meaning," *Ethnomusicology* 34 (winter 1990): 37–73, for a consideration of Simon's album.

16 Elena Oumano, "Island Targets R&B Market with New Album from Kidjo," *Billboard*, May 23, 1998, 1.

17 The term "savage slot" was advanced by Michel-Rolph Trouillot, "Anthropology and the Savage Slot: The Poetics and Politics of Otherness," in *Recapturing Anthropology: Working in the Present*, ed. Richard G. Fox (Santa Fe: School of American Research P, 1991).

18 This is discussed in Taylor, *Global Pop*, chap. 5. For some of the criticisms of Kidjo, see esp. Philip Sweeney, *The Virgin Directory of World Music* (London: Virgin Books, 1991), and Brooke Wentz, "No Kid Stuff," *The Beat* 18 (1993): 42–45, and "Youssou N'Dour: Is He Shaking the Tree or Cutting It Down?" *Rhythm Music*, May/June 1994, 38.

19 Simon Broughton, Mark Ellingham, David Muddyman, and Richard Trillo, eds., *World Music: The Rough Guide* (London: Rough Guides, 1994), 298. The new edition of *World Music: The Rough Guide* is more circumspect, reporting that Kidjo "goes from strength to strength" and that her albums "vary widely in style" (Simon Broughton, Mark Ellingham, and Richard Trillo, eds., *World Music: The Rough Guide*, vol. 1, *Africa, Europe and the Middle East* [London: Rough Guides, 1999], 433, 434).

20 Marcus Breen, ed., *Our Place, Our Music*, vol. 2 of *Australian Popular Music in Perspective* (Canberra: Aboriginal Studies P, 1989), 65.

21 Jocelyne Guilbault, *Zouk: World Music in the West Indies* (Chicago: U of Chicago P, 1993), 150.

22 Jill Stubington and Peter Dunbar-Hall, "Yothu Yindi's 'Treaty': Ganma in Music," *Popular Music* 13 (October 1994): 250.

23 See Leela Gandhi, *Postcolonial Theory: An Introduction* (New York: Columbia UP, 1998), for a similar point about literature.

24 For a discussion of world music on *Billboard*'s charts and in Grammy awards, see Taylor, *Global Pop*. This is not the place to discuss the relative popularity of Indian classical musics; see instead Gerry Farrell, *Indian Music and the West* (Oxford: Clarendon P, 1997); and David Reck, "The Neon Electric Sarswati," *Contributions to Asian Studies* 12 (1978): 3–19. Finally, for a similar argument about the Western success of forms from the margins, see Hannerz, *Transnational Connections*, esp. 78.

25 Homi K. Bhabha, "The Third Space: Interview with Homi Bhabha," in *Identity: Community, Culture, Difference*, ed. Jonathan Rutherford (London: Lawrence and Wishart, 1990), 211. For more of Bhabha's influential writings on these and other issues, see *The Location of Culture* (New York: Routledge, 1994).

26 See James Clifford, *Routes: Travel and Translation in the Late Twentieth Century* (Cambridge: Harvard UP, 1997), esp. chap. 6.

27 Michael Hardt and Antonio Negri, *Empire* (Cambridge: Harvard UP, 2000), 144–146.

28 Broughton, Ellingham, Muddyman, and Trillo, *World Music*; Broughton, Ellingham, and Trillo, *World Music*.

29 There are many examples of uses of the hybridity concept in discussions by South Asians considering bhangra remix. A few: Lavina Melwani, "It's a Party,"

Welcome to Little India, January 1997, 21; and by Sunita Sunder Mukhi, "Forging an Indian American Identity: Guess Who's Coming to Dinner?" *Little India*, May 1996, 49; "Forging an Indian American Identity: Something to Dance About," *Little India*, April 1996, 53; and *Doing the Desi Thing: Performing Indianness in New York City* (New York: Garland, 2000).

30 Bhangra is a folk music of the Punjabis of Northern India and Pakistan, a lively music that celebrates the end of the harvest and that eventually became popular all over the Punjab. Punjabis migrating to England and Canada in the 1960s and 1970s brought bhangra with them. These Punjabis mixed bhangra with the instruments and sounds they found in their new locales, at first using mainly acoustic instruments (such as accordion, violin, and acoustic guitar), then moving to a fairly standard rock-band instrumentation (drum kits, synthesizers, guitars). In the 1980s, bhangra musicians incorporated elements from electronic dance music such as drum machines, which matched the singsong beat of the *dhol* drums, which became the signature sound of bhangra. Later, Caribbean and African American musical influences dominated. While these changes in sound were occurring, in the United Kingdom and other parts of the South Asian disapora, bhangra became a pan–South Asian music that has become extremely popular among diasporic South Asian youths, not just those of Punjabi heritage, but Hindus, Muslims, Sikhs, and Jains alike, uniting all of them into a pan–South Asian ethnic identity. For more on bhangra, see, in addition to the articles cited in the discussion, Sabita Banerji, "Ghazals of Bhangra in Great Britain," *Popular Music 7* (May 1988): 207–213; and Sabita Banerji and Gerd Baumann, "Bhangra 1984–8: Fusion and Professionalization in a Genre of South Asian Dance Music," in *Black Music in Britain: Essays on the Afro-Asian Contribution to Popular Music*, ed. Paul Oliver (Buckingham, U.K.: Open UP, 1990).

31 See Gayatri Gopinath, "'Bombay, U.K., Yuba City': Bhangra Music and the Engendering of Diaspora," *Diaspora* 4 (winter 1995): 303–321; and Nabeel Zuberi, *Sounds English: Transnational Popular Music* (Urbana: U of Illinois P, 2001).

32 Mukhi, "Guess Who's Coming to Dinner?" 49.

33 Mukhi, "Something to Dance About," 53.

34 http://www.cdnow.com/cgi-bin/mserver/SID=1261988902/pagename=/RP/CDN/FIND/album.html/ArtistID=SAGOO*BALLY/ITEMID=630225.

35 Ken Micallef, "Talvin Singh," *Rolling Stone*, August 21, 1997, 36.

36 For some examples of music journalists' use of the term with respect to bhangra remix music, see Neil McCormack, "At the Speed of Sound on Pop," *Daily Telegraph*, February 15, 2001; David Lister, "Mercury Prize," *The (London) Independent*, July 26, 2000; Marty Lipp, "On the Record," *Newsday*, June 11, 2000; Paul H. B. Shin, "Hot New Music Has Some Very Old Roots," *New York Daily News*, February 18, 1998; Lorraine Ali, "Britpop Spiced with Asian Flavor," *New York Times*, October 12, 1997; D. James Romero, "His Drum-and-Bass Is Served with Some Spice," *Los Angeles Times*, July 20, 1997; and Neil Spencer, "Kaftans Are Back but Singh Wants No Part of Any Indian Summer," *The Observer*, February 16, 1997.

37 Sharma, "Sounds Oriental," 25.

38 The best known of these "collaborations" is probably Paul Simon's recording with the South African chorus Ladysmith Black Mambazo on the album *Graceland*.

39 Channi, from Alaap, the first major bhangra band in the United Kingdom, says: "I would not class the music in the bhangra charts as proper bhangra because

they have lost the [South] Asian touch. Bhangra is when you have more authentic sounds like the dhol and the alghoza [flute]" (quoted in Broughton, Ellingham, Muddyman, and Trillo, *World Music*, 231).

40 See Sunaina Marr Maira, *Desis in the House: Indian American Youth Culture in New York City* (Philadelphia: Temple UP, 2002), and "Identity Dub: Second-Generation Indian Americans and Youth Culture," *Cultural Anthropology* 14 (February 1999): 29–60, for extensive treatments of the question of generation among diasporic South Asians.

41 DJ Jiten, interview, http://www.streetsound.com/bhangra/intjiten83.html (accessed in 1999; this URL is no longer active). All quotations from the Internet appear with their original spelling and punctuation unless otherwise noted.

42 Jatender S. Heer, "Revolutionizing Bhangra: Punjabi MC Gives Bhangra a Much Needed Jolt," *Welcome to Little India*, July 1998, 56; www.southall-punjabi.com/coventry/revolutionizing-bhangra.html.

43 Lisa Tsering, "Bally Gets Busy with Bhangra, Film Projects," *India West*, August 1998, http://members.tripod.com/~LisaTsering/index-8.html. (This URL is no longer active.)

44 For more on Sagoo and other U.K.-based South Asian musicians, see Zuberi, *Sounds English*, chap. 5.

45 Liner notes to *What Is Bhangra?* (IRS Records, 7243 8 29242 27, 1994).

46 I would like to thank Steven Feld for his insight on this point.

47 It may be that these musicians are getting back to their roots to combat the appropriation of South Asian sounds and symbols by Westerners. Madonna's 1998 *Ray of Light* album was one culprit here; see Lavina Melwani, "Indian Chic: OM to the Music," *Little India*, April 1998, 20; and Sunaina Maria, "Henna and Hip Hop: The Politics of Cultural Production and the Work of Cultural Studies," *Journal of Asian American Studies* 3 (October 2000): 239–269. Another case concerned Aerosmith's album cover for *Nine Lives*, which was changed after protests by Hindus (see "Hindu Protest Forces Sony to Remake CD," *Hinduism Today*, July 1997, 47). Thanks are due to Irene Nexica for suggesting this line of inquiry.

48 This point is also raised by Aijaz Ahmad, "The Politics of Literary Postcoloniality," *Race and Class* 36 (January–March 1995): 1–20.

49 Maira, "Desis Reprazent: Bhangra Remix and Hip Hop in New York City," *Postcolonial Studies* 1 (1998), 361.

50 Maira, *Desis in the House*, 56–57.

51 See Sengupta, "To Be Young, Indian, and Hip," *New York Times*, June 30, 1996, for a fascinating example of a second-generation South Asian seeking advice from his mother about what Indian film music to sample in his remix.

52 See Clifford, *Routes*.

53 John Castles, "Tjungaringanyi: Aboriginal Rock," in *From Pop to Punk to Postmodernism: Popular Music and Australian Culture from the 1960s to the 1990s*, ed. Philip Hayward (North Sydney: Allen and Unwin, 1992); Philip Hayward, "Music Video, the Bicentenary (and After)," in *From Pop to Punk to Postmodernism*, and "Safe, Exotic, and Somewhere Else: Yothu Yindi, Treaty, and the Mediation of Aboriginality," *Perfect Beat* 1 (January 1993): 33–42; Philip Hayward and Karl Neuenfeldt, "Yothu Yindi: Context and Significance," in *Sound Alliances: Indigenous Peoples, Cultural Politics and Popular Music in the Pacific*, ed. Philip Hayward

(London: Cassell, 1998); George Lipsitz, *Dangerous Crossroads: Popular Music, Postmodernism, and the Poetics of Place* (New York: Verso, 1994); Fiona Magowan, "'The Land Is Our Mäar (Essence), It Stays Forever': The Yothu-Yindi Relationship in Australian Aboriginal Traditional and Popular Musics," in *Ethnicity, Identity, and Music: The Musical Construction of Place*, ed. Martin Stokes (Providence, R.I.: Berg, 1994), and "Traditions of the Mind or the Music Video: Imagining the Imagination in Yothu Yindi's Tribal Voice," *Arena 7* (1996): 99–111; Tony Mitchell, *Popular Music and Local Identity*; Stephen Muecke, *Textual Spaces: Aboriginality and Cultural Studies* (Kensington, NSW, Aus.: New South Wales UP, 1992); Karl Neuenfeldt, "Yothu Yindi and Ganma: The Cultural Transposition of Aboriginal Agenda through Metaphor and Music," *Journal of Australian Studies* 38 (September 1993): 1–11, and "Yothu Yindi: Agendas and Aspirations," in *Sound Alliancesu*, ed. Hayward; Lisa Nicol, "Culture, Custom, and Collaboration: The Production of Yothu Yindi's Treaty Videos," *Perfect Beat* 1 (January 1993): 23–32; Adam Shoemaker, "The Politics of Yothu Yindi," in *Working Papers in Australian Studies* 88–96, ed. Kate Darian-Smith (London: Institute of Commonwealth Studies, 1994), and "Selling Yothu Yindi," in *Republica: All Same As Family in a Big 'Ouse*, ed. George Papaellinas (Sydney: Angus and Robertson, 1994); Stubington and Dunbar-Hall, "Yothu Yindi's 'Treaty'"; Graeme Turner, *Making It National: Nationalism and Australian Popular Culture* (St. Leonards, NSW, Aus.: Allen and Unwin, 1994); and Mandawuy Yunupingu, "Yothu Yindi: Finding Balance," *Race and Class* 35 (April–June 1994): 113–120.

54 Breen, *Our Place*, 121. For more on the importance of Bob Marley and reggae music on Australian and New Zealand Aboriginal popular musics, see also John Dix, *Stranded in Paradise: New Zealand Rock and Roll, 1955–1985* (Wellington, N.Z.: Paradise Publications, 1988); and Lipsitz, *Dangerous Crossroads*. For more on cross-racial or cross-ethnic affiliations, see Juan Flores, "'Que Assimilated, Brother, Yo Soy Asimilao': The Structuring of Puerto Rican Identity in the U.S.," *Journal of Ethnic Studies* 13 (fall 1984): 1–16.

55 See Breen, *Our Place*.

56 Helen Watson, "The Ganma Project," quoted by Neuenfeldt, "Yothu Yindi and Ganma," 1.

57 Thanks to Irene Nexica for pointing this out. For a similar critique, see Turner, *Making It National*.

58 This last point is the main thrust of an important article by Sherry B. Ortner, "Resistance and the Problem of Ethnographic Refusal," *Comparative Studies in Society and History* 37 (January 1995): 173–193.

59 Hutnyk, "Adorno at Womad," 128 (emphasis in original), 129.

60 The best known of the dub poets are probably Linton Kwesi Johnson and Benjamin Zephaniah.

61 Appadurai coined the term "ideoscapes," among others, to describe the kinds of global flows (Arjun Appadurai, *Modernity at Large: Cultural Dimensions of Globalization* [Minneapolis: U of Minnesota P, 1996]).

ALTERNATE ARRANGEMENT FOR
GLOBAL CURRENTS

I

COMPUTER TECHNOLOGY AND INTERNET SPACE

SECTION A: REGULATION

SECTION B: CIRCULATION

NOTES ON CONTRIBUTORS

JÉRÔME BOURDON, formerly a researcher at the Institut national de l' audiovisuel in Paris, has been a senior lecturer in communications at Tel Aviv University since 1996. His current projects include a book on the cultural history of television in Europe and research on the coverage of the Israeli-Palestinian conflict in the Western media.

SANDRA BRAMAN is Professor of Communication and Chair of the Communication Law and Policy Division of the International Communication Association. Her current work includes *Change of State: An Introduction to Information Policy* (forthcoming) and the edited volumes *Biotechnology and Communication: The Meta-technologies of Information* (2004), *The Emergent Global Information Policy Regime* (2003), and *Communication Researchers and Policy-making* (2003).

ANNE CIECKO is Assistant Professor in the Department of Communication at the University of Massachusetts-Amherst. Her work has appeared in such journals as *Asian Cinema*, *Cinema Journal*, *Jump Cut*, and *Post Script*, among others. She recently guest edited a special issue of the *Quarterly Review of Film and Video* on film stars.

ANNA EVERETT is Associate Professor of Film Studies at the University of California at Santa Barbara, where she teaches film, video, and Internet studies. She is the author of *Returning the Gaze: A Genealogy of Black Film Criticism, 1909–1949* (2001).

LENNY FONER holds a Ph.D. from the MIT Media Lab and is the inventor and developer of Yenta, a free, open-source application that finds people with similar interests, automatically forms groups of them, and allows them to talk to each other. Foner's work at the lab has included novel uses of wearable computers for human sensory augmentation, and he is doing research in secure, privacy-protecting, peer-to-peer agent architectures. He is also active in efforts to migrate international human rights NGOs to open-source software.

STEVE JONES is Professor of Communication at the University of Illinois at Chicago. He is the editor of *Virtual Culture: Identity and Communication in Cybersociety* (1997) and *Doing Internet Research: Critical Issues and Methods for Examining the Net* (1998). He is cofounder and president of the Association of Internet Researchers and coeditor of *New Media & Society*, an international journal of research on new media, technology, and culture. He also edits Digital Formations, a series of books on new media, for Peter Lang Publishers.

BRIAN LARKIN is Assistant Professor of Anthropology at Barnard College, Columbia University. He is coeditor (with Faye Ginsburg and Lila Abu-Lughod) of *Media Worlds: Anthropology on New Terrain* (2002). He has published widely on issues of media, urbanization, and globalization in Nigeria.

TOBY MILLER is Professor of Cultural Studies and Cultural Policy at New York University, with appointments in Cinema Studies, American Studies, and Latin American and Caribbean Studies. He is the editor of the journal *Television & New Media* and author and editor of more than twenty books.

SUSAN OHMER teaches media studies at the University of Notre Dame. Her book on George Gallup in Hollywood is being published by Columbia University Press. She has also published articles on film and television history in *Film History*, *Journal of Film and Video*, *Velvet Light Trap*, and *Identifying Hollywood's Audiences*.

TASHA G. OREN is Assistant Professor of Film and Media Studies in the Department of English at the University of Wisconsin-Milwaukee. She is the author of *Demon in the Box: Jews, Arabs, Politics, and Culture in the Making of Israeli Television* (2004) and coeditor of *Asian American Popular Culture* (2004).

PATRICE PETRO is Professor of English and Film Studies and Director of the Center for International Education at the University of Wisconsin-Milwaukee. She is the author of *Aftershocks of the New: Feminism and Film History* (2001) and *Joyless Streets: Women and Melodramatic Representation in Weimar*

Germany (1989) and the editor and coeditor of several volumes, most recently, *Global Cities: Cinema, Architecture, and Urbanism in a Digital Age* (2003).

PETER SANDS is Assistant Professor of English at the University of Wisconsin-Milwaukee, where he teaches graduate and undergraduate courses in rhetoric, American literature, sf/utopia, and writing. He is coeditor of *Electronic Collaboration in the Humanities* (2003), and his articles have appeared in *Academic Writing*, *ACE Journal*, *Kairos*, *Works and Days*, and elsewhere. He is working on a book-length study of rhetoric, utopia, and pedagogy.

ANNABELLE SREBERNY is Director of the Centre for Mass Communication Research at the University of Leicester. She has written widely on international communication, gender, and globalization and is, most recently, the editor of a special issue of *Gazette*, "Mediated Cultures of the Middle East." Her research has been supported by UNESCO, the BBC, the Broadcasting Standards Commission, and the ESRC.

TIMOTHY D. TAYLOR teaches in the Music Department at Columbia University. His publications include *Global Pop: World Music, World Markets* (1997), *Strange Sounds: Music, Technology and Culture* (2001), and numerous articles on various popular and classical musics. His current project is a study of music in advertising from early radio to the present.

INDEX